George Barnett Smith

The United States

From the Earliest Times to the Landing of the Pilgrim Fathers

George Barnett Smith

The United States
From the Earliest Times to the Landing of the Pilgrim Fathers

ISBN/EAN: 9783744666015

Printed in Europe, USA, Canada, Australia, Japan

Cover: Foto ©ninafisch / pixelio.de

More available books at **www.hansebooks.com**

The Romance of Colonization.

THE UNITED STATES.

FROM THE EARLIEST TIMES TO THE LANDING OF THE PILGRIM FATHERS.

BY

G. BARNETT SMITH,

AUTHOR OF "THE HISTORY OF THE ENGLISH PARLIAMENT," BIOGRAPHIES OF WILLIAM TYNDALE, JOHN KNOX, SIR JOHN FRANKLIN, ETC.

NEW YORK:
DODD, MEAD AND COMPANY.
1897.

University Press:
JOHN WILSON AND SON, CAMBRIDGE, U.S.A.

PREFACE.

THERE is probably nothing more surprising in the history of the British Empire than the enormous expansion of its colonial possessions. Long before Canning made his proud boast that he "had called the New World into existence to redress the balance of the Old," England had been adding island after island, and territory after territory, to that empire upon which the sun never sets.

The work of colonization as it has been pursued by various nations in all parts of the world is a study of the deepest interest. Land migrations have had much to do with the settlement of new districts; but the movement has been fostered still more by the growth of merchant navies and the exchange of produce between nations. The Roman Empire furnished one of the most remarkable episodes in the history of colonization; but from that time forward little was done until the extraordinary developments of the colonizing spirit in the sixteenth century. Spain and Portugal took the premier honours in the work; but in this case, as in many others, those who were the pioneers of discovery have been surpassed by their successors.

Mixed motives have formed the basis of nearly all colonizing efforts. National glory and individual ambition have mingled with the love of adventure, the quest after gold, and the missionary spirit. Spain and Portugal desired the conversion of "heretics" as well as the extension of their respective empires, and the acquisition of the wealth of the Indies, in the fitting out of their numerous expeditions. They have long been left behind as colonizers by Holland, England, and France; and it would be a curious speculation to enquire into the causes of the decadence of nations like Spain and Portugal, which once led the vanguard of civilization.

But our purpose in the series of works of which the present forms the initial volume is to trace the romance of colonization in special countries, and chiefly as that colonization has been effected by England. No colonial empire was ever raised of such vast extent as that which acknowledges the sovereignty of Queen Victoria in this Diamond Jubilee year of grace. The great work of acquiring and building up colonies began with us in the seventeenth century; and before the end of the eighteenth Great Britain had become the first power in the world as regards the extent and value of her colonies, and that notwithstanding the serious loss of the United States. The acquisitions during the nineteenth century may not have been so numerous and important as they were in the two preceding centuries, but a greater work has been done in consolidating and strengthening our hold upon the colonies.

A rapid survey of Anglo-Saxon colonization affords much room for congratulation, if our satisfaction is occasionally chastened by a remembrance of the severities which have sometimes accompanied conquest. The premier British colony is Newfoundland, which was annexed by Sir Humphrey Gilbert in 1583; then came the achievements of the East India Company, which was incorporated in 1600; and only a few years later (1607) succeeds the earliest permanent settlement of Virginia. The Pilgrim Fathers began their noble work in 1620; and West Indian colonization was inaugurated with the occupation of Barbadoes in 1625. For three-quarters of a century the work proceeded apace in North America, colony after colony being added to the British Crown. Then other fields began to attract the British, and a new period began with the capture of Gibraltar in 1704. Before the century closed, France had yielded to us in Canada, and also in India, where Clive was more fortunate than Dupleix. The wars with Napoleon succeeded, and Malta, Mauritius, and many West India islands were captured from the French, as well as Ceylon and the Cape of Good Hope from the Dutch. The triumphs of the nineteenth century include the consolidation of India under the Crown; the surprising advance of Australia under the impetus of the gold discoveries; the pacification and opening up of New Zealand; the formation of Canada into a federated dominion; the great extension of British influence through the whole of Africa; the commercial growth of the Chinese and other settlements; and the raising of the British flag over many new protectorates and stations. It is calculated that the population of the British colonies has increased more than fourfold since the Queen came to the throne, while the trade to and from those colonies has multiplied nine or tenfold. In the brief period of fourteen years, 1872 to 1886, although the value of many individual articles had greatly decreased, the imports into the United Kingdom from the British colonies and India increased in amount from £79,372,853 to £81,884,043; and in the same period the exports to British possessions increased from £65,609,212 to £82,067,711. No figures could be more eloquent of colonial progress than these.

Among all the stories of colonization, none possesses a deeper or profounder interest for Englishmen than that of the peopling of the United States. It seems to contain within itself an epitome of all the incidents which have marked the course of colonization elsewhere. It will be the aim of this volume and its successor to follow the course of North American colonization from the earliest times, and all through the chequered periods of development, until the various colonies succeeded in achieving their independence, and forming themselves into a union, as the United States of America. In conclusion, some space will be devoted to an explanation of the Constitution of the United States, and to tracing briefly the later history of the country.

In the preparation of such a work, a writer is necessarily indebted to a great number of authorities; and the author of these volumes has endeavoured always to acknowledge his sources of information in the various chapters of his narrative. The second volume, completing the work, will shortly appear.

At a later date, it is hoped that other volumes will follow, dealing with Canada, Australia, New Zealand, British India, British Africa, and other colonies. Every year that passes only adds to the dignity and importance of our colonial empire, and the record of its manifold developments consequently becomes a study of supreme interest.

G. B. S.

CONTENTS.

CHAP.		PAGE
I.	EARLY HISTORY AND TRADITIONS	11
II.	THE VOYAGES OF COLUMBUS	32
III.	THE CABOTS AND THE FIRST ENGLISH COLONY	87
IV.	HOW AMERICA RECEIVED ITS NAME	115
V.	PORTUGUESE, FRENCH, AND SPANISH EXPLORATIONS	121
VI.	JACQUES CARTIER AND FERDINAND DE SOTO	144
VII.	ENGLISH ADVENTURERS — FROBISHER AND GILBERT	164
VIII.	THE EXPEDITIONS OF RALEIGH AND DRAKE	177
IX.	OPERATIONS OF THE VIRGINIA COMPANY	210
X.	SKETCH OF THE PLYMOUTH COMPANY	250
XI.	COLONIZATION OF MARYLAND	262
XII.	SETTLEMENT OF NEW AMSTERDAM	279
XIII.	THE PURITANS — LANDING OF THE PILGRIM FATHERS	289

THE UNITED STATES.

CHAPTER I.

EARLY HISTORY AND TRADITIONS.

IN the future history of the human race the vast American Continent is destined to play a conspicuous part. Its magnificent possibilities are almost inconceivable. Limitless in its resources, its mighty valleys and fruitful plains are already being opened up by the industry and enterprise of its settlers, while from the sides of its gigantic mountains mineral wealth beyond conception is being extracted. In an incredibly brief space of time splendid cities have risen as by the spell of an enchanter, and civilization already begins to count its teeming and thriving millions of population. "Westward the course of empire takes its way," wrote Bishop Berkeley a century and a half ago, and his utterance now reads like a prophecy of the greatness to which the New World was subsequently to attain.

America is frequently regarded as two distinct continents, connected by the Isthmus of Darien. There is a strange resemblance in the configuration of the two parts: both are very wide in the north, and both gradually taper off as they extend towards the south. Each division has a lofty chain of mountains on the west, and a great central plain declining to the south and the north respectively. The southern part is watered by two gigantic rivers, the La Plata and the Amazon, which may be regarded as the counterparts of the great rivers of the north, the Mississippi and the St. Lawrence. There is little difference between the superficial areas of the two continents, North America embracing no less than seven million four hundred thousand English square miles, and South America six million five hundred thousand English square miles.

It is with the North American Continent that this volume is concerned, and chiefly with the colonization of that portion of it which comes within the definition of the United States territory. America is commonly spoken of as the "New World," but as a matter of fact it is quite as ancient as any other physical section of the planet. Professor L. Agassiz, in his *Geological Sketches*, claims indeed that it is older than any. "First-born among the continents," he remarks, "though so much later in culture and civilization than some of more recent birth, America, so far as her physical history is concerned, has been falsely denominated the New World. Hers was the first dry land lifted out of the waters, hers the first shore washed by the ocean that enveloped all the earth beside; and while Europe was represented only by islands rising here and there above the sea, America already stretched an unbroken line of land from Nova Scotia to the Far

West." With regard to the aboriginal inhabitants, efforts have recently been made to connect their earliest memorials with those of Asia. But while it is within the bounds of possibility that means of communication between the two continents existed in ancient times, the whole question is of so speculative a nature that it would be unprofitable to discuss it here. Humboldt and other geological authorities believed that the summits of the Madeira and the Canary Islands were once the western extremity of the chain of the Atlas Mountains; and other writers have gone so far as to affirm that these islands, and those of the West Indies, are the summits of mountain chains which once crowned an Atlantic continent that was afterwards submerged and disintegrated by some great cataclysm. Among other traditions is that of Plato, who says that an Egyptian priest described to Solon an island called Atlantis, which lay far beyond the Pillars of Hercules. This island, which was inhabited by a warlike and powerful people, was destroyed, said the narrator, by earthquakes and floods nine thousand years before his time.

The aboriginal population of America embraces a great variety of peoples, differing in form, stature, and complexion. Yet one of the eminent physiologists, Blumenbach, places them all under one class, except the Esquimaux, who have close affinity with the inhabitants of Northern Asia. Others, like Dr. Prichard, have denied this; but when all has been said against the theory, there is unquestionably more of a common family character in the American Indians than prevails amongst the indigenous populations of

Asia and Africa. Humboldt remarks that "the Indians of New Spain bear a general resemblance to those who inhabit Canada, Florida, Peru, and Brazil. We have the same swarthy and copper colour, straight and smooth hair, small beard, squat body, long eye, with the corner directed upwards towards the temples, prominent cheek-bones, thick lips, and an expression of gentleness in the mouth, strongly contrasted with a gloomy and severe look. Over a million and a half of square leagues, from Cape Horn to the River St. Lawrence and Behring's Straits, we are struck at the first glance with the general resemblance in the features of the inhabitants. We think we perceive them all to be descended from the same stock, notwithstanding the prodigious diversity of their languages. In the portrait drawn by Volney of the Canadian Indians, we recognize the tribes scattered over the Savannahs of the Apure and the Carony. The same style of features exists in both Americas."

Historians have pointed out that the natives of North America, when first visited by Europeans four centuries ago, belonged as distinctly to the Stone Age as the earliest inhabitants of Europe. Shell-heaps have been discovered along the American coast from Massachusetts to Georgia which Sir Charles Lyell declared to be identical with the kitchen refuse-heaps of ancient Denmark. Human remains pointing to a hoary antiquity have been found at various places, and at various periods, in the United States. The discovery of earth-mounds and temple-mounds in the Valley of the Mississippi and elsewhere points to the existence of a race which peopled the North

American Continent even before the Indian; but however interesting this may be from the ethnological point of view, it does not come within our present purpose to discuss it. Whatever may have been the nature or character of the aboriginal tribes, one thing is universally admitted, that the greater part of the native tribes have never progressed beyond the savage state in civilization. With respect to the vast number of American languages, which amount to something like six hundred, philologists have come to the conclusion that they can all be arranged under eight or ten divisions, or into forty or fifty families, each characterized by affinities sufficiently clear to prove that its component members had sprung from a common parent.

The number of Indians, and persons of partial Indian descent, still remaining in North America, is about six millions; but probably half these consist of Spanish-speaking half-breeds and others in Mexico and the Isthmian republics. The Indians in the United States territory, including Alaska, number about three hundred and fifteen thousand. For many years they were decimated and forced out of existence by very cruel methods; but the American conscience has recently been much disturbed on this painful subject, so that now it is believed the Indians are slowly increasing again in numbers. One-fourth of the United States Indians live in the Indian territory, and one cause of the arrested process of extinction is to be found in the great diminution of inter-tribal warfare.

America was visited by Europeans centuries before

the time of Columbus. In fact, while **King Alfred was displaying his prowess and his enlightenment in Britain, Icelanders settled themselves in Greenland.** There is some little difference about the exact date, but it is a pretty well ascertained fact that this settlement **took place** between 830 and 870 A.D. How extraordinary it seems that such an event should have attracted scarcely any attention! The precise locality of the Norwegian colonies in Greenland cannot now be defined; but Sir Charles Giesecke, who devoted special study to the subject, states that memorials of the settlement exist near the southern point of the peninsula. A visit was likewise paid to the western coast of Greenland; and this fact has been established by an inscription in Runic characters, found on a stone four miles beyond Upernavik, at the seventy-third parallel. This inscription is to the effect that "Erling, the son of Sigvat, and Euride Oddsoen, had cleared that place and raised a hillock on the Friday after Rogation Day." The date on the stone is indistinct; but Professor Rask, the translator of the inscription, fixes it at either 1135 or 1170. In any event the Runic characters prove that the date was anterior to the Reformation, because that mode of writing was afterwards forbidden. In 1828 Professor C. C. Rafn, a Dane, who had been engaged in researches respecting these early voyages, published at Baltimore some interesting facts which he had ascertained from original documents. For example, he announced that America was first discovered in 985, and that it was repeatedly visited by the Icelanders in the eleventh, twelfth, and thirteenth centuries; that the embouchure of the St. Lawrence, and in particular the Bay of Gaspe, was their principal station; that they had penetrated along the coast as far south as Carolina; and that they introduced a knowledge of Christianity amongst the natives. Subsequently, while not altering the general drift of his views, M. Rafn changed his opinion as to the site of the Icelandic colony, fixing it at the mouth of the River Taunton, which falls into the sea in Narragansett Bay, at the north end of Rhode Island. So far as anything can be ascertained with certainty which occurred a thousand years ago, it is now admitted that it was the sons of Eric the Red, an Icelandic rover of the seas, who were the first Europeans to set foot upon the American Continent.

In the year 1001 Markland and Vinland, on the American coast, were visited and named by Norse adventurers. Professor Rafn, in his narrative relating to American antiquities, published by the Antiquarian Society of Copenhagen in 1837, has vividly described this and later Norse voyages. It appears that during the year 1000 Leif, the eldest son of Eric the Red, bought a ship from a fellow-countryman named Bjorni, who had already visited Greenland. Leif besought his father to assume command of the expedition, and at first the old viking consented; but being thrown from his horse on his way to the ship, he exclaimed, "It is not ordained that I should discover any more countries than that which we now inhabit, and we should make no further attempt in company." With that he remained at home, and Leif set forth with a crew of thirty-five men, Bjorni probably acting as pilot. They first reached Newfoundland, which they found to be a plain of flat stones, covered with snow and ice. Leif called it Helluland, from *hella*, a flat stone. Next they visited Nova Scotia. They went on shore, and found a country covered with woods, with low and flat beaches of white sand. Leif said, " This land shall be named after its qualities, and called Markland " — that is, woodland. Setting sail again, they came to a place which must have been on the mainland, and on the coast of New England, but the precise point is unknown.

Some have thought that this landing of the Norsemen was at the Island of Nantucket, but others read it to mean an island and a cape on the outside of Cape Cod. Now, however, it is generally accepted that the voyage resulted in a veritable discovery of the coast of Rhode Island by the Norsemen, and that they landed at some point either in Mount Hope Bay or Narragansett Bay. The narrative states that they went up a river which came through a lake — the very description of the waters in that region. They went ashore, and built a house, in which they passed the winter. By the Scandinavian calendar which they kept, it seems that the shortest day gave the sun as rising at 7.30 a.m. and setting at 4.30 p.m., thus fixing the latitude at a little over 41°, which is equivalent to that of Mount Hope Bay. They reported that there was " no frost in winter, and little did the grass wither there," while " the nature of the country was, as they thought, so good, that cattle would not require house feeding."

One day there was great excitement in Leif's camp.

A German named Tyrker, who was Leif's foster-father, returned from an expedition, gesticulating wildly, and almost beside himself. When he was able to give a rational account of his proceedings, he said, "I have not been much farther off, but still I have something to tell of: I found vines and grapes!" "But is that true, my fosterer?" enquired Leif. "Surely it is true," replied he, "for I was bred up in a land where there is no want of either vines or grapes." The German's statements were verified, and the land was named Vinland, or Vineland. With his vessel full of grapes and timber, Leif returned home in the spring; and because of these discoveries, and his rescue of a shipwrecked crew, the leader was known ever afterwards as Leif the Lucky.

In the following year, 1002, Leif's brother Thorvald set forth on a New England expedition. He pursued his brother's tracks, spent the winter in the booths which his brother had constructed, and in the spring despatched some of his men on explorations to the westward. According to the American historians Messrs. Bryant and Gay, "they spent the summer in this pleasant excursion, coasting along the shores of Rhode Island, Connecticut, and Long Island, the whole length of the Sound, penetrating probably to New York, and finding there another lake, through which a river flowed to the sea. They landed on many islands; they beached their boat many times on the broad, wide, shallow sands, down to the edge of which grew the green grass and the great trees which made this pleasant land seem a very garden to these wanderers from a country all rocks and ice-mountains and fields of snow. But once only did they see any sign of human habitation, and that was a corn-shed built of wood.

"The next spring (1004) Thorvald started for a more extended trip, as he went in his ship. Standing first eastward, he then sailed northward along the sea-coast of Cape Cod, where a heavy storm caught him off a ness (cape), and drove his ship ashore, perhaps at Race Point. Here they remained a long time to repair damages, putting in a new keel; the old one they set up in the sand, and the place they called Kjalarness (Keelness or Kellcape), in commemoration of the disaster. Then they cruised along the opposite shore of what is now Plymouth County, Massachusetts, and sailed into its bays till they came to 'a point of land which stretched out and was covered with wood.' 'Here,' said Thorvald, 'it is beautiful, and here I would like to raise my dwelling.'

"Before the day was out he looked upon his words as prophetic.

"For the first time the Northmen here met with the natives — met them as Europeans so often did in subsequent centuries. Looking about them at this beautiful spot, they saw in a secluded nook three skin-boats set up as tents, beneath which were nine Skraellings, on whom they stole unawares, and captured eight of them. The ninth escaped; the eight they immediately killed in cold blood. This cruel deed done, they lay down to sleep upon the grass under the trees; but it was not to pleasant dreams. There came a shout over them, so that they all awoke.

"Thus said the shout, 'Wake thou, Thorvald! and all thy companions, if thou wilt preserve life, and return to thy ship with all thy men, and leave the land without delay.' It was the savage war-whoops of the enraged Skraellings, come to avenge the murder of their fellows. The Northmen fled to their ship to defend themselves behind their battle-screen.

"'Fight little against them,' was Thorvald's order, mindful now of the mercy he should have shown before. When the fight was over, and the Skraellings had retired, the answer to Thorvald's enquiry as to who was wounded was, 'None.' Then said he, 'I have gotten a wound under the arm, for an arrow fled between the edge of the ship and the shield, in under my arm, and here is the arrow, and it will prove a mortal wound to me. Now counsel I ye, that ye get ready instantly to depart, but ye shall bear me to that cape where I thought it best to dwell; it may be that a true word fell from my mouth, that I should dwell there for a time; there shall ye bury me, and set up crosses at my head and feet, and call the place Krossaness for ever in all time to come.' And it was as he said; he died, and they buried him on the pleasant cape that looked out upon the shores and waters of Massachusetts Bay. At his head and feet they planted crosses, and then sailed back to Vinland to their companions with the heavy tidings of the death of their young commander. In the spring the colony, with another load of grapes and timber, returned to Greenland."

A third son of Eric the Red, Thorstein, sailed for Vinland in 1005, but his expedition was unsuccessful, and he returned to Greenland to die. Two years later a more important venture was made by an Icelandic merchant of much wealth and ancient lineage named Thorfinn. He was surnamed Karlsefne, or the man of promise destined to become great. He had married Gudrid, the widow of Thorstein. An expedition was formed, consisting of Karlsefne's own vessel, a second Icelandic vessel fitted out by three other merchants, and a third vessel commanded by a Greenlander named Thorvard, who had married Freydis, a natural daughter of Eric the Red, and one destined to play a conspicuous part in colonization. The expedition, which consisted of three ships and one hundred and forty men and women, set sail in the spring of 1007, with the evident intention of making a permanent settlement in the new country. They visited Markland and Helluland, and went beyond Cape Cod. Two Scotch scouts were sent out—slaves, fleet of foot, who had been given to Leif the Lucky by the King of Norway—and these returned, bearing respectively a bunch of grapes and an ear of corn. The fleet next reached Nantucket, or Martha's Vineyard, where eider-ducks were found in abundance. During the following winter there was great scarcity of provisions, and one Thorhall, "a bad Christian," who had formerly been steward to Eric the Red, abandoned the expedition, and returned home, inducing nine others to do the same. Thorhall and his companions fared badly, however, for they were driven ashore by a strong gale on the coast of Ireland, and seized by the natives, and sold into slavery. Meanwhile Karlsefne and his companions proceeded to explore the coast of Rhode Island, following in the track of Leif. They spent a winter in Vinland, and it was so mild that there was no snow upon the ground, and the cattle were able to feed upon the green and juicy grasses of the fields. In the spring they went away; but returning in 1009, they began to trade with the natives, the Skraellings. Quarrels at length ensued with the natives, and we read of one great battle in which the wife of Thorvard exhibited great bravery, and caused the Skraellings to flee to their canoes. But the settlers grew weary of the place, and in the spring of 1010 Karlsefne's efforts at colonization were wholly abandoned. Two native boys whom they took with them spoke of a country south of Vinland known as the White Man's Land, which was supposed to extend from Chesapeake Bay to East Florida, and to be peopled by a colony of Irish.

The first European child born on the American continent was Snorri, the son of Karlsefne and Gudrid, who first saw the light in Vinland 1007 A.D. As predicted by Gudrid's former husband, a long line of distinguished descendants sprang from him, and among the later descendants of Snorri were Thorvaldsen, the eminent Danish sculptor, and Finn Magnusson, the distinguished Danish scholar.

In the year 1011 the savage and fearless Freydis, who had long been determined to make another expedition into Vinland, set forth upon a new undertaking with two Icelanders named Helgi and Finnbogi. There were two vessels, each bearing thirty fighting men. The Icelanders first landed, and stored their goods in Leif's booths; but they were dispossessed by the crafty Freydis, who had secreted five more fighting men in her vessel beyond the number agreed upon. Still peace was kept for a time; but in the end the evil machinations of Freydis, who was a kind of Lady Macbeth, led to a terrible tragedy. She made her credulous husband believe that she had been beaten and shamefully used by the Icelanders when she went to negotiate for their vessel, and she spurred Thorvard on to a frightful revenge. He and his people slew Helgi and Finnbogi and all their companions in cold blood. Five women indeed they spared; but when Freydis beheld this, she took an axe and did not rest until she had slain all the women by her own hand. She moreover threatened to kill any of her own band who revealed what had taken place after their return to Greenland. With this ill-fated expedition the colonization by the Northmen in Vinland comes practically to an end.

There are cumulative proofs that the Northmen did effect a settlement on the American coast. Among these are the Icelandic Sagas, whose general drift there is no reason to distrust. Also Adam of Bremen, an ecclesiastical historian, writing about the middle of the eleventh century, has a passage in which he avers that the King of Denmark informed him "that a region called Vinland had been found by many in that ocean, because there vines grew spontaneously, making the best wine; for that fruits grow there which were not planted, we know, not by mere rumour, but by the positive report of the Danes." Further, there are the narratives published by the Northern Antiquarian Society of Denmark, which narratives were originally written between the years 1387 and 1395. These chronicles furnish unimpeachable evidence as to the early discovery of portions of North America.

Of voyages westward before the time of Columbus there are also various traditions in existence. When Lisbon was still held by the Arabs, it is stated that eight hardy and well-instructed Arabian sailors "determined to explore that mighty and mysterious ocean which stretched from the coast of Portugal to the setting sun, on whose western horizon no sail ever crept up against the sky, or disappeared from sight beneath its waters." They navigated the ocean many days, and at last landed upon an island, where they were all made prisoners and taken before the king of the country, who ridiculed their hazardous exploit. Subsequently they were carried out to sea in a boat, and abandoned. They drifted on to the coast of Africa, and ultimately returned to Lisbon, where they became known as "the strayed ones." It is conjectured that these adventurous men must have landed first at the Madeira group of islands, and afterwards on those of Cape Verde.

Another tradition is to the effect that Madoc, a Welsh prince, discovered America about the year 1170. The story rests upon the authority of two Welsh bards, Guttun Owen and Cynfrig ab Gronow, who copied the details from old chronicles of the thirteenth century, which were kept in the Abbeys of Conway and Strat Flur. The assertion that Madoc visited America is not generally accepted as authentic, though a careful writer like Humboldt says of similar traditions, "I do not share the scorn with which national traditions are too often treated, and am of the opinion that with more research the discovery of facts, entirely unknown, would throw much light on many historical problems." Various narratives have been published claiming that traces exist of Welshmen among the Doegs, Mandans, and Mound-builders of North America. They are, however, inconclusive and contradictory, and are partially due to the fact that there was a resemblance between certain Welsh words and others used by the Indians. Madoc is alleged to have proceeded from Wales to the westward, leaving Ireland to the north; and if he really did make the voyage attributed to him, and settled with his companions in a new land, it is probable that it was not Florida—as supposed—but one of the Azores or the West India Islands.

A story of more plausibility and of greater interest is that associated with the names of two Venetians, Nicolo and Antonio Zeno, who are stated to have reached the New World upwards of a century before Columbus. The Zeno family were of noble origin, and had done much valorous service for the State. It is strange, however, that no claim was put forward for the brothers Zeno as American discoverers until the middle of the sixteenth century, when the fame of Columbus and his successors had become well assured. It appears that there was published at Venice in 1558 a volume of letters, edited by one Nicolo Zeno, and purporting to be letters written by his ancestors Nicolo and Antonio Zeno between the years 1380 and 1404. These records were subsequently included in Ramusio's *History of Early Voyages*, but not until after his death, and Hakluyt further translated and adopted them. The opinion of geographers has been very much divided as to whether the story of the brothers Zeno was a fraud or not. Among those who believed the narrative to be genuine, however, was Reinholdt Forster, author of the *Northern Voyages*, and his view has been adopted by Mr. R. H. Major in a work published by the Hakluyt Society.

The narrative is to the effect that in the year 1380 Nicolo Zeno, who was of an adventurous disposition, and wealthy, fitted out a vessel at his own cost, and sailed away northward towards England. He was cast away upon an inhospitable island, where he and his crew were attacked by the natives. They were saved by the king of the neighbouring island of Porland, who invited them to enter his service. This they did, and Nicolo sent home for his brother Antonio. The name of the king was Zichmui, and the island was called Frisland. If it ever existed, it has long ceased to do so; but those who give credence to the narrative suppose that it must have been one of the Faroe Islands. Nicolo remained with Zichmui four years, and then died; but Antonio remained for ten years. Nicolo assisted in subjugating several of the islands in the Icelandic Archipelago, and he also voyaged as far westward as Engroneland, which is taken to refer to Greenland. There he found a monastery of friars of the order of the Preachers, and a church dedicated to St. Thomas. There were also ingenious hot-water works, supplied from a geyser, which provided heat both for cooking and warmth. Strange to say, these facts were corroborated nearly two centuries later by two independent authorities —. Dethmar Blefkins, a German minister sent from Iceland to Hamburg in 1563, and an English sailor, Jacob or James Hall, who was in the service of Denmark, and who made several voyages to Iceland and Greenland.

After the death of Nicolo, there arrived in Frisland an ancient fisherman who related to the king marvellous adventures in foreign lands. Many years before, four fisher-boats from Frisland were driven by a mighty tempest one thousand miles to the westward, and one of them, bearing the narrator and his companions, was wrecked upon an island called Estotiland, supposed to be Newfoundland. The shipwrecked crew lived amongst the natives for five years, and found them to be highly civilized, while the land was a goodly one. To the southward they discovered another great and prosperous country, peopled by a maritime race, who assisted the adventurers in going still farther south to a land called Drogeo. Here, however, the natives were dark, fierce, and cruel, and they have been identified by some as the forerunners of the later Indians in the United States. Farther again to the south-west a more cultured race were found, and these are supposed to have been the people of Mexico, who enjoyed a high degree of civilization. If these statements are to be relied upon, the Norsemen would seem to have travelled down the Atlantic coast, and along the whole of the northern and part of the western coast of the Gulf of Mexico. But such a pre-dating of Columbus and the other great navigators can scarcely be accepted as genuine.

Still, fired by what he had heard, we are assured that Zichmui fitted out a large expedition, which he commanded himself, and which set out for the westward. First, they came to an island called Icaria, the people being named Icari, after the first king of the place, who was alleged to be the son of Dædalus, a king of Scotland. The prince several times attempted to effect a landing, but the people were extremely hostile, and repulsed him. Zichmui consequently left Icaria, and steered farther to the westward. After some days they made a harbour, round a neck of land, which they called Capo di Trin. The people of the land were small in stature, and dwelt in caves. There was an active volcano in the centre of the island. Zichmui determined to remain; but he sent Antonio Zeno back to Frisland, with most of the sailors who had accompanied him. Here all knowledge of the prince ends, and nothing is known as to what became of him.

The geographical objections to this story are regarded as insurmountable. "It is difficult to believe," as Messrs. Bryant and Gay justly remark, "that any actual navigator should have described so many islands that had no existence in the places where he put them, both in the narrative and on a map; and quite as hard to believe that they have all been since sunk in the sea, if they ever had an existence. If it is assumed that the requisite number, and the conquest and discovery of those referred to, may be found by looking for them among the Faroe Islands, the Orkneys, or the Hebrides, it is hard to reconcile such a supposition with the known facts of history: that Norway, at the end of the fourteenth century, was governed, not by a king, but by a queen, Margaret; that the Orkneys and Shetland Isles were never wrested from that crown, but belonged to it till late in the fifteenth century; that Henry Sinclair, Earl of Orkney, held possession of the islands of that name as a loyal subject of Norway at the very time that Zichmui is said to have conquered Frisland; that the Hebrides have been in continual possession of Scotland since the latter part of the thirteenth century. While it is exceedingly difficult to adjust the main statements of the narrative to any reasonable theory consistent with their truth, the meagre information it gives in regard to the Western Continent was possibly accessible from various sources when the letters were published. The most rational conclusion, therefore, seems to be that if the story were not a clumsy attempt to patch up an account of a voyage, some record of which had been retained in mutilated and unintelligible fragments of old letters, then it was a bold, but still clumsy, fabrication, whereby it was hoped that the glory of the great discovery might be snatched from Spain and Columbus. In nothing, in either case, is that clumsiness so apparent as in the adaptation of the Grecian names and fables of Dædalus and Icarus to persons and places in the frozen North."

One more claim to early American exploration — and that more ancient than any which have been discussed — remains to be considered. The Chinese Year-books, in which the events of many centuries are recorded, affirm that a Buddhist priest named Hoei-shin voyaged many thousands of miles in the year 499 A.D., and came to a country which he called Fusang. Conjectures have been raised whether the land referred to was Alaska, Kamtchatka, or Siberia. The traveller found a cultured people, who used as beasts of burden horses, oxen, and stags, which were harnessed to waggons. Copper, gold, and silver were plentiful, but little valued. There was a king entitled Ichi, and a nobility; and the people were peaceable. They were all Buddhists, for they had been converted by five beggar-monks about thirty years before.

While it is quite possible that Chinese navigators may thus early have sailed across the Pacific Ocean, the best Oriental scholars have come to the conclusion that the author of this remarkable narrative was neither more nor less than a Chinese Ananias. Yet there are a few who think it possible that the traveller reached Mexico, while others have fixed the territory described as the Island of Saghalien or Japan. But the whole story is so disjointed and imperfect that it is the wisest policy to regard it as fictitious. Certainly, history must be based upon sounder facts and conclusions than we have here.

Thus far much of our information concerning the exploration of the American Continent is speculative, though there is undoubtedly mixed with it the element of truth. That the Norsemen explored portions of North America in the eleventh and twelfth centuries is unquestionable, but no permanent result followed their labours. The world soon forgot them and their voyages, and nothing more was done until the Spanish Peninsula took the lead by sending its citizens forth into unknown seas, in quest of the El Dorado which was believed to exist beyond the golden gate of the New World.

CHAPTER II.

THE VOYAGES OF COLUMBUS.

IN Christopher Columbus we have one of the great makers of the world's history. Unworthy attempts have sometimes been made to deprive him of the glory due to his name, but they have all signally failed; and it may be assumed that his claims as the first real discoverer of the American Continent will now go down unchallenged till the end of time.

The birthplace of Homer has been warmly contested, and it is a singular circumstance that neither the place of Columbus's nativity nor the year of his birth can be positively and absolutely assigned. But the best authorities, including his descendant the Duke de Veragua, believe that his birth occurred about the year 1436, though other investigators give the date as about ten years later. To the city of Genoa is generally awarded the honour of having given birth to the great discoverer, and this conclusion is supported by the discovery of the will in which Columbus bequeathed part of his property to the Bank of Genoa. "Thence I came, and there was I born," he has himself said.

From the fact that his father was one Domenico Colombo, a wool-comber, his humble origin has always been inferred; and the explorer's son Ferdinand, in his biography of his father, gives very meagre details of his early life. But Sir Arthur Helps has pointed out that the family were not necessarily of very humble origin, seeing that Genoa was a city of traders; and indeed two of Christopher's ancestors were naval commanders of distinction in the maritime service of Genoa and France. No doubt there was but little wealth in the family, but it had honourable traditions. The name of Christopher Columbus is the Latinized form of the Italian Cristoforo Colombo, and when the discoverer went to Spain he adopted the Spanish form of it, Cristobal Colon.

In early life Christopher laboured at his father's trade of wool-combing, but he also attended school for a time, and was likewise for a brief period a student at the University of Pavia, where he was grounded in a knowledge of mathematics and natural science. But the sea was from the first his great object of ambition, and he entered upon his adventurous career when only in his fifteenth year. He was doubtless fired by the deeds of Prince Henry, the famous navigator.

Prince Henry was, up to the appearance of Columbus, the most celebrated of modern explorers. He was a son of John I. of Portugal and Philippa, the daughter of John of Gaunt, Duke of Lancaster. He was born in 1394, and first distinguished himself at the conquest of Ceuta in 1415. But from this time forth his thoughts were taken up with maritime discovery, and it was while prosecuting the war against the Moors of Africa that his sailors reached parts of the ocean heretofore unvisited and unknown. The Prince fixed his abode at Sagres, in Algarve, near Cape St. Vincent, and here he erected an observatory, to which he attached a school for the instruction of sons of the nobility in the sciences necessary to navigation. Many of his pupils were despatched on voyages of discovery, and these resulted at last in the discovery of the Madeira Islands in 1418. But the discovery was not of much value for a long time; for the settlers, in clearing the wood, kindled a fire which burned, it is said, for seven years. The Prince's thoughts were next directed towards the auriferous coasts of Guinea, of which he had gained some knowledge from the Moors; and in 1433 one of his mariners sailed round Cape Nun, until then regarded as the farthest point of the earth, and took possession of the coasts as far south as Cape Bojador.

In 1434 the Prince sent forth a larger vessel than any which he had as yet fitted out. It first touched a point one hundred and twenty miles beyond Cape Bojador, and ultimately, in 1440, Cape Blanco was reached. Henry had up to this period borne all the expense of his undertakings himself; but henceforth self-supporting societies were formed under his patronage and guidance, and the whole nation was at last moved with enthusiasm in a cause which at first was treated with studious neglect. At the same time the Prince did not relax his own efforts, and in 1446 one of his captains, Nuno Tristam, doubled Cape Verde, in Senegambia, while two years later Gonzalez Vallo discovered three of the Azores. The

Pope, Martin V., had already granted to the Portuguese Crown all the possessions which should be conquered from Cape Bojador to the Indies, together with plenary indulgence for those who should die while engaged in such conquests. The terms of this grant, however, were modified after the Spanish discoveries of Columbus and his successors.

Prince Henry always had the Indies in view, as a land of unparalleled wealth and splendour. Visions of it rose before him again and again, but he was not destined to discover the far-famed Khubla Khan. He died in 1460, after learning with satisfaction the news that his mariners had reached as far south as Sierra Leone. One writer remarks that Prince Henry was "hardly a less personage than Columbus. They had different elements to contend in. But the man whom princely wealth and position, and the temptation to intrigue which there must have been in the then state of the Portuguese Court, never induced to swerve from the one purpose which he maintained for forty years, unshaken by popular clamour, however sorely vexed he might be with inward doubts and misgivings ; who passed laborious days and watchful nights in devotion to this one purpose, enduring the occasional short-comings of his agents with that forbearance which springs from a care for the enterprise in hand, so deep as to control private vexation (the very same motive which made Columbus bear so mildly with insult and contumely from his followers),—such a man is worthy to be put in comparison with the other great discoverer who worked out his enterprise through poverty, neglect, sore travail, and the vicissitudes of courts. Moreover, it must not be forgotten that Prince Henry was undoubtedly the father of modern geographical discovery, and that the result of his exertions must have given much impulse to Columbus, if it did not first move him to his great undertaking. After the above eulogium on Prince Henry, which is not the least more than he merited, his kinsmen, the contemporary Portuguese monarchs, should come in for their share of honourable mention, as they seem to have done their part in African discovery with much vigour, without jealousy of Prince Henry, and with high and noble aims. It would also be but just to include, in some part of this praise, the many brave captains who distinguished themselves in these enterprises."

Columbus was imbued by the same idea as Prince Henry. From the first it was the gorgeous Eastern empire which he had in view, and it was his main object, even when his discoveries resulted in a wholly different way from what he anticipated. Returning to the period of his youth, we find that he was a fighting adventurer, like most of the mariners of his time, and among other expeditions he engaged in was one against Naples while in the service of the good King René, Count of Provence. On one occasion he was sent by René to Tunis to intercept a Venetian galley. The crew were unwilling to hazard an engagement when they learnt that the galley was convoyed by three other vessels. Columbus feigned to acquiesce in their view, but he so artfully altered his compass that the vessel succeeded in its purpose, and arrived at Carthagena the following morning, when the crew expected to put in at Marseilles.

There are years in his life concerning which information is scant; but we know that a man of his temperament could never remain idle. As he himself said in middle life, "I have been seeking out the secrets of nature for forty years, and wherever ship has sailed there have I voyaged." In course of time he traversed a large part of the known world, visiting England, and making his way to Iceland and Friesland. For a time Columbus was actually engaged in selling books in Genoa, but about the year 1470 he arrived at Lisbon. His son states that he had sailed with Colombo el Mozo—nephew of the first admiral in the Colon family—on a cruise to intercept some Venetian merchantmen on their way home from Flanders. A battle began at break of day, off Cape St. Vincent, which lasted till nightfall. The vessel on which Columbus held command engaged a huge Venetian galley, which after a desperate struggle caught fire. The flames spread to the privateer, and the combatants on both sides sought safety in the sea. Columbus managed to support himself on an oar, and though almost exhausted he succeeded in gaining the land, which was about six miles distant. As his son remarked, God preserved him for greater things.

A few years after this he met and married Donna Felipa, daughter of an Italian named Parestrello, who had been governor of Porto Santo under Prince Henry. Columbus retired for awhile to this island of Porto Santo, where his wife had inherited a small property, and where their son Diego was born. He studied the papers and maps left by his father-in-law, and was constantly brought into association with persons interested in maritime discovery. The precise date when he conceived the design of discovering, not a new continent, but a western route to Asia, cannot be determined, but it was probably about 1474. We have now to picture him during a period of ten years making proposals of discovery to Genoa, Portugal, Venice, France, and England. His ideas were regarded by several of these governments as the extravagant demands of a mere adventurer. The King of Portugal, however, did incline a favourable ear to him. He referred the project to a maritime junta and his committee of council on geographical affairs; and when both bodies reported it as visionary, he sent out a caravel, under the pretext of taking provisions to the Cape de Verde Islands, but with secret instructions to try the route proposed by Columbus. This act of treachery was due to the Bishop of Ceuta, the chief opponent of Columbus in the council. The pilots, after sailing several days, lost courage, and returned with the report that no indications of land had been seen. The King was still not inclined to give up the scheme, although it had been mercilessly ridiculed by his council and other sceptics.

Columbus, however, perceiving at last that there was no hope, and having lost his wife and property, left Lisbon for Spain, accompanied by his son Diego, the only issue left by his wife Donna Felipa. He applied to the rich and powerful Spanish Dukes of Medina Sidonia and Medina Celi. The latter grandee maintained Columbus for two years in his house, and would have entertained his proposal himself but that he thought it belonged to the Queen to do so. The Duke accordingly gave Columbus a letter to the Queen commending the enterprise, but the times were unpropitious, for Spain was engaged in a deadly war with the Moors. But the adventurer found a friend in the Treasurer of the Household, Alonzo de Quintanilla, who obtained a hearing for him from the Spanish monarchs. Ferdinand and Isabella listened with interest, and the matter was referred to the Queen's Confessor, Fra Hernando de Talavera, who was afterwards Archbishop of Granada. Fra Hernando summoned a junta of cosmographers, which was convened at Salamanca in the summer of 1487. So far everything seemed promising, but the prejudices of centuries were rooted in the breasts of the cosmographers. The members of the junta were chiefly clerical, and they bombarded Columbus with theological objections. They cited Scripture to refute his theory of the spherical nature of the earth, and invoked the Fathers of the Church to overthrow the "foolish idea of the existence of antipodes ; of people who walk, opposite to us, with their heels upwards and their heads hanging down ; where everything is topsy-turvy, where the trees grow with their branches downwards, and where it rains, hails, and snows upwards." Finally, the bigoted junta decided that the project was "vain and impossible, and that it did not belong to the majesty of such great princes to determine anything upon such weak grounds of information."

Ferdinand and Isabella do not seem to have agreed with the junta on the scientific aspect of the question;

and desiring to dismiss Columbus gently, "they merely said that, with the wars at present on their hands, and especially that of Granada, they could not undertake any new expenses; but when that war was ended, they would examine his plan more carefully."

For five weary years, according to some authorities, Columbus waited upon the Court of Spain. He was treated with consideration, although he did not gain his grand object, and he followed the sovereigns in their war movements. He was regarded as a public functionary, and received grants from the treasury for his private expenses. But Las Casas, who knew something of neglect and contumely, speaks of the "terrible, continuous, painful, prolix battle" which Columbus waged with adverse circumstances. His heart, however, was cheered by the devotion of his second wife, Beatriz Enriquez, whom he met and married at Cordova. Their union appears to have been an extremely happy one, and there is no evidence that Beatriz ever attempted to dissuade her husband from his great purpose.

Columbus further met with a powerful friend in Juan Perez de la Marchena, Superior of the Monastery of La Kabida, in Andalusia. This excellent man became so deeply interested in his friend's glorious project that he detained him as a guest, and sent for the learned physician of Palos, Garcia Hernandez, to discuss the scheme. Now, for the first time, it was listened to with admiration, and it also seems to have greatly impressed Alonzo Pinzon, the chief ship-owner of Palos. Dr. Hernandez, who was skilled in physical science, appears to have become a warm admirer of Columbus and his project. Sir Arthur Helps observes :

"It is worthy of notice that a person who appears only once, as it were, in a sentence in history should have exercised so much influence upon it as Garcia Hernandez, who was probably a man of far superior attainments to those around him, and was in the habit of deploring, as such men do, his hard lot in being placed where he could be so little understood. Now, however, he was to do more at one stroke than many a man who has been all his days before the world. Columbus had abandoned his suit at Court in disgust, and had arrived at the monastery before quitting Spain to fetch his son Diego, whom he had left with Juan Perez to be educated. All his griefs and struggles he confided to Perez, who could not bear to hear of his intention to leave the country for France or England, and to make a foreign nation greater by allowing it to adopt his project. The three friends—the monk, the learned physician, and the skilled cosmographer —discussed together the propositions so unhappily familiar to the last-named member of their little council. The affection of Juan Perez and the learning of Hernandez were not slow to follow in the track which the enthusiasm of the great adventurer made out before them; and they became, no doubt, as convinced as Columbus himself of the feasibility of his undertaking. The difficulty, however, was not in becoming believers themselves, but in persuading those to believe who would have power to further the enterprise. Their discussions upon this point ended in the conclusion that Juan Perez, who was known to the Queen, having acted as her confessor, should write to her Highness. He did so, and the result was favourable. The Queen sent for him, heard what he had to say, and in consequence remitted money to Columbus to enable him to come to Court and renew his suit. He attended the Court again; negotiations were resumed, but were again broken off on the ground of the largeness of the conditions which he asked for. His opponents said that these conditions were too large if he succeeded; and if he should not succeed, and the conditions should come to nothing, they thought that there was an air of trifling in granting such conditions at all. And, indeed, they were very large—namely, that he was to be made an admiral at once, to be appointed viceroy of the countries he should discover, and to have an eighth of the profits of the expedition. The only probable way of accounting for the extent of these demands, and his perseverance in making them, even to the risk of total failure, is that the discovering of the Indies was but a step in his mind to greater undertakings, as they seemed to him, which he had in view, of going to Jerusalem with an army and making another crusade. For Columbus carried the chivalrous ideas of the twelfth century into the somewhat self-seeking fifteenth."

Again the negotiations failed, however, and Columbus had resolved to set out for France, when Juan Perez and Alonzo de Quintanilla procured him a hearing from Cardinal Mendoza. The Cardinal favoured the scheme, and Columbus offered to pay an eighth part of the expenses of the expedition, hoping this would conciliate his opponents; but all was in vain. It was now January, 1492; and the great adventurer, seeing his cause to be hopeless in Spain, actually started for France. This at once determined Luis de Santangel, receiver of ecclesiastical revenues of the Crown of Aragon, and one strongly on the side of Columbus, to throw himself at the feet of Queen Isabella. This he did, and addressed her with great fervour, lamenting that her lofty desire for great things should be wanting on this occasion, and hinting that the enterprise might fall under the patronage of other princes. He made light of the vaticinations of the cosmographers, and extolled Columbus as a man of great ideas. Some princes had already acquired lasting fame in this way. Finally, he pointed out that the whole cost of the expedition would only be a million of maravedis— equal to about £308 of the current English coinage —and the undertaking ought not to be abandoned for so small a sum. Quintanilla supported these arguments, and Isabella yielded, but she said that the enterprise must wait until the war drain upon the finances had ceased, or she would pledge her jewels to raise the necessary funds if the scheme must be carried out at once.

Santangel himself agreed to advance the money required, and the Queen despatched a messenger to bring back Columbus to the Court. He was overtaken about two leagues from Granada, and returned to Santa Fé, where the sovereigns were encamped. He was well received by Isabella, though not very warmly by Ferdinand, and an agreement was drawn up by the royal secretary Coloma. King Ferdinand seems to have been imbued with the careful views of Henry VII., who temporized with Christopher's brother, Bartholomew Columbus, when he endeavoured to enlist English sympathy for the same project. Although Bartholomew was unsuccessful, however, there was plenty of English enterprise even before Columbus. A letter written by the Spanish ambassador in London, in July, 1498, stated that merchants of Bristol had for the past seven years sent out annually ships in search of the Island of Brazil and the Seven Cities. If true, this is extremely interesting, for it would show that England was already searching for the New World, though unsuccessfully, before the first voyage of Columbus.

Matters being satisfactorily arranged between Ferdinand and Isabella and Columbus, an agreement to the following effect was concluded:

"The favours which Christopher Columbus has asked from the King and Queen of Spain, in recompense of the discoveries which he has made in the ocean seas, and as recompense for the voyage which he is about to undertake, are the following:

"1. He wishes to be made admiral of the seas and countries which he is about to discover. He desires to hold this dignity during his life, and that it should descend to his heirs.

"*This request is granted* by the King and Queen.

"2. Christopher Columbus wishes to be made viceroy of all the continents and islands.

"*Granted by the King and* Queen.

"3. He wishes to have a share, amounting to a tenth part, of the profits of all merchandise, be it pearls, jewels, or any other things, that may be found, gained, bought, or exported from the countries which he is to discover.

"*Granted by the King and Queen.*

"4. He wishes in his quality of admiral to be made sole judge of all mercantile matters that may be the occasion of dispute in the countries which he is to discover.

"*Granted by the King and Queen, on the condition, however, that this jurisdiction should belong to the office of admiral, as held by Don Enriquez and other admirals.*

"5. Christopher Columbus wishes to have the right to contribute the eighth part of the expenses of all ships which traffic with the new countries, and in return to earn the eighth part of the profits.

"*Granted by the King and Queen.*

"SANTA FÉ, IN THE VEGA OF GRANADA,
"*April* 17, 1492."

This agreement is signed by the secretary Coloma and written by Almazan.

Then there is a sort of passport or commendatory letter, intended for presentation to the Grand Khan, Prester John, or any other Oriental potentate at whose territories Columbus might arrive:

"FERDINAND AND ISABELLA TO KING ——,

"The sovereigns have heard that he and his subjects entertain great love for them and for Spain. They are, moreover, informed that he and his subjects very much wish to hear news from Spain; and send, therefore, their admiral, Christopher Columbus, who will tell them that they are in good health and perfect prosperity.

"GRANADA, *April* 30, 1492."

In redeeming his promise, Santangel, in May, 1492, advanced one million one hundred and forty thousand maravedis, "being the sum he lent for paying the caravels which their Highnesses ordered to go as the armada to the Indies, and for paying Christopher Columbus, who goes in the said armada." The municipality of Palos was requisitioned for two vessels, being in disgrace with the council, and a proclamation of immunity from civil and criminal process was issued to persons taking part in the expedition. This addition of criminals and runaway debtors to his crew formed in itself a difficulty for Columbus. Then the mariners of Palos of the better class held aloof, and it required all the persuasion of Juan Perez and the Pinzons before the undertaking was completed. At length three vessels were manned with ninety mariners, and provisioned for a year. The ships were small, probably not exceeding one hundred tons burden each—light craft with which to brave the dangers of the Atlantic. Columbus commanded the *Santa Maria*, which was the only vessel decked throughout; and the others were the *Pinta*, commanded by Martin Alonzo Pinzon, and the *Niña*, commanded by Vicente Yanez Pinzon.

It must have been a memorable day when the crews, having been confessed, set sail on the 3rd of August, 1492, from the Bar of Saltes, with the intention of making for the Canary Islands. The ideas of the commander were unfathomable to many of the men, and distrusted by others. The convoy safely reached the Canary Islands; but here the admiral—for such henceforth Columbus is styled—was obliged to remain for some time, refitting the *Pinta*, which had unshipped her rudder, etc. But on the 6th of September the squadron set sail from Gomera. In the course of a week the variations of the needle began to cause the crews much concern, and they were further disturbed by having to cut their way through immense plains of seaweed. Columbus was sometimes obliged to use subterfuge to keep them on their course. Land was occasionally seen; but as the admiral believed it to belong only to a group of islands, he determined to press on for the Indies. Yet some of the sailors had already come to the conclusion "that it would be their best plan to throw him quietly into the sea, and say he unfortunately fell in, while he stood absorbed in looking at the stars." Las Casas reports Columbus as saying, " Very needful for me was this contrary wind, for the people were very much tormented with the idea that there were no winds on these seas that could take them back to Spain."

Then there came delusive signs of land, which the presence of birds and fish served to intensify. But no land appeared, and the mariners began to give way to despair. Columbus is found saying on the 3rd of October, "that he did not choose to stop beating about last week during those days that they had such signs of land, although he had knowledge of there being certain islands in that neighbourhood, because he would not suffer any detention, since his object was to go to the Indies; and if he should stop on the way, it would show a want of mind." It was a time of severe trial for Columbus, who was surrounded by a mocking band on the verge of mutiny. "At last came the 11th of October, and with it indubitable signs of land. The diary mentions their finding on that day a table-board and a carved stick, the carving apparently wrought by some iron instrument. Moreover, the men in one of the vessels saw a branch of a haw tree with fruit on it. Now, indeed, they must be close to land. The sun went down upon the same weary round of waters which for so long a time their eyes had ached to see beyond, when, at ten o'clock, Columbus, standing on the poop of his vessel, saw a light, and called to him, privately, Pedro Gutierrez, a groom of the King's Chamber, who saw it also. Then they called Rodrigo Sanchez, who had been sent by their Highnesses as overlooker. I imagine him to have been a cold and cautious man, of the kind that are sent by jealous states to accompany and curb great generals, and who are not usually much loved by them. Sanchez did not see the light at first, because, as Columbus says, he did not stand in the place where it could be seen; but at last even he sees it, and it may now be considered to have been seen officially. It appeared like a candle that went up and down, and Don Christopher did not doubt that it was true light, and that it was on land; and so it proved, as it came from people passing with lights from one cottage to another."

A pension of ten thousand maravedis had been promised by Ferdinand and Isabella to the man who should first sight land. The *Pinta* being the foremost vessel, it was from her deck, at two in the morning, that one Rodrigo de Triana first saw land. For some reason or other this poor fellow did not get the reward, and it is said that he afterwards went to Africa in a fever of disappointment, and became a Mahometan. The pension was awarded to the admiral, and it was religiously paid him to the day of his death. Herrera, the historian, remarks that Columbus "saw light in the midst of darkness, signifying the spiritual light which was introduced among these barbarous people, God permitting that, the war being finished with the Moors, seven hundred and twenty years after they had set foot in Spain, this work (the conversion of the Indians) should commence, so that the Princes of Castile and Leon might always be occupied in bringing infidels to the knowledge of the Holy Catholic Faith."

This language is similar to that which Columbus himself used in a general sense, in an address to Ferdinand and Isabella, which prefaces his diary. After referring to the conclusion of the Moorish War, he reminded their Highnesses how that he had given them information of the lands of India, and of a prince called the Grand Khan, who had sent ambassadors to Rome, praying for doctors to instruct him in the faith, but that none had been sent, so that people were perishing in idolatry. He added, "Your Highnesses, as Catholic Christians and princes, lovers and furtherers of the Christian Faith, and enemies of the sect of Mahomet, and of all idolatries and heresies, thought to send me, Christopher

Columbus, to the aforesaid provinces of India to see the aforesaid princes, the cities and lands, and the disposition of them, and of everything about them, and the way that should be taken to convert them to our holy Faith." The writer likewise referred to the expulsion of the Jews from Spain as another evidence of the zeal of the Queen for the Catholic Faith. Even in the matter of slavery he perceived the same religious spirit, which permeated all the actions of Isabella. Sincere, but lamentably mistaken in some things, must be the verdict passed upon her.

Friday, the 12th of October, 1492, was an epoch-making day in the history of the human race. On that day Columbus first set foot upon one of the islands belonging to the New World. It was one of the Bahama group of islands which was thus discovered, but as to which particular island there was long great difference of opinion. Humboldt thought it was Cat Island, called by the natives Guanahavi, and by the Spaniards San Salvador. Other writers have claimed that it was on that beautiful spot where Columbus wished to be buried, and where his remains reposed for centuries—the island of St. Domingo. Later investigations certainly showed that Columbus landed on Cat, Samana, or Watling's Island. These investigations, pursued chiefly in the explorer's log-book, indicated somewhat strongly that the admiral's landing-place was the last-named island, which is regarded as the true San Salvador. There is now no reason to suppose that the world will ever arrive at a more accurate knowledge of the landing of Columbus on the American Continent.

The admiral, clad in complete armour, and carrying in his hand the royal banner of Spain, was the first to descend upon the shore of the island, which he found to be very fruitful and like a garden full of trees. The other captains closely followed him, each also bearing a banner with a green cross depicted upon it, and with the initials of Ferdinand and Isabella surmounted by their respective crowns. The islanders must have stood in silent amazement before such a visitation. We are assured that, on touching land, Columbus and all the Spaniards who were with him fell upon their knees, and with tears expressive of the deepest joy, poured forth their "immense thanksgivings to Almighty God." Then the great-hearted Columbus pardoned and comforted those who had caused him such sorrow and suffering during the voyage, and who were now filled with remorse for their murmurings and reproaches.

With all due legal formalities, Columbus took possession of the island in the name of the Spanish monarchs, and called it San Salvador. The Indians were astonished at the looks of the Spaniards and the whiteness of their skins; and more than all they marvelled at the leader of the expedition, who formed an imposing figure as he stood with a crimson scarf thrown over his armour. In giving his impressions afterwards of the islanders, Columbus wrote: "Because they had much friendship for us, and because I knew they were people that would deliver themselves better to the Christian Faith, and be converted more through love than by force, I gave to some of them some coloured caps, and some strings of glass beads for their necks, and many other things of little value, with which they were delighted, and were so entirely ours that it was a marvel to see. The same afterwards came swimming to the ships' boats where we were, and brought us parrots, cotton threads in balls, darts and many other things, and bartered them with us for things which we gave them, such as bells and small glass beads. In fine, they took and gave all of whatever they had with goodwill. But it appeared to me they were a people very poor in everything. They went totally naked, as naked as their mothers brought them into the world." The Indians were well made, yellow in colour, and of good countenances, but they painted themselves. They had no knowledge of arms; and when swords were shown to them, they took hold of them by the blades and cut themselves. Columbus came to the conclusion that "they ought to make faithful servants, and of good understanding, for I see that very quickly they repeat all that is said to them, and I believe they would easily be converted to Christianity, for it appeared to me that they had no creed."

More tractable and intelligent still were the natives found upon another island, and the admiral's scouts reported that their houses were the best they had yet seen. They were constructed like pavilions, "very large, and appeared as royal tents, without an arrangement of streets, except one here and there, and within they were very clean, and well swept, and their furniture very well arranged. All these houses were made of palm branches, and were very beautiful. Our men found in these houses many statues of women, and several heads fashioned like masks, and very well wrought. I do not know whether they have these for the love of the beautiful, or for purposes of worship." The Indians had excellent nets and fishing tackle, and there were tame birds and dogs which did not bark. Columbus adds that mermaids were found on the coasts, but they were " not so like ladies as they are painted."

This voyage resulted in a knowledge being acquired of that weed which has ever since been a source of delight to the individual and of profit to almost every European nation. Since tobacco was introduced, Europeans have cheerfully paid the taxation involved by its consumption. It appears that two discoverers whom the admiral sent out from the Puerto de Mares found the natives indulging in a peculiar kind of fumigation. They absorbed into the mouth through a charred stick the fumes of certain herbs wrapped in a dry leaf, which outer covering was called " tabaco." The Indians told Las Casas that the process took away fatigue, and he came across Spaniards addicted to the same habit on the Island of Hispaniola, who told him that they were not able to leave it off. This discovery of tobacco proved eventually more productive to the Spanish Crown than the gold discoveries of the Indies.

Columbus never lost sight of his idea of discovering Khubla Khan, the Khan of Khans. When the Indians told him of a king in the south who had much gold, and kept repeating the word "Cubanacan, Cubanacan," he concluded that they referred to the great Khan, whereas they were only speaking of the middle of Cuba. The fact is he was full of his Marco Polo and other travellers, and he determined to push his way farther south in quest of India. First he discovered a group of islands, to which he gave the name of Santa Maria de la Concepcion; then he discovered Cuba, and coasted along its north-eastern shores; and next he came to Hispaniola, which the natives called Hayti, and here he was cordially received by King Guacanagari. Hispaniola formed a central point of discovery, not only for the West Indies, but for the whole of the New World.

On one occasion, while the admiral was taking a sound and much-needed sleep on board his own vessel, the ship was allowed to drift until it grounded on a shoal. Some of the cowardly crew left by the boat, and Columbus did what he could in the emergency, until assistance arrived from the king, who was moved to tears by the misfortune. Every one was rescued, and the natives behaved most honourably in taking nothing. The admiral was much moved by the kindness of the Indians, and said, "They are a loving, uncovetous people, so docile in all things, that I assure your Highnesses I believe in all the world there is not a better people, or a better country; they love their neighbours as themselves, and they have the sweetest and gentlest way of talking in the world, and always with a smile."

Columbus determined on founding a colony in this land, "having found such goodwill and such signs of gold." The *Santa Maria*, being entirely disabled, was broken up, and with her timbers the admiral built a fort, calling it La Navidad, because he entered the port close by on Christmas Day. But he could not remain behind himself; he was naturally anxious to return to Spain, and to be the herald of his own wonderful discoveries. He left a body of his followers, to the number of forty, to guard the fort, and he charged them to do no violence, but to act as Christians.

On the 4th of January, 1493, he set sail for home in the *Niña*; but he had not gone far before he was joined by the *Pinta*, and the two vessels put into the Bay of Monte Christo together. Pinzon explained that he had been parted from Columbus by the bad weather, which had driven the *Pinta* out of sight of its leader; and the admiral, not desiring a quarrel, accepted the explanation. He was, however, convinced in his own mind of Pinzon's bad faith. The wily Pinzon had heard of an island where all the gold was, and he wanted to secure the profits of this El Dorado on his own account. He failed in his scheme, though he did secure a considerable quantity of gold through barter.

When they had refitted, the vessels set out again, coasting to the eastward of St. Domingo as far as the Gulf of Samana. Here there was a brush with the natives, which Columbus peacefully composed, compelling Pinzon at the same time to set free six natives whom he had seized for the purpose of selling into slavery. On the 16th of January the vessels resumed their course, Columbus hoping to find the island which Marco Polo had described as being peopled by Amazons. But this hope was abandoned, for the crews were homesick, and in deference to the universal wish the admiral was obliged to make for Europe. The passage was very rough, and the vessels were in danger, owing to want of ballast; but the commander, by a happy thought, ordered all the empty casks on board to be filled with water. As the weather remained tempestuous, he first invoked the aid of Heaven, and then lots were drawn as to who should perform a pilgrimage to the Shrine of Our Lady of Guadaloupe if they reached land in safety. Twice the lot fell upon the admiral, and he and all the crew made a vow to go in a penitential procession to the first church dedicated to the Virgin which they should meet with after reaching land. So violent were the gales that Columbus wrote a brief account of his voyage on parchment, which he enclosed in wax, and placed in a cask that was committed to the waves. Happily he survived to tell his own story.

On the 18th of February the vessels cast anchor off the Island of St. Mary, one of the Azores, belonging to the Portuguese. In fulfilment of their vow, the crew went barefooted and in their shirts on a pilgrimage to the Chapel of St. Mary. The governor, thinking such a seizure would gratify the Portuguese monarch, captured the whole band. Great difficulties ensued, but in the end the governor gave up his prisoners, and on the 24th the *Niña* again steered for Spain. Boisterous weather once more ensued, and the violence of the gale was such that Columbus said, "I escaped by the greatest miracle in the world." However, on the 4th of March he succeeded in anchoring in the Tagus; and having received an invitation to visit the Portuguese Court, he was received by the King with the highest honours. The latter put in a claim to the newly found countries, on the strength of the old **Papal Bull**, but Columbus repudiated it. A few days later the admiral left the Tagus for the Bar of Saltes, and reached his original starting-point at Palos on the 15th of March.

Great was the enthusiasm manifested by the inhabitants of Palos, who regarded even the humblest of the adventurers as a hero. Columbus sent a letter to Ferdinand and Isabella, who were then at Barcelona, announcing the success of his mission, and stating that he should soon present himself in person to their Highnesses. But Pinzon, the commander of the *Pinta*—which had been separated from the *Niña*—had already despatched a letter from Bayonne to the sovereigns, announcing *his* discoveries, and ignoring Columbus, whom he probably believed to have been lost at sea. The monarchs, however, sent a reply, commanding him not to appear at Court without the admiral, and this so preyed on his mind that he took to his bed and died of a broken heart.

The details furnished by the historian Herrera show what a magnificent reception was accorded to Columbus, who now " entered into the greatest reputation." Nothing could be talked of or thought about save the admiral's wonderful success. One of his biographers thus describes the memorable scene of his appearance before the Spanish monarchs :

" The Court prepared a solemn reception for the admiral at Barcelona, where the people poured out in such numbers to see him that the streets could not contain them. A triumphal procession like his the world had not yet seen ; it was a thing to make the most incurious alert, and even the sad and solitary student content to come out and mingle with the mob. The captives that accompanied a Roman general's car might be strange barbarians of a tribe from which Rome had not before had slaves. But barbarians were not unknown creatures. Here, with Columbus, were beings of a new world. Here was the conqueror, not of man, but of nature, not of flesh and blood, but of the fearful unknown, of the elements, and, more than all, of the prejudices of centuries. We may imagine the rumours that must have gone before his coming. And now he was there. Ferdinand and Isabella had their thrones placed in the presence of the assembled Court. Columbus approached the monarchs, and then, 'his countenance beaming with modest satisfaction,' knelt at the King's feet, and begged leave to kiss their Highnesses' hands.

"They gave their hands; then they bade him rise and be seated before them. He recounted briefly the events of his voyage—a story more interesting than the tale told in the Court of Dido by Æneas, like whom he had almost perished close to home—and he concluded his unpretending narrative by showing what new things and creatures he had brought with him.

"Ferdinand and Isabella fell on their knees, giving thanks to God with many tears, and then the choristers of the Royal Chapel closed the grand ceremonial by singing the Te Deum. Afterwards men walked home grave and yet happy, having seen the symbol of a great work, something to be thought over for many a generation.

"Other marks of approbation for Columbus were not wanting. The agreement between him and the sovereigns was confirmed. An appropriate coat of arms, then a thing of much significance, was granted to him in augmentation of his own. In the shield were conspicuously emblazoned the Royal Arms of Castile and Leon. Nothing can better serve to show the immense favour which Columbus had obtained at Court by his discovery than such a grant; and it is but a trifling addition to make, in recounting his new honours, that the title of Don was given to him and his descendants, and also to his brothers. He rode by the King's side; was served at table as a grandee; 'All hail!' was said to him on state occasions; and the men of his age, happy in the fact, had found out another great man to honour.

"The more prosaic part of the business had then to be attended to. The sovereigns applied to the Pope, Alexander VI., to confer on the Crowns of Castile and Leon the lands discovered and to be discovered in the Indies. To this application they soon received a favourable answer. The Pope granted to the Princes of Castile and Leon, and to their successors, the sovereign empire and principality of the Indies, and of the navigation there, with high and royal jurisdiction and imperial dignity and lordship over all that hemisphere. To preserve the peace between Spain and Portugal, the Pontiff divided the Spanish and Portuguese Indian sovereignties by an imaginary line drawn from pole to pole, one hundred leagues west of the Azores and the Cape de Verde Islands."

The nine Indians brought by Columbus were baptized at Barcelona; and as one of them died immediately afterwards, he was spoken of as the first of the Indian nation to enter heaven. A special department for the control of colonial affairs was constituted, with an eminent ecclesiastic, Juan de Fonseca, as director; but Fonseca was ill-fitted to take charge of a Christian office of this kind. He was hard, worldly, and unscrupulous, and inflicted great miseries upon the Indian race, instead of reconciling them to the sovereignty of their new masters.

Ferdinand and Isabella, moved partially by jealousy of Portugal, now hastened forward the preparations for Columbus's second voyage. On the 29th of May, 1493, he received his instructions, which ordered him to labour in all possible ways to bring the dwellers in the Indies to a knowledge of the Holy Catholic Faith. Gentleness and forbearance were to be exercised; and if any person or persons were found treating the natives harshly, they were to be severely chastised.

The new expedition was a very imposing one, for it consisted of seventeen ships and seventeen hundred men. With this armada under his command, Columbus sailed from Cadiz on the 25th of September, 1493. The ships had a fair and prosperous voyage, and sighted land on the 3rd of November, having accomplished the passage "by the goodness of God, and the wise management of the admiral, in as straight a track as if they had sailed by a well-known and frequented route." As it was Sunday, the name of Dominica was given to this first island touched at. A second island to the northward was named Maria Galante, after the admiral's flag-ship; while a third and much larger one was called Guadaloupe, after a monastery in Estremadura. This island was thickly wooded, and peopled by cannibals. Sailing then to the north-westward, Columbus passed and named in succession Montserrat, Antigua, St. Martin, and Santa Cruz. Arriving later at a lovely and fruitful island, he called it St. John, but it afterwards became known as Porto Rico. On reaching La Navidad, he was profoundly moved on discovering that the colony which he had planted had entirely disappeared. King Guacanagari told him that the Spaniards had fallen into evil courses, and quarrelled amongst themselves, so that they fell an easy prey to a neighbouring Indian chief named Caonabó, who had destroyed the fort and slain the garrison. Guacanagari was willing for another settlement to be effected, but Columbus decided upon finding another site, as the Indians, who had at first hailed the white men as angels from heaven, came to look upon them as debased profligates and disturbers of the peace.

It was on the coast of Hayti, and about forty miles to the east of Cape Haytien, that Columbus planted his new settlement, which he called Isabella, after his royal mistress. Unfortunately it was now that his troubles and anxieties began, and it was written by the finger of fate that they were only to end with his life. Disease and fatigue began to tell upon the colonists; provisions and medicines began to fail; while there was no prospect of that golden harvest which they were promised on leaving Spain. The admiral himself was made ill by his anxieties. He sent home an account of the state of the colony in January, 1494. It was placed in charge of Antonio de Torres, the Receiver of the Colony, who was to lay it before the Court of Spain and explain its details. Many of the suggestions which Columbus made were excellent, and these were at once approved by Ferdinand and Isabella. But when he went on to recommend the initiation of a slave traffic, to the eternal honour of the sovereigns they declined to accede to it. Columbus desired no doubt to improve the health and morals of the natives by capturing them and sending them abroad. "The Catholic sovereigns would have been very glad to have received some money from the Indies: money was always welcome to King Ferdinand. The purchase of wine, seeds, and cattle for the colonists had hitherto proved anything but a profitable outlay; the prospect of conversion was probably dear to the hearts of both these princes, certainly to one of them; but still this proposition for the establishment of slavery was wisely and magnanimously set aside."

Meantime the new colony soon fell into a deplorable condition. What with illness, hard work, and poor living, complaints developed into open mutiny, and Columbus was in sore straits. A rising under Bernal Diaz, a man in high authority, was summarily quelled, and Diaz was sent prisoner to Spain, there to undergo his trial. The admiral now founded a mining settlement in the district of Cibao, which he named the Fort of St. Thomas; but the mines were inefficiently worked, and proved disappointing. Knowing that the Spanish monarchs were eager for further discoveries, Columbus determined to go still farther afield. He therefore appointed a Council of Government, with his brother Don Diego as President, and Don Pedro

Margarite as Captain-General; and having done this, he sailed from Hispaniola on the 24th of April, 1494.

During this new voyage Columbus made the important discovery of Jamaica, and a number of other islands. Navigation was so dangerous that he is reported never to have slept for a whole month. Then, after leaving an island named La Mona, he fell into what his biographers call a pestilential drowsiness, which completely deprived him of his senses for a time. It was no doubt partly the result of anxiety, privation, and sickness. As the admiral's chief object in making for the Island of San Juan was to capture cannibals, Las Casas regards this lethargical attack as a judgment upon him for his arbitrary efforts in introducing Christianity. Ill and helpless, the admiral returned to Isabella on the 29th of September, and here he remained for five months, unable to move. He appears to have found consolation in the presence of his brother Bartholomew. His family affections generally indeed were very strong; and in a letter to his son Diego, exhorting him to make much of his half-brother Ferdinand, he remarked, "Ten brothers would not be too many for you. I have never found better friends, on my right hand and on my left, than my brothers."

Things looked a little brighter at Isabella when Antonio de Torres returned from Spain with provisions and other necessaries for the colony, as well as with despatches for Columbus. But this agreeable change did not last long, for the internal affairs of the colony were disorganized, and the Indians were at war with the Spaniards. Don Pedro Margarite, who had been appointed captain-general in the admiral's absence, had devastated the country in filibustering expeditions. He had been commissioned to explore the islands with four hundred men, but told to treat the Indians kindly and yet justly, and to capture Caonabó the chief, and his brothers, either by force or artifice. Margarite interpreted his instructions in the worst sense; and rapine and injustice marked his footsteps, until the Indians passed from terror to despair, and became strongly hostile towards the colonists. Having done all this mischief, Margarite had now returned to Spain, with Father Buil and other prominent men, in the same vessel which took back Bartholomew Columbus.

But difficulties only kindled the energies of Christopher Columbus. Learning that a hostile chief named Guatiguaná was besieging the Fort of Magdalena, within only two days' march of Isabella, Columbus at once went out, and defeated him. The whole of the province was reduced to order, and the admiral took a large number of the inhabitants as slaves. These were despatched to Spain in four vessels, which sailed from Isabella in February, 1495. At a later period, on the broad plains of the Vega Real, Columbus defeated with great slaughter an immense body of Indians, whose numbers are placed by some historians at one hundred thousand. There was a fearful carnage, and many of those who escaped death were condemned to slavery. Caonabó, the formidable hostile chief, was amongst those who escaped, and stratagem was now resorted to in order to entrap him. He fell into the snare, and was conveyed manacled to Columbus, who sent him to Spain for trial, but he died on the voyage.

These events were of great significance; for, as Sir Arthur Helps has observed, they must be looked upon as the origin of West Indian slavery. "We have seen," he says, "that the admiral, after his first victory, sent off four ships with slaves to Spain. He now took occasion to impose a tribute upon the whole population of Hispaniola.

"It was thus arranged. Every Indian above fourteen years old, who was in the provinces of the mines, or near to these provinces, was to pay every three months a little bellful of gold; all other persons in the island were to pay at the same time an arroba of cotton for each person. Certain brass or copper tokens were made—different ones for each tribute time—and were given to the Indians when they paid tribute; and these tokens, being worn about their necks, were to show who had paid tribute. A remarkable proposal was made upon this occasion to the admiral by Guarioneux, cacique of the Vega Real—namely, that he would institute a huge farm for the growth of corn and the manufacture of bread, stretching from Isabella to St. Domingo (*i.e.* from sea to sea), which would suffice to maintain all Castile with bread. The cacique would do this on condition that his vassals were not to pay tribute in gold, as they did not know how to collect that. But this proposal was not accepted, because Columbus wished to have tribute in such things as he could send over to Spain.

"This tribute is considered to have been a most unreasonable one in point of amount, and Columbus was obliged to modify his demands upon these poor Indians, and in some instances to change the nature of them. It appears that, in 1496, service instead of tribute was demanded of certain Indian villages; and as the villages were ordered to make (and work) the farms in the Spanish settlements, this may be considered as the beginning of the system of *repartimientos*, or *encomieodas*, as they were afterwards called.

"We must not, however, suppose that Indian slavery would not have taken place by means of Columbus, even if these uprisings and defeats of the Indians in the course of the year 1495 had never occurred. Very early indeed we see what the admiral's views were with regard to the Indians. In the diary which he kept of his first voyage, on the 14th of October, three days after discovering the New World, he describes a position which he thinks would be a very good one for a fort; and he goes on to say, 'I do not think that it (the fort) will be necessary, for this people is very simple in the use of arms (as your Highnesses will see from seven of them that I have taken in order to bring them to you, to learn our language and afterwards to take them back); so that when your Highnesses command, you can have them all taken to Castile, or kept in the island as captives.'

"Columbus was not an avaricious nor a cruel man; and certainly he was a very pious one; but early in life he had made voyages along the coast of Africa, and he was accustomed to a slave trade. Moreover, he was anxious to reduce the expenses of these Indian possessions to the Catholic sovereigns, to prove himself in the right as to all he had said respecting the advantages that would flow to Spain from the Indies, and to confute his enemies at Court."

When the slaves reached Spain, Ferdinand and Isabella were anxious to have it decided whether they were prisoners of war, for they were opposed to slavery, as we have seen. They consequently referred the matter to Bishop Fonseca, who had charge of Indian affairs, instructing him to withhold receiving the money for the sale of these Indians, until their Highnesses should be able to inform themselves from men learned in the law, theologians and canonists, whether with a good conscience the Indians could be sold or not. It seems doubtful whether the point was ever decided. The Indians who remained in Hispaniola, and who were supposed to be free, had a worse fate even than those who were deported. They thought by refusing to till the soil that they should starve the Spaniards out; but this policy only reacted upon themselves, and they perished of hunger, sickness, and misery in great numbers.

Meanwhile, the Court of Spain was being moved against Columbus by the representations of Margarite, Father Buil, and others. The result was that a royal commissioner was sent out to Hispaniola in the person of Juan Aguado, a Gentleman of the Chamber, who arrived at Isabella in October, 1495. His action in the colony, coupled with the fear of a hostile report, quickened the admiral in his desire to return to Spain to defend himself. Aguado had obtained a good deal of evidence from the Spaniards touching the despotic rule of Columbus, his harsh treatment of the hidalgoes, his expensive mania for discovering new lands, and other matters; and the Indians, hoping to reap benefit from a change, likewise turned against him. Accordingly, he left Isabella on the 10th of March, 1496, in the *Niña*, Aguado himself returning in another caravel. A number of the colonists returned with them. The voyage was a wretched one, and the greatest privations were endured before the vessels safely entered the Bay of Cadiz, on the 11th of June. A month later the admiral obeyed a summons from the Court to proceed to Burgos. His journey was not so much of a triumphal procession as his first one, although he displayed gold and natives as before. But the sovereigns received him kindly, and listened sympathetically to the story of his troubles, and his defence from the charges levelled against him by his enemies. His defence was practically accepted by the sovereigns.

Columbus now remained in Spain for two years, and the course of events during that period must be briefly traced. Don Bartholomew Columbus, who was still conducting affairs in Hispaniola, sent home in 1496 three hundred slaves, who were supposed to be rebels. In 1497 the sovereigns, on the advice of Columbus, issued two objectionable edicts—one authorizing the judges to transport criminals to the Indies, and the other giving an indulgence to all those who had committed any crimes (with the exception of heresy, treason, and a few others) to go out at their own expense to Hispaniola, there to serve for a time under the orders of the admiral.

Columbus had reason to repent giving this advice, for only three years afterwards we find him writing, "I swear that numbers of men have gone to the Indies who did not deserve water, from God or man." Yet Las Casas, speaking of these same colonists, said, "I have known some of them in these islands, even of those who had lost their ears, whom I always found sufficiently honest men."

Letters patent were next issued by the sovereigns, authorizing the admiral to grant *repartimientos* of the lands in the Indies to the Spaniards. No mention was made of the Indians themselves at this time: the Spaniard who received a grant of land was "to have, and to hold, and to possess," etc., and he was empowered "to sell, and to give, and to present, and to traffic with, and to exchange, and to pledge, and to alienate, and to do with it and in it all that he likes or may think good." This oppressive legislation was supplemented by the equally oppressive deeds of Don Bartholomew, the *adelantado*, or deputy, of Hispaniola. He traversed many of the islands, subduing the chiefs and people either by force or stratagem, and compelling them to pay tribute. His activity was such that the Spaniards began to complain of the labours imposed upon them, while the Indians constantly rose against their masters. An insurrection broke out among the Spaniards, headed by Roldan, Chief Justice of Hispaniola, who was anxious to return to Spain as Margarite had done. He and his adherents left Isabella in a body, and it was with great difficulty that Don Bartholomew could keep a sufficient number of men faithful to him.

Guarionex, one of the disaffected Indian chiefs or caciques, fled to the territories of Maiobanex, the chief of a hardy hill tribe near Cabron. Don Bartholomew pursued the fugitive, and demanded his surrender, but Maiobanex refused to give him up. Even when his own people counselled the surrender, the chief made the noble reply that "Guarionex was a good man, and deserved well at his hands, for he had given him many royal gifts when he came to him. . . . Wherefore he would be party to no treaty to desert Guarionex, since he had fled to him, and he had pledged himself to take care of the fugitive, and would rather suffer all extremities than give detractors a cause for speaking ill, to say that he had delivered up his guest." Loyally and manfully he stood by his brother chief to the last, for both were ultimately captured and thrown into prison.

We now come to the third memorable voyage of Columbus. His instructions on this occasion were to bring the Indians into peace and quietude, their subjection being accomplished amicably or "benignantly." They were also to be converted to the Holy Catholic Faith, and have the sacraments administered to them. The expedition set sail from the port of San Lucar on the 30th of May, 1498. It consisted of six vessels and two hundred men, in addition to the sailors who were necessary to navigate the ships. On reaching the Canary Isles, Columbus sent three of his ships direct to Hispaniola, telling their commanders that he was going to the Cape Verde Islands, and thence "in the name of the Sacred Trinity" to the south, until he should arrive under the equinoctial line, in the hope of being "guided by God to discover something which may be to His service, and to that of our Lords, the King and Queen, and to the honour of Christendom; for I believe," he added, "that no one has ever traversed this way, and that this sea is nearly unknown."

This declaration shows that Columbus had a clear and definite object in view in going south, and that he expected to come upon a greater land than any he had hitherto encountered. On the 27th of June he reached the Cape Verde Islands. Leaving them on the 4th of July, after experiencing dense fogs, he steered for the south-west. He sailed for upwards of one hundred and twenty leagues, and then experienced eight days of such intolerable heat that if the remaining seven had been clear and cloudless like the first not a man would have been left alive. Not until Thursday, the 31st of July, was land observed. On that day Alonzo Perez, a mariner of Huelva, and a follower of the admiral, chanced to go aloft upon the maintop-sail of the admiral's ship, and suddenly saw land towards the south-west, about fifteen leagues away. Columbus named the land Trinidad, and the sailors sang the Salve Regina and other pious hymns in honour of God and in thankfulness for the new discovery. From the shores of the island, Columbus saw the South American Continent for the first time; but imagining it to be only a large island, he gave it the name of Zeta. He next came to the Gulf of Paria, and wherever he went he found the coasts fruitful and well cultivated. In coasting up the gulf, the admiral invariably met with friendly treatment from the natives. From the immense amount of fresh water which was brought down by the rivers into the Gulf of Paria, he came to the conclusion that a tract of land which he had named Gracia was not an island, but a continent, and this supposition was correct. He thought he had reached the gates of the earthly Paradise, and that this was the beginning of that golden continent of the East which had for years been a settled conviction with him.

One of his biographers writes: " Columbus did not forget to claim, with all due formalities, the possession of this approach to Paradise for his employers, the Catholic sovereigns. Accordingly, when at Paria, he had landed and taken possession of the coast in their names, erecting a great cross upon the shore, which, he tells Ferdinand and Isabella, he was in the habit of doing at every headland, the religious aspect of the conquest being one which always had great influence with the admiral, as he believed it to have with the Catholic monarchs. In communicating this discovery, he reminds them how they bade him go on with the enterprise, if he should discover only stones and rocks, and had told him that they counted the cost for nothing, considering that the Faith would be increased, and their dominions widened.

" It was, however, no poor discovery of mere 'rocks and stones' which the admiral had now made. It will be interesting to see his first impressions of the men and the scenery of this continent which he had now, unconsciously, for the first time, discovered. He says, 'I found some lands, the most beautiful in the world, and very populous.' The lands in the Island of Trinidad he had previously compared to Valencia, in Spain, during the month of March. It is also noticeable that he had observed that the fields were cultivated. Of the people he says, 'They are all of good stature, well made, and of very graceful bearing, with much and smooth hair'; and he mentions that on their heads they wore the beautiful Arab head-dress (called *keffeh*), made of worked and coloured handkerchiefs, which appeared in the distance as if they were silken."

Columbus said nothing to the Spanish monarchs of his discovery of pearls. It is conjectured that he wished to keep this secret for awhile, lest the fruits of his enterprise should be snatched from him; but of course the knowledge could not long be suppressed, and the Pearl Coast soon became a favourite field for adventurers.

The admiral himself had not the time to push to the utmost the advantages to be derived from his discoveries, for he was anxious to return to Hispaniola. He arrived there on the 30th of August, and found the colony in a deplorable condition. He sent off five ships from St. Domingo laden with six hundred slaves. In his letters to the Spanish Court, he spoke of the intended adoption, on behalf of private individuals, of a system of exchange of slaves for goods wanted from the mother country. This plan, which was a new kind of *repartimiento*, he proceeded to carry into effect without waiting for the necessary authority. After a long series of negotiations with Roldan, he confirmed him in his chief-justiceship, and rewarded his friends with lands and slaves, making the Indians till the lands for the new possessors. Those adherents of Roldan who preferred to return to Spain he permitted to do so, giving each of them a certain number of slaves.

Queen Isabella was very angry when she learnt that Columbus had thus been giving her new vassals away. She therefore ordered proclamations to be made at Seville, Granada, and elsewhere, commanding all persons who were in possession of Indians, given to them by the admiral, to send back those Indians to Hispaniola, under pain of death—"and that particularly they should send back those Indians, and not the others who had been brought before, because she was informed that the others had been taken in just war." The Spanish sovereigns appear to have eased their consciences by accepting the dictum that Indians taken in open warfare could be justifiably made slaves of; yet there was practically no difference between these slaves and those ordered to be returned.

Fate now began to press heavily against Columbus. His enemies increased in numbers and bitterness, and Don Ferdinand thus graphically describes the attitude of his father's foes: "When I was at Granada, at the time the most serene Prince Don Miguel died, more than fifty of them (Spaniards who had returned from the Indies), as men without shame, bought a great quantity of grapes, and sat themselves down in the court of the Alhambra, uttering loud cries, saying that their Highnesses and the admiral made them live in this poor fashion on account of the bad pay they received, with many other dishonest and unseemly things, which they kept repeating. Such was their effrontery, that when the Catholic King came forth they all surrounded him, and got him into the midst of them, saying, 'Pay! pay!' and if by chance I and my brother, who were pages to the most serene Queen, happened to pass where they were, they shouted to the very heavens, saying, 'Look at the sons of the admiral of Mosquitoland, of that man who has discovered the lands of deceit and disappointment, a place of sepulchre and wretchedness to Spanish hidalgoes': adding many other insulting expressions, on which account we excused ourselves from passing by them."

Ferdinand and Isabella now began to consider the question of the suspension of Columbus. But before doing this they resolved to send out to Hispaniola an official with full civil and judicial authority. Accordingly, on the 21st of March, 1499, they authorized Francis de Bobadilla "to ascertain what persons have raised themselves against justice in the Island of Hispaniola, and to proceed against them according to law." Two months later they conferred upon him the government, and signed an order that all arms and fortresses in the Indies should be given up to him. Then, on the 26th of May, they entrusted him with this letter to Columbus:

"Don Christopher Columbus, our Admiral of the Ocean: We have commanded the Comendador Francis de Bobadilla, the bearer of this, that he speak to you on our part some things which he will tell you: we pray you give him faith and credence, and act accordingly.

"I THE KING, I THE QUEEN.
"By their command,
"MIGUEL PEREZ DE ALMAZAN."

Bobadilla did not arrive in Hispaniola until the 23rd of August, 1500; but he at once began to act in an arbitrary spirit, and one which could not have commended itself to the sovereigns. He took possession of the admiral's house at St. Domingo, and summoned the admiral, who was then at La Concepcion, to appear before him. The accusers of Columbus gained courage at Bobadilla's coming, and charges multiplied in a manner that was equally rapid and contemptible. Bobadilla put Columbus and his brothers in chains, and sent them to Spain. When the captain of the ship offered to free Columbus from his fetters, he proudly replied, "No, I will wear them as a memento of the gratitude of princes." He declared that he would never have them taken off, except by royal command, and he ordered them to be buried with him. There was great indignation throughout Spain at the outrage; and when the sovereigns heard of it, they disclaimed the proceeding, and ordered him to be immediately liberated. He was directed to proceed to the Court at Granada, and money was forwarded to enable him to make the journey in a style befitting his rank. On his arrival, he was received with every mark of distinction: their Highnesses dismissed the charges against him as unworthy of investigation, and promised him redress and compensation. Yet Ferdinand was jealous of his power over the colonies, and the wealth that might possibly accrue to him, and he was resolved not to reinstate him in his viceroyalty.

The Queen granted Columbus a private audience, and received him very graciously. The admiral told the story of his difficulties and grievances with much eloquence, and showed that he was obliged to strike out a path for himself under the untoward circumstances which presented themselves. Isabella made full allowance for this, and expressed her appreciation of his services; but then she went on to say: "Common report accuses you of acting with a degree of severity quite unsuitable for an infant colony, and likely to excite rebellion there. But the matter as to which I find it hardest to give you my pardon is your conduct in reducing to slavery a number of Indians who had done nothing to deserve such a fate. This was contrary to my express orders. As your ill fortune willed it, just at the time when I heard of this breach of my instructions everybody was complaining of you, and no one spoke a word in your favour. And I felt obliged to send to the Indies a commissioner to investigate matters, and give me a true report; and, if necessary, to put limits to the authority which you were accused of overstepping. If you were found guilty of the charges, he was to relieve you of the government and to send you to Spain to give an account of your stewardship. This was the extent of his commission. I find that I have made a bad choice in my agent; and I will take care to make an example of Bobadilla, which shall serve as a warning to others not to exceed their powers. I cannot, however, promise to reinstate you at once in your government. People are too much inflamed against you, and must have time to cool. As to your rank of admiral, I never intended to deprive you of it. But you must bide your time and trust in me."

Bobadilla was superseded, and a new governor named Ovando appointed, who was to hold his post at their Highnesses' will and pleasure. His instructions stated that "all the Indians in Hispaniola should be free from servitude and be unmolested by any one, and that they should live as free vassals, governed and protected by justice, as were the vassals of Castile." They were to pay tribute, but they were to receive daily wages for their assistance in getting gold. No Jews, Moors, or new converts were permitted to go out to the colonies; but "negro slaves born in the power of Christians were to be allowed to pass to the Indies, and the officers of the royal revenue were to receive the money to be paid for their permits." These instructions, issued in 1501, thus give the first intimation with regard to negroes going to the Indies. Ovando proved to be a cruel and tyrannical deputy, who thought nothing of devastating provinces and massacring the inhabitants.

Having been to a considerable extent restored to favour, Columbus conceived a scheme for a passage from the neighbourhood of St. Domingo to those regions in Asia from which the Portuguese were now beginning to reap profit, and which he believed must be near the El Dorado of his dreams. He appealed to the sovereigns to allow him to go forth once more, and Ferdinand granted his request, at the same time reiterating his confidence in him. So on the 9th of May, 1502, Columbus set sail from Cadiz with his brother Bartholomew and his second son Fernando. There were four caravels, and it was the admiral's intention to explore the Gulf of Mexico. Martinique was reached on the 13th of June. The largest vessel was in a dangerous state, and he desired to run into St. Domingo to refit; but as he had been forbidden in his instructions to visit St. Domingo, Ovando would not permit him to land. He therefore went forward, passing Jamaica on the 14th of July, and afterwards coasting Honduras. To one place, touched at on the 12th of September, he gave the name of Cape Gracias a Dios. Some weeks later he explored several bays on the Isthmus of Panama, but he could learn nothing of the kingdom of the Khan or of the strait which he believed led to it.

In December the little expedition encountered terrible storms; but after eight days' tossing about, a small harbour was made at the mouth of a river, which the admiral named Bethlehem, because he entered it on the day of the Epiphany. Here he found much gold, and formed a little settlement for collecting it. But the natives were very hostile, and threatened the extinction of the settlers, so Columbus was obliged to take them all on board again. He had now lost one of his worm-eaten vessels, and the others were in a crazy condition. With great difficulty he managed to steer for Jamaica, however, and in the harbour of Santa Gloria his voyage came to a conclusion. As his vessels could float no longer they were run ashore, and he constructed huts on the decks for his men, forbidding them to go on shore, so as to avoid all quarrel with the natives.

But Columbus could not rest here, and he sent a letter to Ovando—which was taken by Diego Mendez in a canoe—asking him to forward a relief vessel to take off the crews. He also forwarded a despatch to the sovereigns, giving a detailed account of his voyage and a glowing description of the riches of Veragua. This despatch was a strange commingling of faith and enthusiasm. The passage in which he described his emotions during the storm at the mouth of the River Bethlehem was most extraordinary, and ran as follows: "Wearied and sighing, I fell into a slumber, when I heard a piteous voice saying to me, 'O fool and slow to believe and serve thy God, who is the God of all! What did He more for Moses, or for His servant David, than He has done for thee? From the time of thy birth He has ever had thee under His peculiar care. When He saw thee of a fitting age, He made thy name to resound marvellously throughout the earth, and thou wert obeyed in many lands, and didst acquire honourable fame among Christians. Of the gates of the ocean sea, shut up with such mighty chains, He delivered to thee the keys; the Indies, those wealthy regions of the world, He gave thee for thine own, and empowered thee to dispose of them to others, according to thy pleasure. What did He more for the great people of Israel, when He led them forth from Egypt? Or for David, whom, from being a shepherd, He made a king in Judæa? Turn to Him, then, and acknowledge thine error: His mercy is infinite. He has many and vast inheritances yet in reserve. Fear not to seek them. Thine age shall be no impediment to any great undertaking. Abraham was above a hundred years when he begat Isaac: and was Sarah youthful? Thou urgest despondingly for succour. Answer! Who hath afflicted thee so much and so many times—God, or the world? The privileges and promises which God hath made to thee He hath never broken, neither hath He said, after having received thy services, that His meaning was different, and to be understood in a different sense. He fulfils all that He promises, and with increase. Such is His custom. I have shown thee what thy Creator hath done for thee, and what He doeth for all. The present is the reward of the toils and perils thou hast endured in serving others.' I heard this," adds Columbus, "as one almost dead, and had no power to reply to words so true, excepting to weep for my errors. Whoever it was that spoke to me finished by saying, 'Fear not! All these tribulations are written in marble, and not without cause.'"

No doubt this exordium was intended to rouse the sympathies of the sovereigns. Twice did Mendez make efforts to reach Hispaniola and invoke the succour of Ovando, and at length the latter authorized him to proceed to St. Domingo to purchase a caravel on behalf of Columbus. In the interim the admiral was having a bad time of it at Santa Gloria, and in January, 1504, his men broke out into open mutiny. The disaffected, finding that they were unable to return to Spain in canoes, roamed over the Island of Jamaica, committing excesses wherever they went.

The natives retorted, but Columbus regained his power over them by predicting that the moon would change her colour in testimony of the evils which would fall upon the people. It was fortunate that Columbus knew of an eclipse at this time, for it brought the natives in terror and submission to his feet. The mutiny among the admiral's own men was quelled at last by a sharp and sanguinary action.

On the 28th of June, 1504, two relief caravels arrived at Santa Gloria, one sent by Mendez and the other by Ovando. Columbus and his men at once embarked, but they did not reach St. Domingo until the 13th of August. A month after that the admiral set sail for Spain; and after suffering great hardship and famine, as well as being prostrated by sickness, he reached San Lucar on the 7th of November, 1504. Here he lay sick for many months, during which period his truest friend, Queen Isabella, passed away. On his recovery Columbus proceeded to the capital, but it was only to have his claim finally rejected by the King.

Columbus died at Valladolid on the 20th of May, 1506, his last words being, "Into Thy hands, O Lord, I commit my spirit." Infirm of body, but in full possession of all his faculties, and yet so poor that he could not frequently pay for his sustenance, the discoverer of a new world expired in a small apartment of a modest house, with a few faithful friends and followers standing by his bedside. A small tablet has been placed on the front of the building—now some six hundred years old—which briefly states, "Here died Columbus."

The remains of the great discoverer were buried at Valladolid, but afterwards removed to Seville. Here they were not allowed to remain, however, for in 1536 they were taken with great pomp to St. Domingo, and interred in the Cathedral. In 1796 they were once more removed, and buried in the Cathedral of Havana with imposing ceremonies, though some authorities assert that the remains were not those of Columbus, but of his son Diego. But the Duke of Veragua, the only remaining descendant of Columbus in the female line, on being appealed to on this point, and also as to whether the discoverer was a native of Calvi, in Corsica, wrote, "I do not think any of the historians or writers have been successful in their attempts to deprive Genoa of the honour of being the birthplace of Columbus, or in taking from Havana the glory of possessing his ashes." The last legitimate descendant of Columbus in the male line died in 1578.

A remarkable letter by Columbus, never before published, appears in the sketch of the explorer written by General J. Grant Wilson for *The Cyclopædia of American Biography*. It was written in Spanish, and addressed to Agostino Barberigo, Doge of Venice, to whom Columbus had previously made unsuccessful proposals of exploration. Penned two days before the admiral set sail from Saltes on his first great expedition, it lay for nearly four hundred years in the Venetian Archives undiscovered. The letter runs as follows:

"MAGNIFICENT SIR,—Since your Republic has not deemed it convenient to accept my offers, and all the spite of my many enemies has been brought in force to oppose my petition, I have thrown myself in the arms of God, my Maker, and He, by the intercession of the Saints, has caused the most clement King of Castile not to refuse to generously assist my project toward the discovery of a new world. And praising thereby the good God, I obtained the placing under my command of men and ships, and am about to start on a voyage to that famous land, grace to which intent God has been pleased to bestow upon me."

The four hundredth anniversary of the discovery of America by Columbus was celebrated in Europe and the United States with great rejoicings in 1892. At Huelva the festivals began on the 31st of July, and vessels were sent by Great Britain, France, the United States, Austria, Greece, Portugal, the Argentine Republic, and Mexico. The caravel *Santa Maria*, constructed as an exact reproduction of the vessel in which Columbus sailed, set sail over the Bay of Cadiz, bound for Huelva, where she was moored off Palos, on the very spot where her great original was anchored. On the 2nd of August she went out to sea, and returned amidst salutes from the lines of ships in the bay. A congratulatory telegram from the Alcalde of Huelva was despatched to President Harrison, who suitably responded. In October the Queen Regent of Spain and the young King visited Cadiz, when the most brilliant celebrations occurred. At Huelva the *Niña* and *Pinta* were received by the Spanish and foreign war-ships, twenty-three in number. The town and shipping were brilliantly illuminated on the evening of the 10th. The 12th of October being the anniversary of the day when America was first seen from the ships of Columbus, the day was observed throughout the principal cities of Spain, and especially at Valladolid, where the great explorer died.

At Genoa, the birthplace of Columbus, two gold medals were struck, one for the Queen of Spain and one for the King of Italy. The Municipal Palace was thronged by a brilliant assemblage in the evening, including the King and Queen of Italy, the ministers, ambassadors, officers of the fleet, etc. In the port of Genoa were war-ships representing fifteen nations. At a later date there was a Columbus Exhibition and a historical procession representing the return of Columbus. There was also an Exhibition at Madrid, and one of its most interesting features was a facsimile reproduction of the first chart on which the American Continent was delineated. The original was traced by Juan de la Cosa, the pilot of Columbus, in 1500. A grand historical cavalcade was subsequently witnessed by the royal family and their guests, the King and Queen of Portugal.

At New York there was a grand naval parade in the harbour, by vessels of all nations, early in October. The 12th was observed as a general holiday; and the Columbus statue, sent as a present from Italy to America, was unveiled. A noble statue by a Spanish sculptor was also unveiled in the Central Park. Reproductions of the three vessels with which Columbus first went out were exhibited; and after being taken first to Havana and then to the Chicago Exhibition, they were formally presented to the United States Government, to be preserved as relics.

Accounts differ as to the details of the personal appearance of Columbus, but all agree in stating that he had a commanding presence. He was above the middle height, with a long countenance, rather full cheeks, an aquiline nose, and light grey eyes full of expression. His hair, naturally of a light colour, turned white when he was quite a young man.

He had many fine qualities of character, and was magnanimous and benevolent, though also impetuous and irritable. While practical in action, he was a man of ardent impulses and strong imagination. Sometimes he lacked the iron nerve of a leader; and although he was sincerely and earnestly religious, his conduct in the capture and sale of slaves can never be inherently justified, though it was countenanced by the jurists and divines of his time. He desired to obtain revenues for the Crown by his new discoveries, and to Christianize the slaves; but it is the worst way in the world to attempt to convert a man by first taking his freedom from him. The full value of his discovery he never lived to realize, and at his death he believed that the land which he had discovered was the long-sought-for Indies. But with all his failings and limitations, he was one of the world's truly great men; and as such his glory can never fade.

CHAPTER III.

THE CABOTS AND THE FIRST ENGLISH COLONY.

THE first discoverer of the mainland of North America was John Cabot, and it is to his remarkable adventures, as well as to those of his more celebrated son Sebastian Cabot, that we must now direct attention.

Neither the time nor the place of John Cabot's birth can be definitely fixed. The first authentic information concerning him appears in the Venetian Archives, where it is stated that he was accorded the rights of a citizen on the 28th of March, 1476, after the required fifteen years' residence. Yet, according to other authorities, some time before the latter year Cabot had left Venice for London, there to follow the trade of merchandise. Instead of staying in London, however, he made his way to Bristol, then the second city in the kingdom. As, being a foreigner, he was not permitted to settle in the city itself, he took up his abode in one of the suburbs. This was probably a district now known as Cathay, so-called after the Indies, and a large Indian trade is still carried on in its midst. Here at least two of John Cabot's sons were born, Sebastian and Sanctus.

Sebastian told a contemporary of his that he was

born in Bristol, and that when he was four years old he was taken by his father to Venice. After remaining there for some years, he was again conveyed to England, and these facts gave rise to the impression that he was born in Venice. The date of his birth has been placed between 1474 and 1477. Both father and son seem to have been fired with an adventurous zeal, to which they were stimulated by the deeds of Columbus, a man whom they warmly and reverently admired.

In the year 1495 John Cabot was residing at Bristol, and doubtless had been for some years. Under date of March 5, 1495 (Old Style), Henry VII. granted a patent licensing Cabot and his three sons—Lewis, Sebastian, and Sanctus—or either of them, their heirs or assigns, to search for islands, provinces, or regions, in the eastern, western, or northern seas; and, as vassals of the King, to occupy the territories that might be found, with an exclusive right to their commerce, on paying the King a fifth part of all the profits. This interesting document runs thus:

"HENRY, by the grace of God, etc., etc.

"Be it known to all, that we have given and granted, and by these presents do give and grant, to our well-beloved John Cabot, citizen of Venice, to Lewis, Sebastian, and Sanctus, sons of the said John, and to their heirs and deputies, full and free authority, leave, and power to sail to all parts, countries, and seas of the East, of the West, and of the North, under our banners and ensigns, with five ships, of what burthen or quality soever they be, and as many mariners and men as they will take with them in the said ships, *upon their own proper costs and charges*, to seek out, discover, and find whatsoever Isles, Countries, Regions, or Provinces of the Heathen and Infidels, whatsoever they be, and in whatsoever part of the world, which before this time have been unknown to all Christians. We have granted to them and every of them and their deputies, and have given them our licence, to set up our banners and ensigns in every village, town, castle, isle, or mainland of them newly found; and that the said John and his sons and their heirs may subdue, occupy, and possess all such towns, cities, etc., by them found, which they can subdue, occupy, and possess as our vassals and lieutenants, getting to us the rule, title, and jurisdiction of the said villages, towns, etc.

"Yet so that the said John and his sons and their heirs, of all the fruits, profits, and commodities growing from such navigation, shall be held and bound to pay to us, in wares or money, *the fifth part of the capital gain* so gotten for every their voyage, as often as they shall arrive at our port of Bristol (at which port they shall be obliged only to arrive), deducting all manner of necessary costs and charges by them made; we giving and granting unto them and their heirs and deputies that they shall be free from all payments of customs on all such merchandise they shall bring with them from the places so newly found. And, moreover, we have given and granted to them and their heirs and deputies that all the firm land, islands, villages, towns, etc., they shall chance to find, may not, without licence of the said John Cabot and his sons, be so frequented and visited, under pain of losing their ships and all the goods of them who shall presume to sail to the places so found.

"Willing and commanding strictly all and singular our subjects, as well on land as on sea, to give good assistance to the said John and his sons and deputies, and that as well in arming and furnishing their ships and vessels as in provision of food and buying victuals for their money, and all other things by them to be provided necessary for the said navigation, they do give them all their favours and assistance.

"Witness myself at Westminster, 5th March, in the eleventh year of our reign, or 1495 A.D."

There are accounts of a hypothetical voyage said to have been made by the Cabots in 1474—that is, long before Henry VII.'s first charter. This idea would seem to be supported by Sebastian Cabot's map now in the Bibliothèque Impériale, Paris. Barrow, in his *History of Voyages*, and other writers, also support the view. Yet there would certainly be some more definite information on the subject if such a voyage had actually been made, and it had resulted in important consequences. As facts remain, however, historians and biographers begin their dating of the Cabot discoveries with Henry's charter of 1495.

For some reason or other, although the King's patent was granted in March, 1495, John Cabot and his son Sebastian did not set sail from Bristol until May, 1497. The adventurers held a westward course for an estimated distance of seven hundred leagues. On the 24th of June land was sighted, which John Cabot believed to be part of the dominions of the Grand Cham, or Khan, but which was really Cape Breton Island and

Nova Scotia. This shore he coasted for three hundred leagues, finding no traces of human habitation, and then he set sail for home, reaching Bristol in August.

A letter written by one Lorenzo Pasqualigo to his brother, and dated London, August 23, 1497, thus describes the voyage and John Cabot's return and reception in England:

"The Venetian, our countryman, who went with a ship from Bristol in quest of new islands, is returned, and says that seven hundred leagues hence he discovered land, the territory of the Grand Cham; he coasted for three hundred leagues and landed; saw no human beings, but he has brought hither to the King certain snares which had been set to catch game, and a needle for making nets; he also found some felled trees, wherefore he supposed there were inhabitants, and returned to his ship in alarm.

"He was three months on the voyage, and on his return he saw two islands to starboard, but would not land, time being precious, as he was short of provisions.

"He says that the tides are slack, and do not flow as they do here. The King of England is much pleased with this intelligence.

"The King has promised that in the spring our countryman shall have ten ships armed to his order, and at his request has conceded him all the prisoners, except such as are confined for high treason, to man his fleet.

"The King has also given him money wherewith to amuse himself till then, and he is now at Bristol with his wife, who is also a Venetian, and with his sons.

"His name is Juan Cabot, and he is styled the Great Admiral; vast honour is paid him; he dresses in silk; and these English run after him like mad people, so that he can enlist as many of them as he pleases, and a number of our own. The discoverer of these places planted on his new-found lands a large cross, with one flag of England and another of St. Mark, by reason of his being a Venetian, so that our banner has floated very far afield. August 23, 1497."

Sebastian Cabot is entitled to be honoured as well as his father for this first successful expedition to the North American Continent. The recent scholarly researches by Mr. Rawdon Brown among the Venetian Archives have furnished irrefragable proof that this expedition of the Cabots, under the auspices of Henry VII., in 1497, resulted in the discovery of the continent, and its being taken possession of for England.

Owing mainly to the discoveries of Columbus, the theory that the earth is a sphere had been generally accepted by advanced thinkers, and it was believed that the shortest route to the Indies lay westward. Cabot's discovery, therefore, created great excitement in England and Europe. A portrait of Sebastian Cabot was subsequently painted by Holbein, and Cabot's map was reproduced by Clement Adams. Several other maps and charts are supposed to have been given up by a friend of Cabot, after the latter's death, to Philip of Spain. The portrait by Holbein was painted at a time when Sebastian was the Worshipful Governor of the Merchant Adventurers' Company, and when he had under him in his official capacity the Lord High Admiral, the Lord Steward, the Lord Treasurer, and other State dignitaries.

One report alleges that John Cabot was knighted, but the matter is very doubtful. If it took place, it must have been on the admiral's return from his great voyage. It is further possible that his death ensued close upon his knighthood, which would account for the lack of definite information on the subject. He probably died in the year 1498, and it is known that he left his son Sebastian very rich, and full of ambition.

A second charter was granted by Henry in February, 1498, not long before the death of John, and Sebastian Cabot went forth upon this expedition alone. This new charter was really only an extension of the first, which it did not in any way set aside, and which still remained valid. The supplementary charter gave Cabot extra powers to press ships at the same rate of payment which the King gave for his own service, and to enlist men for the venture; there was in it no bar to his trading or granting licences, no empowering other persons to trade independently of the Cabot family, and no release from the one-fifth tribute which, under the first charter, they were to pay to the King out of their profits.

It was in May, 1498, that Sebastian Cabot sailed from Bristol in command of two ships, manned by volunteers, in search of a north-west passage. He went so far north that in the early part of July daylight was almost continuous. The sea, nevertheless, was so full of icebergs that he worked southward, and discovered what is generally believed to have been

Newfoundland. Proceeding farther, he reached the mainland, made several landings, dealt with the natives, and followed the coast southward as far as Chesapeake Bay. Yet notwithstanding this discovery of a wide domain under the Temperate Zone, the voyage was not successful in its original object—that of opening up the passage to the Indies. But we are struck with admiration at what Cabot did achieve; for from the 68° N. latitude to the 30°, or from the northernmost part of Hudson's Bay to the Gulf of Mexico, he was the first European who surveyed its coasts, or attempted to colonize its deserted shores.

It is thought that Cabot landed a portion of his men at about Davis's Inlet or Port Manvers, and they were to colonize the country; but the settlement proved abortive. In *Stow's Annals*, 1498, there is a passage which shows that, among other objects in this voyage, Cabot had in view trade and colonization as well as discovery; that the King shared in the expense, probably fitting out one ship and giving help to the men; that the coast, inhabitants, beasts, fishes, and birds observed prove that the scene of their principal operations was the country now known as Labrador, but then called by Cabot "the land of the *baccalaos*" (cod-fish); and that Cabot was the first man who discovered Hudson's Bay, which he afterwards more thoroughly explored.

Cabot tendered his services to Henry VII. in 1499 for another voyage; but as the English sovereign was at this time fully occupied with threatening domestic troubles, his offer failed to meet with a favourable reception. Nevertheless, Seyer, the historian of

Bristol, states that Cabot set forth from that western port and made great discoveries. One Hojeda, a Spanish navigator, found an Englishman and his crew at Caquibaco at the close of 1499, and it is conjectured that the traveller was Cabot. He had probably taken up his explorations where he had suspended them before, on the coast of Florida, and proceeded southwards, arriving at the place where Hojeda met the English. There is a further tradition to the effect that Cabot afterwards went north, and was engaged in colonizing Newfoundland and the neighbourhood. On the other hand, Rymer considers that it was the Portuguese and certain other merchants who sailed in 1502 and visited Newfoundland.

At this time the contemporary achievements of Vasco di Gama were so much more brilliant that the exploits of the Cabots were outshone, and they were so careless of their chartered rights that the patent giving them exclusive privileges was lost or mislaid.

After the death of Henry VII., Ferdinand V. of Spain wrote to Lord Willoughby, Captain-General of the King of England, to send over Sebastian Cabot, he having heard of his ability as a seaman. In September, 1512, accordingly, Cabot went to Spain; and after being appointed one of the "Council of the New Indies," Ferdinand's successor named him pilot-major of the kingdom, a liberal salary was apportioned him, and his residence was fixed at the city of Seville. Peter Martyr saw much of him there, and states that his first voyage was arranged to take place in March, 1516. Unfortunately, the King died in January of that year, and the order for the expedition was countermanded, owing to the jealousy of the Spaniards against foreigners. Cabot thereupon returned to England, and found immediate employment under Henry VIII.

In 1517 he set forth on a voyage the object of which was to find an opening through Hudson's Bay to the back of Newfoundland. Hakluyt states that Cabot "sailed very far westward, with a quarter of the north, on the north side of Labrador, on the 11th of June, until he came to the septentrional latitude of $67\frac{1}{2}°$; and finding the sea still open, might and would have gone to Cathay, if the mutiny of the master and mariners had not been." Another report says that it was one of his captains, Sir Thomas Pert, whose faint heart was the cause that the voyage took none effect. There seems to be no question that Cabot was on the very verge of a great discovery, having attained to the straits which lead to the magnetic pole, and within a short distance of the passage whose existence McClure, McClintock, and others have verified in the nineteenth century.

Although this voyage produced excellent scientific results, cowardice robbed it of what might have been its greatest glory. Cabot returned dispirited to England, only to find the country being ravaged by that terrible scourge, the sweating sickness. All commerce was at a standstill; so when Charles V. visited England in 1520, he took Cabot back with him, and the latter now entered upon his duties as pilot-major. But Cabot desired more active work; and as Spain was at this time very jealous of England, he now opened up negotiations with Venice with a view to employment. It is to be regretted that Cabot swerved from the truth in conducting these negotiations, which after all seem to have come to nothing.

In April, 1524, a conference of geographers assembled at Badajoz. Cabot was president, and the son of Columbus had a seat at the board. Portugal retired from the conference in high dudgeon, when it was decided that the coveted Spice Islands were declared to be within Spanish waters by twenty degrees. Portugal prepared a fleet to enforce her claims; and Spain, anxious to secure the treasures of the East, formed an exploring company in the ensuing September. The Council of the Indies gave permission to Cabot to take the command, and he entered into a bond for the faithful execution of his trust. The Emperor Charles sanctioned a squadron of three vessels, of not less than one hundred tons, and one hundred and fifty men. A small caravel was added by a private individual—probably Robert Thorne, merchant of Bristol, who was then at Seville—and the title of captain-general was conferred on Cabot. The Emperor was to receive four thousand ducats and a share of the profits. The object of the expedition was to find a direct south-west passage to Asia, by way of the Straits of Magellan.

Owing to Portuguese intrigues, the expedition did not set sail until April, 1526, and even then the rival power sent out a spying squadron after it. Cabot made for the Brazils, by way of the Canaries, Cape de Verde, and Cape Augustine; but he was soon hampered by difficulties. Mendez, the second in command, was inefficient, and sealed orders had been given to each ship as to the succession in command, which practically put a premium upon the murder of the commanders. Provisions ran short, and there was a mutiny; but Cabot, who stood almost alone, courageously seized the mutineers, and landed them at the first point touched at, where they were afterwards taken up by the Portuguese commander Garcia. Cabot sent home two of his friends, who made satisfactory explanations to the Emperor. Still, calumnies were circulated to his disadvantage; but their value may be gauged from the fact that when Cabot returned to Spain Charles V. at once reinstated him in his high and honourable office of pilot-major.

After quelling the mutiny, Cabot proceeded to the great river La Plata, which had been previously discovered by his immediate predecessor as pilot-major, De Solis, who lost his life on one of the islands at the mouth of the river. Cabot had now only two ships and a caravel, one vessel having been lost on the voyage. He pushed up the inlet of the La Plata, and came to an island which he named St. Gabriel, a name it still bears. Leaving his ships here for the boats, he explored seven leagues up the stream until he reached another river, and a port which he named St. Salvador.

The stream he was now exploring was the Rio Navanjos, or the lower branch of the mouth of the Parana, near its confluence with the Uruguay. He sent for his vessels, and erected a fort upon one of the islands. Avoiding the Uruguay, he now proceeded westward up the Parana, and built another fort at Terceiro. In both the forts he left garrisons. He ultimately reached the Parana's junction with the

Paraguay, and pursued the course of the latter for thirty-four leagues. In describing this voyage, he said, "I found an exceedingly large and great river, named at this present time the Rio de la Plata—that is, the river of silver—into which I sailed, and followed it into the firme land more than one hundred and twenty leagues, finding it everywhere very faire, and inhabited with infinite people, which, with admiration, came running daily to our ships. Into this river run so many other rivers that it is in manner incredible."

The natives were of a superior class, who cultivated the soil. But they were also lawless, and seized three Spaniards who had strayed to gather the fruit of the palm tree. Cabot hastened to their succour, and a severe battle ensued. Three hundred natives were slain, and Cabot had the misfortune to lose twenty-five out of his small forces. He sent down his wounded, and apprised his faithful adherent Caro, governor of one of the constructed forts, of his loss and their danger. Garcia soon afterwards arrived at Fort Sanctus Spiritus, and summoned Caro to surrender in the name of the Emperor. Caro nobly replied that he held the fort in the name of the Emperor and Sebastian Cabot, and would never surrender it, though he was quite willing to give Garcia a welcome. He begged Garcia to look out for wounded Spaniards on his way up the river; but the latter heartlessly neglected to do so, and pursued his own course. Cabot and Garcia eventually met, but no record exists of their interview.

Cabot had now reached a point where he was in sight of the mountains of Peru, and he was hoping to reap the fruit of his labours, when once more the cruel hand of Fate was against him. The events which succeeded are thus described by Mr. Nicholls in his sketch of Cabot:

"Charles V. had outrun his exchequer, and was afflicted with a disease very prevalent in modern days, impecuniosity. His Cortes refused him money. He had mortgaged the Moluccas to Portugal, and his treasury was empty.

"Just then Pizarro, overflowing with ambition, well known at Court, personally importunate, but asking for no money, only for the government of the countries which he might conquer, assailed the Emperor continually.

"Cabot was shelved; Pizarro succeeded. Of his successful but infamous career we need say no more than this, that if Cabot had achieved the conquest of Peru, the blackest page in the history of Spanish America would never have been written.

"Whilst waiting, sick at heart, with hope deferred, Cabot erected forts, administered justice, and reduced all the surrounding natives to obedience to the Emperor. Ever active, when no supplies came from Spain, he set the whole party to work, rapidly raised sufficient food, made experiments on the fertility of the soil, carefully noting the results, which, with great minuteness, he afterwards reported to the Emperor.

"He classified also the various productions of the country, and graphically describes the marvellous fecundity of the swine, and also of the horses, both of which they had imported from Spain: these latter became the parent stock whence sprang the vast wild hordes which scour the Pampas to this day.

"A clever wit of the last generation said of a certain nobleman that he was ready to take the helm of the State or the command of the Channel fleet at an hour's notice. It was witty, but not new; for here we actually have the greatest commander and navigator of his age organizing a nation from the most discordant elements, and developing its powers under manifest disadvantages.

"We are naturally proud of the Bristol mariner whose personal agency gave to England and her sturdy offspring their valuable possessions in the north, and to Spain the rich and well-watered regions in the south of the American Continent; and if any one should be at all curious to see his monument in his native city, let them know that it lies with Sir Thomas Lawrence's, in the vast limits of futurity.

"In the midst of his labours—and, remember, they extended over five years in this region—the same evil genius which had followed him across the Atlantic was constantly marring his efforts, and finally struck a well-nigh fatal blow to the expedition.

"Garcia had swept the country, and sailed with his spoil; but he had left behind him a party of his followers, who held themselves amenable to no law. These men, located at Sanctus Spiritus, were guilty of some acts of atrocity towards the natives, which roused their wildest resentment.

"It is expressly stated that with this act, whatever it was, Cabot had nothing at all to do; but the fierce and sanguinary Indians made no distinction.

"Secret meetings were held, a plan of action was decided upon, and it was determined to cut off every white man in the country.

"A little before daybreak the enraged nation burst, with one fell swoop, down on and carried the entrenchments of Sanctus Spiritus, putting the feeble garrison to the sword.

"Here Caro, the faithful, probably perished in command, for we henceforth lose sight of him.

"Maddened with success, they rapidly traverse the intervening country, and try the same tactics at Fort Salvador.

"But better watch and ward is kept here. 'Defence, not Defiance,' is the Bristol man's motto, or rather, as on his portrait, 'Spes una in Deo est'; but he watches as well as hopes, fights as well as prays, and beats the enemy off.

"Sad faces come down the river a few days afterwards; reinforcements, sent to alarm and put the advance garrison on their guard, return dispirited; they had found Sanctus Spiritus desolate, a ruin, and their friends and companions slain to a man. So Cabot ships the requisite supplies, dismantles the fort, embarks the remnant of his people, and quits for ever the ill-omened shore."

Cabot returned to Spain in 1531, and resumed the functions of his high office; but after some years he longed to return to Bristol, which he regarded as his home. Strype tells us that in pursuance of this desire he came to England, and settled in Bristol in 1548, the first year of Edward VI., and the beginning of a reign of toleration in religion. Cabot seems to have been a man of deep piety, for we find him eschewing the vices and follies of the time, advising morning and evening prayers daily, and recommending that "the Bible be daily read devoutly and Christianly to God's honour, and for His grace to be obtained by humble and hearty prayer."

Not long had Cabot been resident in Bristol when the Spanish Ambassador preferred a demand before the English Council for his return to Spain, on the ground that he was a servant of the Emperor and received a pension from him. Cabot had no quarrel with the Emperor, but he refused to go either into Spain or Flanders, though he was willing to give the Emperor all the information he desired. When the Emperor learnt his decision, he struck off his pension; but Edward VI. immediately gave him another one of two hundred and fifty marks, or £166 13s. 4d.—a considerable sum in those days.

The nature of Cabot's employment under the English Government seems to have been as a kind of superintendent of the naval affairs of the kingdom. He examined and licensed pilots, etc., and he assisted the King in his studies in navigation, explaining to him the variation of the compass and other matters. He also constructed a number of invaluable charts and maps, which have unfortunately been destroyed. An edition of Ptolemy's *Geographia*, published at Rome in 1508, shows that Cabot had ascertained exactly the position of the magnetic pole, and pointed out the spot where the ship's compass lost its specific property. The adventurer was thoroughly practical in his plans and aims, and taught others to follow in his train and continue his investigations.

In the year 1551 Cabot brought to fruition an important project which had long occupied his thoughts; it at the same time crushed an extensive monopoly, and established Cabot's title to be regarded as one of the fathers of free trade. Letters of incorporation were issued on the 13th of December, 1551, declaring that, " in consideration of his being the chiefest setter forth of this journey or voyage, therefore we make, ordain, and constitute him, the said Sebastian Cabot, to be the first and present governor during his natural life, without removal." The company thus founded was that of the Merchant Adventurers, and in December, 1552, the Bristol branch of it was incorporated under a separate charter.

We read that, "at the very outset of the society, it was to encounter a difficulty which would have appalled a man of small mental calibre, and led him to give it up in despair.

"The German cities, Antwerp and Hamburg, held exclusive possession of the trade of Northern and Central Europe. By gifts or bribes they had obtained large concessions in the duties and customs of England.

"They paid much less, for instance, when they exported English cloth, than the native manufacturer, if he chose to export, had to pay.

"In importing goods at a favoured and lower rate for themselves, they also furtively introduced large quantities, as their own (for a consideration), at the low rate of duty.

"Having thus secured the command of the English

market, as well as the monopoly of the foreign, they set their own value on goods, and actually brought English wool down to eighteenpence per stone; employed no English ships; and with their joint stocks playing into each other's hands, crushed the English merchants. They were called the Stilliard (Steelyard) merchants.

"Cabot's genius rose to the occasion. He saw no reason why, these impediments once removed, England should not become the manufactory of the world, and her ships the carriers of its produce.

"The father of free trade, he set himself against this monopoly, and manfully did he battle with it.

"By the King's entries in his private journal, we see the deep interest that Edward felt in a matter that so seriously concerned the welfare of his subjects; these entries are continued over five months, and are often of considerable length.

"At last, on February 23, A.D. 1551, success crowned Cabot's persevering efforts, and a result so auspicious to commerce as the breaking up of the close monopoly and so advantageous to the public revenue was not forgotten.

"In March 'Sebastian Cabot, the great seaman, had £200, by way of the King's Majesty's reward.'

"This huge obstacle removed, the merchant adventurers set to work in earnest to open the way and passage to the northern seas.

"New ships are ordered to be built, strong and well-seasoned planks are selected for the purpose, and, to guard against worms, 'which many times pierceth and eateth through the strongest oake,' it is resolved to 'cover the keel of the shippe with thinne sheets of leade.'

"This was the introduction of sheathing into the British marine; the art had been practised in Spain, and Cabot, if not the original inventor, must be allowed the honour of introducing it into England."

Strype affirms that this famous expedition set out from Bristol, where Cabot lived, and where likewise the ships were probably built. The gallant Sir Hugh Willoughby was appointed to the command, and Richard Chancellor—who had been brought up with Sir Philip Sidney—was named pilot-major to the expedition, with command of one of the vessels. Chancellor, who was an intimate friend of Cabot, was a keen, observant man, who noted with remarkable insight the customs, religious habits, manners of the people, and the laws of the country visited. Chancellor's sailing master was Stephen Burroughs, afterwards chief pilot of England.

Cabot drew up a book of instructions for the guidance and government of the expedition, and these instructions were ordered to be read publicly on board each ship once a week. Nothing could more clearly show Cabot's foresight as a navigator than this book of rules, while they also reveal much of the inner character of the man. It is of great interest to note the chief points in the instructions, which ran as follows:

"Ordinances, instructions, and advertisements of and for the direction of the intended voyage to Cathay, compiled, made, and delivered by the right worshipful M. Sebastian Cabota, Esqr., Governour of the Mysterie and Companie of the Merchants Adventurers, for the discoverie of regions, dominions, islands, and places unknowen, the 9th day of May, in the yere of our Lord God 1553, and in the 7 yere of the reigne of our most dread sovereigne Lord Edward VI., by the grace of God King of England, France, and Ireland, defender of the faith, and of the Church of England and Ireland, in earth, supreme head.

"7 item. That the merchants and other skilful persons, in writing, shall daily write, describe, and put in memorie the navigation of each day and night, with the points and observations of the lands, tides, elements, altitude of the sunne, course of the moon and starres, and the same so noted by the order of the master and pilot of every ship to be put in writing; the captaine-generall assembling the masters togethe) once every weeke (if winde and weather shall server to conferre all the observations and notes of the said ships, to the intent it may appeare wherein the notes do agree and wherein they dissent, and upon good debatement, deliberation, and conclusion determined to put the same into a common leger, to remain of record for the companie; the like order to be kept in proportioning of the cardes, astrolabes, and other instruments prepared for the voyage, at the charge of the companie.

"12 item. That no blaspheming of God, or detestable swearing, be used in any ship, nor communication of ribaldrie, filthy tales, or ungodly talke to be suffered in the company of any ship, neither dicing, tabling, nor other divelish games to be frequented, whereby ensueth not only povertie to the players, but also strife, variance, brauling, fighting, and oftentimes murther, to the utter destruction of the parties, and provoking of God's most just wrath and sword of vengeance. These and all such like pestilences and contagions of vices and sinnes to be eschewed, and the offenders once monished, and not reforming, to be punished at the discretion of the captaine and masters as appertaineth.

"13 item. That morning and evening prayer, with other common services appointed by the King's Majestie, and lawes of this realme, be reade and saide in every ship daily by the minister or the Admirall, and the merchant or some other person learned in other ships; and the Bible or paraphrases to be read devoutly and Christianly to God's honour and for His grace to be obtained and had by humble and hearty prayer of the navigants accordingly.

"23 item. Forasmuch as our people and shippes may appear unto them strange and wonderous, and theirs also to ours, it is to be considered how much they may be used, learning much of their natures and dispositions by some one such person as you may first either allure or take to be brought aboard your shippes, and there to learn as you may, *without violence or force*, and no woman to be tempted or intreated to incontinence or dishonestie.

"26 item. Every nation and region to be considered advisedly, and not to provoke them by any distance, laughing, contempt, or such like; but to use them with prudent circumspection, *with all gentleness and courtesie*; and not to tarry long in one place until you shall have obtained the most worthy place that may be found in such sort, as you may returne with victuals sufficient prosperously."

In the 32nd item he refers to the difficulties experienced from timidity and incredulity; and speaks of the "obstacles which had ministered matter of suspicion in some heads that this voyage could not succeed, for the extremitie of the North Pole, lacke of passage, and such like, which have caused wavering minds and doubtful heads, not only to withdraw themselves from the adventures of this voyage, but also dissuaded others from the same," etc., etc.

"33rd item of instructions. No conspiracies, part-takings, factions, false tales, untrue reports, which be the very seedes and fruits of contention, discord, and confusion by evil tongues, to be suffered, but the same and all other ungodliness to be chastened charitably with brotherly love, and always obedience to be used and practised by all persons in their degrees, not only for duty and conscience' sake towards God, under whose merciful hand navigants, above all other creatures, naturally be most high and *vicine*, but also for prudent and worldly policy and publicke weale, considering and always having present in your minds that you be all our most loyal King's subjects, and naturally with daily remembrance of the great importance of the voyage, the honour, glory, praise, and benefit that depend of and upon the same toward the common wealth of this noble realme, the advancement of you the travelers therein, your wives and children, and so to endeavour yourselves as that you may satisfy the expectation of them who, at their great costes, charges, and expenses, have so furnished you in good sort and plenty of all necessaries as the like was never in any realme seen, used, or known, requisite and needful for such an exploit, which is most likely to be achieved and brought to good effect, if every person in his vocation shall endeavour himself according to his charge and most bounden duty, praying the living God to give you His grace to accomplish your charge to His glory, whose merciful hand shall prosper your voyage and preserve you from all dangers. In witness whereof I, Sebastian Cabota, Governor aforesaid, to these present ordinances have subscribed my name and put my seal the day and year above written."

The expedition sailed on the 20th of May, 1553, and as it passed Greenwich it was viewed by the Court, the King being unable to do so on account of sickness. The vessels were parted during a great storm at sea, but Chancellor reached the rendezvous in Norway in safety. Having waited some days in vain for the other ships, he set sail, rounded the North Cape, and reached the White Sea. He landed on the spot where Archangel now stands; and having soon tranquillized the natives, he was provisioned by them. Chancellor safely returned home by the overland route to Moscow, where he established a trade which is still carried on between that city and England.

Willoughby's expedition, on the contrary, met with a tragic fate. His two vessels became frozen up in the ice. These were discovered long afterwards, but all traces of the crew had disappeared, and the only thing known of the gallant but unfortunate adventurers is that some of them were alive in January, 1554.

While Chancellor and Willoughby were still pursuing their voyages, Cabot organized yet another expedition. In this he was assisted by Sir George Barnes (the Lord Mayor), Sheriff Garnett, York, Wyndham, and other adventurers. Guinea was its destination, and the expedition sailed in August, 1553. The King lent two ships, the *Primrose* and the *Lion*, for this voyage. There does not seem to be a record of the fortunes of the expedition. If one existed, it may have been lost with other documents and maps.

In the company of which he was Governor, Cabot had associated with him as members such celebrated men as the Marquis of Winchester, Lord High Treasurer; the Earl of Arundel, Lord Steward; the Earl of Bedford, Lord Privy Seal; Lord Howard of Effingham, Lord High Admiral; the Earl of Pembroke, etc.

After the accession of Mary, England was embroiled in a war with France, and all Cabot's schemes of exploration and colonization had to be abandoned. He secured, however, through Chancellor a charter to trade with Russia. The last voyage which Chancellor, now grand pilot, was destined to make was one in 1556-7, on the occasion of his conveying the Russian Ambassador to England. His vessel was driven on the rocks at Pitsligo, on the Scottish coast, and the noble and intrepid Chancellor lost his life in saving that of the ambassador.

The last attempt to induce Cabot to return to Spain

was made by Charles V. soon after Mary's accession. The veteran navigator preferred to remain under English colours, and he was rewarded by additional emoluments.

The trade with Russia soon increased greatly. Four ships were despatched thither in 1557, one of them being the *Primrose*. The English who went out taught the Russians rope-making, and took apprentices to learn the duties of agents. Among other trade directions which Cabot drew up was one advising the underselling all other nations. The whaling trade with Spitzbergen had its origin at this period. Great impulse was given to commerce in all directions, and this was due entirely to the energy and genius of Cabot. Among other things, a mission was sent out to Persia, which resulted in the opening up of an excellent trade with that far-off country.

Cabot's biographer, Nicholls, thus describes the last authentic glimpse we have of the indefatigable navigator:

"Stephen Burroughs, who had been with Chancellor, was again despatched to the north, in 1556, in a pinnace called the *Seathrift*, and in his journal he gives us a glimpse of the anxious supervision of Cabot, and of his unwillingness to quit them until the very last moment of their sailing.

"We catch the genial smile, marvel at the wonderful unbroken spirit, and note how the wise old man gauged and understood the character of those who surrounded him, and knew how to leave a lasting impression on their minds that there would ever be a feeling of warm and loving sympathy cherished for them, though far, far away, by those who were compelled to stay at home.

"On the 27th of April, being Monday, the Right Worshipful Sebastian Caboto came aboard our pinnesse at Gravesend, accompanied with divers gentlemen and gentlewomen, who, after that they had viewed our pinnesse, and tasted of such cheere as wee could make them aboarde, they went on shore, giveing to our mariners right liberal rewardes. And the goode olde gentleman, Master Caboto, gave to the poore most liberall almes, wishing them to pray for the good fortune and prosperous successe of the *Seathrift* our pinnesse.

"And then, at the sign of the Christopher, he and his friends banketted, and made me and them that were in the companie great cheere; and, for very joy that he had to see the towardnesse of our intended discovery, he enter'd into the dance himself, amongst the rest of the younge and lusty company; which, being ended, hee and his friends departed, most gently commending us to the governance of Almighty God."

Philip of Spain came to England in May, 1557. He was no friend to Cabot, who had refused his father's overtures. Consequently, we are not surprised that on the 27th of May, 1557, Cabot was compelled to resign his position and pension. Two days later he was reinstated; but one William Worthington was associated with him, taking half his pension, and, what is worse, being given the custody of Cabot's "maps, charters, and discourses, written with his own hand." The fate of these documents, and whether they are in the Spanish Archives or not, is not known.

8

When Hakluyt tried to get sight of this precious collection twenty years after Cabot's death, he was met with repeated and peremptory refusals by Worthington.

It is strange that neither the date of the birth nor the death of so distinguished a man as Sebastian Cabot is known, nor even the place where his ashes found burial. Richard Eden, his faithful and attached friend, saw him die; and in a work to be found in the King's Library of the British Museum he records how the ruling passion was strong in death: "As the spirit struggles with the clay, he speaks flightily about a divine revelation to him of a new and infallible method of finding the longitude, which he could not disclose to any mortal."

So sailed out into the unseen the spirit of Sebastian Cabot, who was practically the creator of the British Navy. In addition to that, he was the discoverer of a very large portion of both American continents. His genius, his discoveries, his multifarious labours, and his high and honourable character make up the sum of one of Britain's heroes, and one to whom much of her commercial greatness is due.

CHAPTER IV.

HOW AMERICA RECEIVED ITS NAME.

It is one of the most extraordinary incidents in the history of maritime discovery that the name of the American Continent owes its origin either to a fraudulent misrepresentation or a very singular misapprehension. The weight of opinion has generally favoured the former hypothesis.

Amerigo Vespucci, or, to give another form of the name, Americo Vespucio, is the navigator round whom the controversy has raged, and his partizans have not scrupled to affirm that he took precedence both of Columbus and of the Cabots in the discovery of the mainland of America. As we shall presently see, however, the claim is totally unfounded. Vespucci came of a wealthy family of merchants, and was born at Florence on the 9th of March, 1451. He received his education from his uncle, Giorgio Antonio Vespucci, a Dominican friar, and a friend and colleague of Savonarola. Amerigo early engaged in commerce, first in Florence and afterwards in Seville. In the latter city he met Columbus, probably as early as the year 1493. In 1497 he was engaged in fitting out the ships with which Columbus sailed on his third voyage, and a year before that he had been engaged in fitting out a fleet for the Spanish Government. These undisputed facts entirely dispose of the allegation, erroneously made by himself or others, that he had made a voyage to America in 1497.

The fact is that the first expedition in which Vespucci took part was that under the command of Alonzo de Ojeda, which sailed on the 20th of May, 1499. Ojeda was one of those who accompanied Columbus in his first voyage, and his patron now was the Bishop of Fonseca, the enemy of Columbus, who treacherously procured for him the charts which the great navigator had sent home, and gave him a licence for his voyage, although there was a royal order that none should go without permission within fifty leagues of the lands Columbus had last discovered. Vespucci claimed to have the command of two caravels in Ojeda's fleet. The expedition visited the neighbourhood of Cape Paria, explored several hundred miles of coast as far as Cape de la Veda, and returned in June, 1500.

In May, 1501, Vespucci entered the service of the King of Portugal, and participated in an expedition that visited the coast of Brazil. Here again he only went where others had preceded him, for in 1500 three Spanish expeditions had visited Brazil, under the command respectively of Vicente Yanez Pinzon, Diego de Lepe, and Rodrigo de Bastidas; while a Portuguese fleet, under Pedro Alvarez de Cabral, had accidentally discovered the country and taken possession of it in the name of Portugal. Still, "the expedition of Vespucci was a bold one, and made important additions to astronomical science" by its leader's "observations of the heavenly bodies of the southern firmament, especially of the 'Southern Cross,' and to the knowledge of geography in his exploration of the southern continent and sea of the Western Hemisphere. After leaving Cape Verde, he was sixty-seven days at sea before he made land again at 5° south, off Cape St. Roque, on the 17th of August. Thence he sailed down the coast, spending the whole winter in its exploration, till in the following April he was as far south as the fifty-fourth parallel, farther than any navigator had been before. The nights were fifteen hours long; the weather tempestuous and foggy and very cold. The last land he saw is supposed to be the Island of Georgia, where, finding no harbours, and seeing no people along its rugged shores, the little fleet turned to escape from these savage seas, where perpetual winter and almost perpetual darkness seemed to reign. They reached Lisbon again in 1502."

In May, 1503, Vespucci commanded a caravel in a squadron that sailed for the discovery of Malacca. But he parted company from the rest, and finally made his way to the coast of Brazil, where he discovered the Bay of All Saints. Here he remained for two months, and then ran two hundred and sixty leagues farther south, where he built a fort near Cape Frio; and leaving a colony there, he returned to Lisbon in June, 1504.

Abandoning now the service of Portugal, early in 1505 he obtained letters of naturalization from King Ferdinand of Spain, and on the 22nd of March, 1508, was appointed pilot-major of the kingdom. This office he held until his death, taking charge of the preparation of a general description of coasts and accounts of new discoveries, and also superintending the construction of charts and the examination of pilots. Vespucci died at Seville on the 22nd of February, 1512.

With regard to Vespucci's claim to be the discoverer of America, it is both important and significant that none of the original letters of Amerigo bearing on the subject are extant, except in translations, and these differ greatly among themselves, and contain inconsistencies of fact and date. It is not even known in what language the letters were written. An account by Amerigo of his voyage of 1499, said to have been written on the 18th of July, 1500, was published by Bandini in 1745. A letter of Vespucci to Lorenzo Piero de Medici of Florence, a cousin of Lorenzo the Magnificent, describing the voyage of 1501, was published in various editions, some in Latin, others in German; and in 1789 a new text, in Italian, was discovered by Bartolozzi. The first edition of the letter to Lorenzo Piero de Medici was published at Augsburg in 1504, and round this letter great interest centres. "No wonder that, as it was probably the first printed narrative of any discovery of the mainland of the new continent, it should excite unusual attention. Several editions appeared, in the course of the next four years, in Latin and Italian, and among them one at Strasbourg in 1505 under the editorship of one Mathias Ringmann, a native of Schlestadt, a town in the lower department of the Rhine, twenty-five miles from Strasbourg. So earnest an admirer of Vespucci was this young student, that he appended to the narrative of the voyage a letter and some verses of his own in praise of the navigator, and he gave to the book the title of *Americus Vesputius: De Ora Antarctica per Regem Portugalliæ pridem inventa* (Americus Vespuccius : concerning a Southern Region recently discovered under the King of Portugal). Here was the suggestion of a new southern continent as distinct from the northern continent of Asia, to which the discoveries hitherto mainly north of the Equator were supposed to belong. And this supposition of such a new quarter of the globe gave rise, two years afterward, to a name, all growing naturally enough out of the enthusiasm of this Ringmann for Vespucci, and communicated by him to others."

In 1507 a *Cosmographiæ Introductio* was published at the little College of St. Dié in Lorraine. This college was established and conducted by Walter Lud, secretary of the Duke of Lorraine. It enjoyed the distinction of having one of the new printing-presses then being set up, and Ringmann was appointed to the important post of proof-reader, while he also held the collegiate professorship of Latin. The work above mentioned, the *Cosmographiæ Introductio*, was the composition of Martin Waldseemüller, and it was published under his Greco-Latinized name of "Hylacomylus." Waldseemüller was teacher of geography in the college. To his little work was appended an account by Amerigo of his voyages, purporting to be addressed to René II., Duke of Lorraine. Here it was asserted that four voyages were made, the date of the first being fixed in May, 1497. If this had been true, Amerigo would have reached the mainland a week or two earlier than Cabot, and about fourteen months earlier than Columbus. It was also suggested in the book that Amerigo was entitled to give his name to the continent he had discovered.

But the claim was groundless, and considerable doubt has been thrown on the whole of Vespucci's narrative. Many have charged him with deliberate falsification, and most of his apologists have contented themselves with defending his character rather than the truth of his narrative, ascribing the inconsistencies of the latter to the errors of translators and copyists. In his *Researches*, Santarem says he could find no mention at all of Vespucci in the Royal Archives of Portugal; and it is very important to note that his reputed discovery of the mainland was not used as evidence by the Spanish Government in an action at law in 1512, when it would have been clearly in their favour to do so. On the contrary, Ojeda distinctly asserted that the mainland was discovered by Columbus.

The name of America, however, soon began to be used as the designation of the whole of the Western Hemisphere; and it was not until the publication of Schoner's *Opusculum Geographicum* in 1533 that doubt began to be thrown upon its propriety. Now it is known to be clearly untrue that Vespucci was the first discoverer of the Western Continent. But it would be useless, we presume, to advertise in the daily newspapers that on and after such a date America would henceforth be called and known as Columbia, as it really ought to be. The name of America has taken root, and will no doubt continue to be used till the end of time.

CHAPTER V.

PORTUGUESE, FRENCH, AND SPANISH EXPLORATIONS.

WITH the advent of the sixteenth century, expeditions to the Western Hemisphere became very frequent, France, Spain, Portugal, and England all contributing their quota of adventurers. The leading explorers will be dealt with in separate chapters, while men like Hernando Cortes, the conqueror of Mexico, do not come within the purview of this work.

Confining ourselves now to the minor Portuguese, French, and Spanish explorers, we come first upon the name of Gaspar Cortereal, a native of Lisbon. In 1500, by appointment of Manuel, King of Portugal, he left the mouth of the Tagus with two ships, well equipped at his own cost, and went as far as the regions since known as Canada. He reached 60° N., and imposed upon many places purely Portuguese names, such as Labrador. After his return from this voyage, he again left Lisbon, with two caravels, for the Arctic regions in May, 1501. Cortereal ranged the coast of North America for about seven hundred miles, till he was blocked by ice when approaching the fiftieth degree. The country by which he passed had excellent verdure, and the explorer admired the stately forests in which pines, large enough for masts and yards, promised profitable commerce. Yet he filled his ships with men instead of timber, taking on board fifty Indians to be sold as slaves. The name of Labrador, which was transferred from the territory south of the St. Lawrence to a region farther north, is the only permanent survival of Portuguese exploration in North America. Cortereal never returned from his second voyage; and although two rescue expeditions were sent out, nothing was discovered as to his fate.

The French were early in the field as North American colonizers. In 1504, seven years only after the discovery of the continent, Bretons and Normans were fishing in Newfoundland. The former gave their name to the Island of Cape Breton. In 1506 a map of the Gulf of St. Lawrence was drawn by John Denys of Honfleur, who had explored the gulf. There are many records of private French fishing enterprises. One Thomas Aubert, a pilot of Dieppe, visited Cape Breton Island, and carried some of the natives thence to France. But the most remarkable expedition for some years was the voyage of Giovanni di Verrazano in 1523. Verrazano, though a native of Florence, had been trained under Aubert. Originally he went out with four vessels, but three were lost, leaving only his own ship, the *Dauphine*. In a letter which he sent to King Francis I., it is believed that we get for the first time a passing glimpse, by actual description, of much of the long stretch of the Atlantic coast of North America now within the boundaries of the United States. His vessel is supposed to have been the first to enter New York Harbour; and Verrazano is further believed to have visited what are now known as

Narragansett Bay and the shores of New England and Maine. His fate is unknown, but "the credit belongs to him, not only of having first explored with some care the Atlantic coast of the United States, but of first promulgating the true theory of the size of the globe in contradistinction to that of the old cosmographers, which Columbus had adopted and believed in to the day of his death."

Leaving for the present the great work of Jacques Cartier, we must now briefly sketch the painful but romantic story of the celebrated Admiral Coligny's attempt at colonization in North America. The admiral despatched from Havre, in the King's name, in February, 1562, two ships under the command of Captain John Ribault, "to discover and view a certaine long coast of the West Indies called La Florida"—a coast which really included the whole of the Atlantic side of the United States from the Rio Grande to the Canadian line. Ribault was a tried commander, and a man of faith and truth, brave also and experienced. Besides his seamen, he had under him a band of soldiers, and a number of gentlemen, whose object was to build up the Reformed Protestant Church in the wilderness to the glory of God.

Ribault's expedition safely reached the coast of Florida, and entered a river which they called the River of May, but which is now known as the St. John. Thanks were given to God for their success, and a pillar was set up with the arms of France, this being the first boundary on the south of the French King's dominions in the New World. The land seemed fair and fruitful, "and pleasantest of all the world."

It abounded in all kinds of fruits, birds, and fishes. Proceeding northward, on the 30th of May the expedition entered the harbour of Port Royal, where a navy might ride in safety. Here it was proposed to found a colony; and Ribault, calling his men together, delivered a speech to them full of noble sentiments. Those whom Ribault left behind to establish a colony, under Albert de la Pierria as leader, erected a fort, which was called Charles Fort. It was on a little island on the Chenonceau stream, now known as Archer's Creek, about six miles from Beaufort, South Carolina.

Improvidence and idleness on the part of the colonists led to mutiny and bloodshed. Captain Albert was deposed for his severity, and a worthy man named Nicholas Barre was chosen as his successor. But although peace was secured, the pangs of hunger could not be allayed, and the colonists built a vessel, on board which they embarked for France. Terrible privations were experienced during the voyage, and the remnant who were left were taken by an English captain, the feeblest being sent to France, and the others conveyed as prisoners to England.

As no news had been received of Ribault in France, in April, 1564, Coligny despatched a new expedition under Captain René de Laudonnière, who had four vessels under him. Laudonnière reached the River of May in June, and was received with enthusiastic transports by the natives. The captain made a most glowing report of the country He built a triangular fort, which he named Fort Caroline, on a spot now known as St. John's Bluff, on the bank of the St.

John River. The greed for gold and silver, however, soon set in amongst the colonists, and disaffection and insubordination followed. The mutineers seized the vessels, but speedily quarrelled amongst themselves, with the result that three of the vessels fell into the hands of the Spaniards, while the fourth was brought back to Fort Caroline, where Laudonnière punished the ringleaders with death. But famine next attacked the colony, which was aggravated by conflicts with the natives. In August, 1565, an English fleet arrived, under Sir John Hawkins, who succoured the colonists. They were next engaged in making preparations to return to France, when on the 28th of August seven ships arrived under the command of Ribault himself. Unjust complaints had been made to Coligny against Laudonnière, and the latter was told that he must return to France to answer them, Ribault being appointed to take command of the colony in his place.

A Spanish fleet shortly afterwards arrived in the River of May, under the command of Pedro Menendez, whose mission was to burn and destroy all Lutheran Frenchmen whom he might meet with. Menendez was a treacherous, bloodthirsty bigot. Against the advice of Laudonnière, Ribault sailed with all the larger vessels and most of the effective men at his command, intending to attack the enemy at the mouth of the River of Dolphins; and he left behind him at Fort Caroline only about two hundred and forty persons, including the sick, the women, and the children. Learning these facts, Menendez marched on Fort Caroline, which fell an easy prey, and the poor colonists were ruthlessly slaughtered without any consideration for age or sex. A few persons escaped, including Laudonnière; and these got on board vessels in command of a nephew of Ribault, who sailed away for France.

As the other men on board Ribault's ships had been wrecked on Anastasia Island, a little to the southward, Menendez proceeded thither; and although the poor creatures appealed to his humanity, he put nearly all of them to the sword, as they were of the Reformed religion. Ribault himself, with the remnant of his force, next fell into the hands of the butcher; and they also were diabolically murdered, Menendez fiendishly reporting to the King of Spain that he judged this "to be expedient for the service of God our Lord, and of your Majesty." The place of this fearful massacre is still called "the bloody river of Matanzas." There were still a few French colonists left, and when these were captured a few were killed and the majority sent to the galleys.

Menendez now erected a fort at the mouth of the River of Dolphins. "It was the first permanent European settlement within the present boundaries of the United States, and called by Menendez 'St. Augustine,' because on the festival day of that saint—the 28th of August—the Spanish fleet had come in sight of the coast of Florida, and run into the mouth of the river." The foundation of this Spanish colony marked the end of the French colony.

When the news of the Spanish cruelties reached France, great indignation was excited amongst the people; yet the Catholic King and his infamous mother Catherine took no steps to avenge the wrong because the Frenchmen slain were Lutherans. However, a few years later, that is, in the spring of 1568, three French vessels appeared off the mouth of the River of May, commanded by one Dominique de Gourgues. De Gourgues was a soldier of high repute, who had vengeance to work out on his own account against the Spaniards, as well as to punish them for the Matanzas massacre. His followers eagerly entered into his projects, and they were warmly welcomed by the Indians. An alliance was formed with the friendly chief Satouriona, and a desperate assault was made on the fort one morning at daybreak. The Spaniards were completely surprised, and in a few moments only fifteen of them were left alive.

De Gourgues now embarked his men, and made for the other side of the river, where he furiously attacked the bewildered Spaniards in that quarter. The port of San Mateo, with a force of nearly three hundred men, was next assaulted and taken, almost every Spaniard being left for dead. "But the massacre of Fort Caroline was not even yet atoned for. The flag of France once more floated over its ramparts of earth; the bodies of nearly four hundred Spaniards lay unburied on the shores of the River of May; but there were prisoners still alive. De Gourgues ordered them to be brought before him, in the presence of his own men and his Indian allies. He was there, he told them, to avenge acts which were as heinous an insult to France as they were atrocious crimes against humanity; although such deeds could not be punished as they deserved, the perpetrators should, at least, be made to suffer all the retaliation that could be inflicted by an honourable enemy. Near by were still standing the trees on which Menendez had hanged his prisoners, beneath the inscription : 'I do this not as to Frenchmen, but as to Lutherans.' To the same trees the French captain ordered the Spaniards to be led for execution ; and over their heads were the words, burned into a plank with a hot iron : 'I do not this as unto Spaniards, nor as unto Maranes ; but as unto traitors, robbers, and murderers.'"

As De Gourgues's whole force numbered less than three hundred men, he was not sufficiently strong to attack St. Augustine, so he left Florida and returned home. The King of Spain sent a small fleet to capture him off the French coast ; but he eluded their pursuit, and lived in retirement until 1579.

Among the early French voyagers to the coast of Maine was André Thévet, the traveller and cosmographer, who had been a member of Villegagnon's Huguenot colony in South America. In 1536 he visited the Grand River (Penobscot), and entered into traffic with the natives, who were most friendly. The Abnakis, who, with the Micmacs, were the aboriginal inhabitants of Maine, inhabited the territory from the Penobscot, north of Canada, and through New Hampshire, and dwelt in five permanent villages. They were brave, hospitable, and faithful people ; and coming under the influence of the French missionaries, they soon became attached to the French, who kept them strongly hostile to the English.

Under the title of Nouvelle France, the French proclaimed their authority over the whole of the region which included Maine, though for many years they did little towards colonizing it. In 1598 the Marquis de la Roche, a nobleman of Brittany, secured an ample commission from Henry IV., and made a futile attempt at a settlement. He scoured the French prisons, and took out their inmates to the desolate Isle of Sable; but after suffering great hardships, a small remnant were glad to return to France, when they received a pardon.

De Chauvin, an experienced sea officer, next obtained a commission similar to that granted to De la Roche. He had associated with him in the enterprise Pontgrave, a merchant of St. Malo. Chauvin made two profitable voyages, and was preparing for a third when his sudden death intervened.

But the work of French colonization was destined to be effected by Samuel Champlain, who has not unjustly been styled "the Father of New France." He was a native of Brouage, and was an able marine officer and a man of science. In 1603 he was selected to command an expedition manned by a company of merchants of Rouen, which had been founded by the Governor of Dieppe. Champlain is described as by his natural disposition "delighting marvellously in these enterprises." The American historian George Bancroft observes that Champlain had for a season, in the last year of the sixteenth century, "engaged in the service of Spain, that he might make a voyage to regions into which no Frenchman could otherwise have entered. He was in Porto Rico and St. Domingo and Cuba, visited the city of Mexico, and showed the benefits of joining the two oceans by a canal to Panama. He now became the father of New France. He possessed a clear and penetrating understanding with a spirit of cautious inquiry, untiring perseverance with great mobility, indefatigable activity with fearless courage. The account of his first expedition to Canada gives proof of sound judgment, accurate observation, and historical fidelity. It is full of details on the manners of the savage tribes, not less than the geography of the country; and Quebec was already selected as the appropriate site for a fort.

"In November, 1603, just after Champlain had returned to France, an exclusive patent was issued to a Calvinist, the able, patriotic, and honest De Monts. The sovereignty of Acadia and its confines, from the fortieth to the forty-sixth degree of latitude, that is, from Philadelphia to beyond Montreal; a still wider monopoly of the fur trade; the exclusive control of the soil, government, and trade; freedom of religion for Huguenot emigrants,—these were the privileges which his charter conceded.

"In March, 1604, two ships left the shores of France not to return till a permanent settlement should be made in America. The summer glided away while the emigrants trafficked with the natives and explored the coasts. The harbour called Annapolis, after its conquest, by Queen Anne, an excellent harbour, though difficult of access, possessing a small but navigable river, which abounded in fish and is bordered by beautiful meadows, so pleased Pontrincourt, a leader in the enterprise, that he sued for a grant of it from De Monts, and, naming it Port Royal, determined to reside there with his family. The company of De Monts made their first attempt at a settlement on the Island of St. Croix, at the mouth of the river of the same name. Yet the island was so ill-suited to their purposes that, in the spring of 1605, they removed to Port Royal.

"For an agricultural colony a milder climate was more desirable. In view of a settlement at the south, De Monts in the same year explored and claimed for France the rivers, especially the Merrimac, the coasts, and the bays of New England, as far at least as Cape Cod. The numbers and hostility of the savages led him to delay a removal, since his colonists were so few. Yet the purpose remained. Thrice, in the spring of 1606, did Dupont, his lieutenant, attempt to complete the discovery. Twice he was driven back by adverse winds, and at the third attempt his vessel was wrecked. Pontrincourt, who had visited France and returned with supplies, himself renewed the design; but meeting with disasters among the shoals of Cape Cod, he too returned to Port Royal."

Henry IV. confirmed the possessions of Pontrincourt in 1607; Marie de Medici contributed to support the missions which the Marquise de Guercheville protected; in 1610 the Jesuits were granted an impost on the fisheries and fur trade; and in the following year a number of Jesuit priests arrived to begin the work of converting the natives. In a very short time the tribes between the Penobscot and the Kennebec became the firm allies of France. A French colony was founded in 1613, under the auspices of De Guercheville and Marie de Medici, when De Saussaye raised the entrenchments of St. Sauveur on the eastern shore of Mount Desert Isle. The Indians now gathered round the Christian cross as raised by the Jesuits, and they looked upon the Jesuit leader Father Biart as a messenger from heaven. But while this was taking place, the monopoly of De Monts had been revoked through the influence of French merchants. Champlain, who was filled with the ambition of founding a state, succeeded in forming a company of merchants of Dieppe and St. Malo, and under their auspices he raised the French flag over Quebec on the 3rd of July, 1608.

Champlain, with a mixed party consisting of Hurons and Algonkins, and two Europeans, undertook, in 1607, an expedition against the Iroquois, or Five Nations, in the north of New York. He explored the lake which now bears his name, and fought a successful battle near Ticonderoga. After the death of Henry IV., the Prince of Condé became Viceroy of New France, and through him the merchants of St. Malo, Rouen, and La Rochelle obtained a colonial patent from the King in 1615. Champlain, who was then in France, again went out to the New World, and unsuccessfully invaded the territory of the Iroquois. Wounded and dispirited, he wandered about the forests until he reached a village of Algonkins, near Lake Nipissing.

In 1620 Champlain carried out the wishes of the new viceroy, Montmorenci, by beginning the construction of the strong Castle of St. Louis. It was completed in 1624, on a commanding elevation, and it long formed the place of council against the Iroquois and against New England. Difficulties arose between the Jesuits and the Calvinists in the French settlements; but Champlain finally established the authority of the French on the banks of the St. Lawrence. This enterprising navigator died at Quebec on Christmas Day, 1635.

With regard to the Spanish explorations, they were of a stirring and romantic character. First in order come those of Vasco Nuñez de Balboa, who discovered the Pacific Ocean in September, 1513; but as his exploits do not come within our scope, we pass on to the discoverer of Florida, Juan Ponce de Leon. This Ponce de Leon was a fellow-voyager of Columbus in his second expedition. For a time he was governor of Porto Rico. When removed from this post, although he was getting into years, he resolved on an expedition to the north. Accordingly, on the 3rd of March, 1513, he sailed from Porto Rico with three vessels, fitted out at his own expense. He cruised among the Bahamas, and on the 27th of March anchored off the mainland near the point now called Fernandina. He took possession of the land in the name of Spain; and as the day was Easter Sunday —called by the Spaniards *Pascua de Flores*—he named the newly discovered territory Florida. The land, moreover, was brilliant with flowers. Ponce doubled Cape Florida; and in addition to giving Spain a new province, he opened up for Spanish commerce a new channel through the Gulf of Florida. The King of Spain ordered him to colonize the new land, and appointed him its governor; and Ponce had thus the distinction of being the first governor of territory within the limits of the present United States. After being absent in Europe for some years, Ponce de Leon returned to Florida in 1521. He was engaged in selecting a site for a new colony, when the Indians fell furiously upon the Spaniards, and Ponce, who was mortally wounded by an arrow, returned to Cuba to die.

Between Ponce de Leon's discovery of Florida and his death other travellers visited the coast. In 1516 Diego Miruelo, a sea captain, landed and traded with the natives; in 1517 Hernandez de Cordova did the like, but was mortally wounded; in 1518 his pilot conducted another squadron to the same shores; and in 1519 Francisco de Garay, a companion of Columbus, and now governor of Jamaica, landed on the shore, but was attacked by the Indians and lost most of his men. He returned the next year, and he was the first thorough explorer of the gulf coast of the United States. He found that Florida was not an island, as was supposed; and he was believed also to have made the first discovery of the Mississippi, which appears in the earliest charts as the Rio del Espiritu Santo, or River of the Holy Ghost.

The next important discoverer was Lucas Vasquez de Ayllon, who in 1520 explored the coasts of South Carolina, which was then called Chicora. The name of the Jordan was given to the Combahee River, and that of St. Helena, given to a cape, now belongs to the sound. Vasquez treacherously kidnapped a number of Indians, whom he intended to sell as slaves for the gold-mines and plantations of the islands. But of his two vessels, one foundered at sea and all on board perished, and only a few of the Indians remaining on the other ship lived to reach Hispaniola. The Emperor Charles V. rewarded Vasquez, and appointed him to the conquest of Chicora. In 1525 Vasquez set forth again with a formidable expedition. He appears to have explored the territory which is now represented by the States of Georgia, the Carolinas, Virginia, and Maryland; but sickness and the Indians decimated his force, so that out of six hundred soldiers and sailors who formed the expedition not more than one hundred and fifty returned to Hispaniola. Vasquez himself died from sickness.

Stephen Gomez, an able Portuguese seaman in the service of Spain, sailed from Corunna with a single vessel only, in February, 1525, to find a passage to Cathay, which he believed to lie between Florida and the Baccalaos, or Newfoundland. He voyaged from north to south on the American coast, and discovered the Hudson, which he named the St. Antony. It would seem that he got to about the latitude of New York, but no positive record remains of his voyage. He returned to Spain, however, with a freight of furs and Indians.

A story of the deepest interest is that relating to the formidable but disastrous expedition of Pamphilo de Narvaez, who obtained from Charles V. the contract to explore and reduce all the territory from the Atlantic to the River Palmas. Narvaez was a wealthy man, who risked all his treasure upon his conquests. He sailed from Spain in 1527 with five ships and about five hundred men. Many Spaniards of noble birth were in his train, and one, Alvar Nuñez Cabeza de Vaca, will have a permanent place in the records of discovery as treasurer and historian of the expedition. During the winter of 1527-8 the expedition, amidst storms and losses, passed from port to port on the southern side of Cuba. In the spring Cape San Antonio was doubled; but a strong south wind setting in, the fleet was driven upon the American coast. On the 14th of April Narvaez anchored in or near the outlet of the Bay of the Cross, now Tampa Bay. This was the day before Good Friday, and two days afterwards the governor landed, and in the name of Spain took possession of Florida. Against the advice of Cabeza de Vaca, Narvaez, with three hundred men, struck into the interior of the country, being allured by the prospect of gold. Nature everywhere they found to be most beautiful, and the trees, birds, deer, etc., elicited admiration; but they discovered no gold.

The further fate of the expedition is told in detail by many historians; but as the narrative by Mr. Bancroft is perhaps the most graphic, we quote from it the following passage: "When on rafts and by swimming they had painfully crossed the strong current of the Withlochoochee, they were so worn away by famine as to give infinite thanks to God for lighting upon a field of unripe maize. Just after the middle of June, they encountered the Swanee, whose wide, deep, and rapid stream delayed them till they could build a large canoe. Wading through swamps, made more terrible by immense trunks of fallen trees, that lay rotting in the water, and sheltered the few but skilful native archers, on the day after Saint John's they came in sight of Appalachee, where they had pictured to themselves a populous town and food and treasure, and found only a hamlet of forty wretched cabins.

"Here they remained for five-and-twenty days, scouring the country round in quest of silver and gold, till, perishing with hunger, and weakened by fierce attacks, they abandoned all hope but of an escape from a region so remote and malign. Amidst increasing dangers, they went onward through deep lagoons and the ruinous forest in search of the sea, till they came upon a bay, which they called Baia de Caballos, and which now forms the harbour of St. Mark's. No trace could be found of their ships. Sustaining life, therefore, by the flesh of their horses, and by six or seven hundred bushels of maize, plundered from the Indians, they beat their stirrups, spurs, crossbows, and other implements of iron into saws, axes, and nails; and in sixteen days finished five boats, each of twenty-two cubits, or more than thirty feet in length.

"In calking their frail crafts, films of the palmetto served for oakum, and they payed the seams with pitch from the nearest pines. For rigging, they twisted ropes out of horsehair and the fibrous bark of the palmetto; their shirts were pieced together for sails, and oars were shaped out of savins; skins flayed from horses served for water-bottles; it was difficult in the deep sand to find large stones for anchors and ballast. Thus equipped, on the 22nd of September about two hundred and fifty men—all of the original party of five hundred whom famine, autumnal fevers, fatigue, and the arrows of the savage bowmen had spared—embarked for the River Palmas.

"Former navigators had traced the outline of the coast, but among the voyagers there was not a single expert mariner. One shallop was commanded by

Alonzo de Castillo and Andres Dorantes, another by Cabeza de Vaca. The gunwales of the crowded vessels rose but a hand-breadth above the water, till, after creeping for seven days through shallow sounds, Cabeza seized five canoes of the natives, out of which the Spaniards made guard-boards for their five boats. During thirty days more they kept on their way, suffering from hunger and thirst, imperilled by a storm, now closely following the shore, now avoiding savage enemies by venturing out to sea. On the 30th of October, at the hour of vespers, Cabeza de Vaca, who happened to lead the van, discovered one of the mouths of the river now known as the Mississippi, and the little fleet was snugly moored among islands at a league from the stream, which brought down such a flood that even at that distance the water was sweet. They would have entered the 'very great river' in search of fuel to parch their corn, but were baffled by the force of the current and a rising north wind.

"A mile and a half from land they sounded, and with a line of thirty fathoms could find no bottom. In the night following a second day's fruitless struggle to go up the stream, the boats were separated; but the next afternoon Cabeza, overtaking and passing Narvaez, who chose to hug the land, struck boldly out to sea in the wake of Castillo, whom he descried ahead. They had no longer an adverse current, and in that region the prevailing wind is from the east. For four days the half-famished adventurers kept prosperously towards the west, borne along by their rude sails and their labour at the oar. All the 5th of November an easterly storm drove them forward;

and, on the morning of the 6th, the boat of Cabeza was thrown by the surf on the sands of an island, which he called the Isle of Malhado—that is, of misfortune. Except as to its length, his description applies to Galveston; his men believed themselves not far from the Panuco. The Indians of the place expressed sympathy for their shipwreck by howls, and gave them food and shelter. Castillo was cast away a little farther to the east; but he and his company were saved alive. Of the other boats, an uncertain story reached Cabeza: that one foundered in the gulf; that the crews of the two others gained the shore; that Narvaez was afterwards driven out to sea; that the stranded men began wandering towards the west; and that all of them but one perished from hunger.

"Those who were with Cabeza and Castillo gradually wasted away from cold and want and despair; but Cabeza de Vaca, Dorantes, Castillo, and Estevanico, a blackamoor from Barbary, bore up against every ill, and, though scattered among various tribes, took thought for each other's welfare. The brave Cabeza de Vaca, as self-possessed a hero as ever graced a fiction, fruitful in resources, and never wasting time in complaints of fate or fortune, studied the habits and the languages of the Indians, accustomed himself to their modes of life, peddled little articles of commerce from tribe to tribe in the interior and along the coast for forty or fifty leagues, and won fame in the wilderness as a medicine man of wonderful gifts. In September, 1534, after nearly six years' captivity, the great forerunner among the path-finders across the continent inspired the three others with his own marvellous fortitude, and, naked and ignorant of the way, without so much as a single bit of iron, they planned their escape. Cabeza has left an artless account of his recollections of the journey; but his memory sometimes called up incidents out of their place, so that his narrative is confused. He pointed his course far inland, partly because the nations away from the sea were more numerous and more mild, partly that, if he should again come among Christians, he might describe the land and its inhabitants. Continuing his pilgrimage through more than twenty months, sheltered from cold, first by deer-skins, then by buffalo robes, he and his companions passed through Texas as far north as the Canadian River; then, along Indian paths, crossed the water-shed to the valley of the Rio Grande del Norte; and borne up by cheerful courage against hunger, want of water on the plains, cold and wearisome, perils from beasts and perils from red men, the voyagers went from town to town in New Mexico, westward and still to the west, till in May, 1536, they drew near the Pacific Ocean at the village of San Miguel, in Sonora. From that place they were escorted by Spanish soldiers to Compostella; and all the way to the city of Mexico they were entertained as public guests."

After his return to Spain in 1537, Cabeza de Vaca published an account of his expedition. He was subsequently appointed administrator of La Plata, but was shipwrecked in going out on the coast of Paraguay, and became the first explorer of that country. In 1544 he was taken to Spain, and on certain charges affecting his administration was banished to Africa. Recalled by the King in 1552, he was pardoned and made judge of the Supreme Court of Seville, dying seven years later.

The news originally brought by Cabeza de Vaca of the existence of half-civilized tribes far to the north led to expeditions in that region. The first was sent out under Marco de Niza in 1539. On its return a more important expedition was fitted out under Francisco Vasquez de Coronado, governor of New Galicia. It departed from Culiacan, on the Pacific coast, in April, 1540. Coronado passed up the entire length of what is now the State of Sonora to the River Gila. Crossing this, he penetrated the country beyond to the Little Colorado, and visited the famed cities of Cibola mentioned by De Vaca and De Niza. He states that he found seven cities in the kingdom; but the country was too cold for cotton, although the people wore mantles of it, and cotton yarn was found in their houses. He also found maize, guinea-cocks, peas, and dressed skins. From Cibola, Coronado travelled eastward, visiting several towns, similar to the existing villages of the Pueblo Indians, till he reached the Rio Grande; and from there journeyed three hundred leagues to Quivira, the ruins of which are well known, being near lat. 34° N., about one hundred and seventy miles from El Paso. There he found a temperate climate, with good water and an abundance of fruit. The people were clothed in skins. On his way back in March, 1542, Coronado fell from his horse at Tiguex, near the Rio Grande, and is said to have become insane. Mendoza, the viceroy, desired a colony to be founded in the regions visited; but the commander of the expedition did not wish to leave any of his party in so poor a country and at so great a distance from succour. It appears that the narrative of this expedition furnishes the first authentic account of the buffalo, or American bison, and the great prairies and plains of New Mexico. Drawings of the cities and houses, built by the Indians, were sent to Spain with Coronado's report.

An expedition under Don Tristan de Luna, a scion of a noble family in Aragon, sailed from Vera Cruz on the 14th of August, 1559, for Florida. It was a large and imposing fleet, for Tristan had with him an army of fifteen hundred men, besides many friars bent on Indian proselytizing, and a number of women and children, the families of the soldiers who were to colonize the new dominion. The expedition arrived safely at a good harbour, which Tristan named the Santa Maria, now known as Pensacola Bay. Within a few days, however, a great storm arose, and all the ships were driven on shore and destroyed. The leader sent out a detachment of soldiers to explore the country. After a march of forty days, they came upon an Indian town, and found provisions abundant. The sergeant-major sent back a party of sixteen to De Luna, who, with his train of one thousand men, women, and children, set out for the Indian town, which was safely reached. But the provisions which at first seemed so abundant were soon exhausted, and De Luna sent out a second search party. As his people began to die of hunger, however, he led them back by a weary and painful march to Santa Maria. De Luna despatched from the port two small vessels to the viceroy, asking for succour, which fortunately arrived, and the colonists were borne away. The commander was recalled, and returned to Mexico in 1561, chagrined at the failure of the most promising attempt ever made by the Spaniards for the colonization of Florida.

Pedro Menendez, who had already founded St. Augustine, likewise made an attempt in 1566 to establish a post on the shores of the Bay of St. Mary, or Chesapeake Bay, or upon one of its tributary rivers. The expedition was unsuccessful; but four years later Menendez persuaded the General of the Order of the Jesuits to found a missionary station at Axacan, as a portion of Virginia was called. A band of priests, led by an Indian convert named Don Luis, afterwards landed on the banks of the Potomac—then called the Espiritu Santo—and travelled on foot to the Rappahannock, near which river they put up a chapel. But Don Luis soon forgot his Christianity, and returned to his savage Indian instincts, and the priests were massacred. Menendez returned from Spain, and exacted vengeance for the deed. For more than thirty years longer, nevertheless, St. Augustine remained the only European colony within the present limits of the United States. In 1586 Sir Francis Drake, on entering the River of Dolphins, found the Spanish settlement under the command of Pedro Menendez, a nephew of the founder, who had also continued his relative's explorations on the coast of Florida. To Spain thus belongs the honour of discovering Florida and the Mississippi; but the path of the explorers was unfortunately too often stained by treachery, cruelty, and bloodshed.

CHAPTER VI.

JACQUES CARTIER AND FERDINAND DE SOTO.

AMONG the early pioneers of North America, Jacques Cartier is entitled to a very prominent place. This distinguished explorer was born in the French town of St. Malo in December, 1494. He led a seafaring life, and made several fishing voyages to the great banks of Labrador, until he entered upon his first real voyage of discovery in 1534. It was Philip Chabot, Admiral of France, who initiated the expedition. He had urged the King to establish a colony somewhere in the north-west, and the enterprise was entrusted to Cartier, who already enjoyed high repute as an experienced mariner.

Cartier, who had only two ships of sixty tons each, with a total of one hundred and twenty-two men, sailed from St. Malo in April, 1534. Steering for Newfoundland, he passed through the Straits of Belle Isle into the Gulf of Chaleurs, and planted a cross at Gaspé, decorated with the arms of France, and bearing the inscription, *Vive le Roi de France!* The native Indians, whom he described as being in a lamentable condition, objected through their chief to this proceeding; but Cartier deceived them by saying that it " was only set up to be as a light and leader which ways to enter into the port." He further conciliated them by trifling presents, and persuaded the chief to allow him to take his two sons back to France with him. During this voyage Cartier discovered the Great River of Canada, and ascended its channel until he could perceive land on either side. When he returned home, his native city and France were filled with the fame of his discoveries.

The consequence was that, in the ensuing year, a new expedition was decided upon, the King himself providing three well-furnished vessels, the largest, however, being of only one hundred and twenty tons. It solemnly set forth in May, 1535, Cartier's object being, not only to find the way to Cathay, but to plant French colonies in new lands, where whole nations were to be converted to the Holy Catholic Faith. Steering westward along the coast of Labrador, Cartier entered a small bay opposite the Island of Anticosti, which he called the Bay of St. Lawrence. He proceeded cautiously up the river, past the Saguenay and Cape Tourmente, and anchored off a wooded and vine-clad island. On account of the rich clusters of grapes he called this island Bacchus (afterwards known as the Island of Orleans); and after friendly converse with the Indians, notably with Donnacona, their chief, he came upon the majestic site of the modern Quebec, then called Stadaconé. He next went in a boat up the St. Croix River (now the St. Charles); and understanding that many days' journey up the River Hochelaga (for by that name the Indians called the St. Lawrence) there was a large town of the same name, he resolved to proceed thither. The Indians were averse to his going, and tried to frighten him by sending three of their number, disguised as devils, with blackened faces and "horns on their heads more than a yard long." But Cartier only ridiculed the devils, and declared the Indian god Cudruaigny to be "but a fool and a noddie." Christ would defend from the cold all who believed in Him; and though he (the French captain) had not himself talked with Jesus upon this subject, his priests had, and received from Him a promise of fair weather. The Indians felt themselves defeated, and Cartier proceeded on his way. On the 2nd of October, 1535, his vessels lay in the stream off Hochelaga, the modern Montreal.

The stirring scene which followed the arrival of Cartier and his companions is thus described by one historian: "When they landed below the Rapids of St. Mary, a thousand Indians, men, women, and children, came down to the strand to welcome them. With great pomp and circumstance, Cartier, 'very gorgeously attired,' marched with his companions to the royal residence. It was in a village of about fifty huts, surrounded with a triple row of palisades, in the midst of wide fields where the brown dried leaves of the Indian corn waved and rustled in the autumn winds. On this spot now stands Montreal, and a hill near by which Cartier called Mont Royal gave a name to the future city.

"In the centre of Hochelaga was a public square, where all the people gathered. The women and the maidens came with their arms full of children, begging that they might even so much as be touched by these wonderful white men from some far-off country. The 'lord and king,' Agouhanna, a man of fifty years, helpless from palsy, was brought in by his attendants stretched upon a deer-skin. Upon his head, instead of a crown, he wore 'a certain thing made of the skinnes of hedgehogs like a red wreath,' but otherwise his apparel did not distinguish him from his subjects. He prayed that relief might be given him from the disease with which he was afflicted. Cartier with his own hands rubbed the shrunken limbs of the royal sufferer, who bestowed upon him in return his crown of coloured porcupine quills. It seemed to these poor heathen 'that God was descended and come downe from heaven to heale them'; and the halt, the lame, the blind, the impotent from age—so old, some of them, 'that the hair of their eyelids came downe and covered their cheekes'— were brought forward to be healed. The best the good captain could do was to pray; he read the first chapter of the Gospel of St. John and the passion of Christ from his service-book, and besought the heavenly Father that He would have mercy upon these benighted savages, and bring them to a knowledge of His holy Word. The Indians were 'marvellously attentive,' looking to heaven as the Christians did, and imitating all the gestures of devotion; but they better understood, and were overwhelmed with joy, when, the prayers being finished, the distribution of hatchets, knives, beads, rings, brooches of tin, and other trifles was begun.

"Cartier and his companions soon returned to their winter quarters at the mouth of the St. Charles, where those they had left behind had meanwhile built a rough fort. The river within a few weeks was covered with solid ice, and their ships were buried in four feet of snow. With the increasing cold, one of those pestilences so common among the Indians broke out; and whether it was contagious, or whether it was superinduced by exposure to the severity of the climate, it soon attacked the French. Twenty-four of the company died, and the rest were so enfeebled that only three were capable of any exertion. To the fear of death from sickness was added suspicion of the Indians, who, they were afraid, would take advantage of the weakness of the strangers and exterminate those whom the pestilence spared. The natives were ordered to keep away from the fort and the ships under pretence of precaution against infection; and when any of them approached, Cartier ordered his sick men to beat with hammers and sticks against the side of their berths that the noise might be mistaken for sounds of busy industry. But where they looked for danger came succour. From the Indians they learned that a decoction of the leaves and bark of a certain tree was a specific for that malady under which they were fast perishing. The squaws brought branches of the tree, and taught them how to prepare and use this sovereign medicine, which in a few days, not only did all that was promised for it, but also cured the sick of some old chronic difficulties.

"Their suspicions of the Indians, nevertheless, continued. When Donnacona had gone on a hunting expedition, the French had feared it was to gather a force sufficient for an attack upon the fort and ships. A certain shyness the Indians showed on their return, and an unwillingness to part, except at a high price, with provision they needed for their own support, confirmed the apprehensions. Suspicion on the one side undoubtedly begot it on the other; but that the natives had the most ground for it was shown in the end. When Cartier, in the spring, was ready to sail, he enticed Donnacona, with nine others, on board his ships, seized and confined them, and, heedless of the cries and entreaties of their countrymen, carried them to France. In July, 1536, the fleet arrived at St. Malo; and when, four years later, another expedition returned to Canada, Donnacona and his companions, excepting one little girl, were all dead. They had been baptized and received into the bosom of the Church, however, before they died—compensation enough, it was thought, for enforced loss of liberty, country, and friends."

Cartier made such a report to King Francis of the natural wealth of Canada, that in 1540 Jean François de la Roque, Lord de Roberval of Picardy, was made viceroy and lieutenant-governor in Canada, Hochelaga, Saguenay, Newfoundland, and all the other French-American territories. Cartier was appointed his captain-general, and went out before De Roberval, leaving St. Malo on the 23rd of May, 1541. He had five vessels with him. When he reached Stadaconé, Cartier announced the death of Donnacona, and spread the false report that the other chiefs had married in France and dwelt in great affluence.

De Roberval's expedition was, says the historian already quoted, barren of any permanent results, like those preceding it. "A new fort was begun a few miles above the site of the old one, at the mouth of the St. Croix River; some little land was sowed; something which they took to be gold was gathered; something else, probably crystals of quartz, they supposed were diamonds—for they were so 'faire, polished, and excellently cut,' that in the sunlight they 'glister as it were sparkles of fire.' Two ships were sent home in the autumn with tidings of good progress. It was determined, nevertheless, to abandon the adventure. The Indians soon became troublesome, for probably they were not in the least imposed upon by the story of Jacques Cartier, that their kidnapped countrymen—except Donnacona, who, it was acknowledged, was dead—were all married in France, and living there as 'lords.' And the next summer Roberval, on his way out with an addition to the colony of two hundred men and women, met Cartier in the harbour of St. John, Newfoundland, with his three remaining vessels bound homeward. Roberval indignantly ordered him to return to the St. Lawrence. In the morning his lieutenant was far out to sea on his way to France, having quietly slipped off in the darkness of the night. Perhaps it was not fear of the Indians, nor the hopelessness of a longer struggle with the difficulties and hardships of settling a new country, that alone influenced Cartier and his companions. For, says the old narrative, they were moved, as it seemeth, with ambition, because they would have all the glory of the discovery of those parts themselves. Roberval continued his voyage, weakened but not dismayed by the desertion of his lieutenant. Of the colony he planted little is known except its failure, after at least one winter's experience of the hardships of the wilderness. According to one account, Cartier was sent to bring the survivors home. At any rate they returned. Roberval, it is said, undertook another expedition with a brother in 1549, which was lost at sea; but it is also asserted that this could not be, as he was killed in Paris. Cartier died about 1555."

Cartier called the St. Lawrence "the River of Hochelaga," or "the Great River of Canada," and limited the designation of "Canada" to a stretch of country from the Isle des Coudres to a point above Quebec. He said that the Indians called the country above Quebec "Hochelaga," and that below the city "Saguenay." "Canada," according to him, was an Indian word, signifying a town; and in this Indian origin of the word he was sustained by other early French authorities, one of whom, however, rendered it *terre*, that is, land, while another called it an Indian proper name of unknown meaning.

One of the most ambitious of all the North American explorers was Ferdinand de Soto, a Spaniard of Xeres. He had distinguished himself under Pizarro, sharing in the wealth thus acquired, and, returning to Spain, was desirous of rivalling the exploits of Cortes and Pizarro in a new field. Consequently, he applied to Charles V. for permission to conquer Florida at his own cost. The Emperor, familiar with his past renown, conferred upon him the government of Cuba, with absolute power over the whole of the region to which the name of Florida was given.

Upon this, noble and wealthy Spaniards flocked to

Court, to enrol themselves under his banner; many even selling their estates to take part in his adventures. Even a number of brave Portuguese enlisted in the service. The muster at the port of San Lucar of Barrameda furnished a remarkable scene, the Portuguese glittering in burnished armour, and the Castilians being "very gallant with silk upon silk." Soto made choice of six hundred men for his purposes, all in the bloom of life, and the very pick of the Peninsula. Some have said that he had several hundreds more than this in his expedition, which was fitted out with the double purpose of conquest and colonization. The fleet consisted of nine vessels, ships, caravels, and pinnaces; and in addition to the soldiers and crews, they carried nearly three hundred horses, a large herd of swine, and a number of bloodhounds.

The expedition safely reached Cuba, where De Soto began his preparations for the conquest of Florida. He left his wife to govern Cuba, and on the 18th of May, 1539, sailed from Havana. After a good passage, the fleet anchored at Tampa Bay in about twelve days. The adventurers at once began their march into the interior, following practically the route of Narvaez some years before. De Soto early fell in with a Spaniard who had long been held in captivity by the Indians. The historians Bryant and Gay observe that "the romantic story of John Smith and Pocahontas was in part anticipated in the experience of this man, Juan Ortiz. When first captured by a band whose chief was named Ucita, he was bound hand and foot to stakes, stretched at length upon a scaffolding, beneath which a fire was kindled. The smoke had enwreathed the victim, and the forked flames were leaping to seize the naked flesh, when the intended holocaust was suddenly interrupted by the prayers of a daughter of the chief. She besought her father to spare the life of the Christian; one such, she urged, if he could do no good, at least could do no harm; and she made a cunning appeal to the vanity of the chief, by suggesting how great a distinction it would be to hold a white man as a captive. Her prayers were listened to; Ortiz was lifted from the scaffold and unbound, to serve henceforth as a slave. What the feeling was which the sight of the pale stranger had aroused in the bosom of the dusky maiden, or what the relation which may have afterward existed between them, we are not told; but whether it was on her part mere pity for a stranger, or a tenderer and deeper sentiment, the service was not forgotten. Three years later Ucita was defeated in a petty war with another chieftain, and there was danger that Ortiz would be sacrificed to propitiate the devil whose anger, Ucita believed, had brought this misfortune upon him and his people. Then the princess came again to the rescue of the stranger, and saved him from probable death. Warning him of his danger, and leading him secretly and alone in the night-time beyond the boundaries of her father's village, she put him in the way to find the camp of the victorious chieftain who had just triumphed over her father, and would protect, she knew, the Christian slave. Ortiz, when years afterwards he heard that his countrymen had arrived in Florida, was glad enough to welcome them, while he did not forget that he had some cause of gratitude to his Indian friends.

As a horseman rode at him, not distinguishing him from the savages, he cried out, 'Do not kill me, cavalier; I am a Christian! Do not slay these people; they have given me my life!' Fortunately his appeal was heard in time, and to him the expedition was more indebted than to any other man, next to De Soto himself; for through him alone was it possible to hold any intelligent communication with the Indians, whether for peace or war. His death, which occurred not long before that of the governor, was a source of deep perplexity, and a 'great cross to his designs.'"

To ensure his men remaining with him, De Soto had sent his ships back to Cuba before leaving the coast, so that his followers were now obliged to press forward with him. He played upon their avarice as well as their religious feelings in his march. But after wandering for three months—July to October, 1539—and discovering no gold at Appalachee as promised, and finding, moreover, the journey to be full of dangers and the Indians hostile, the whole company grew dispirited. They begged their leader to return, but he replied, "I will not turn back till I have seen the poverty of the country with my own eyes." Indians were captured, and made to grind the maize and carry the baggage. One exploring party discovered Ochus, the harbour of Pensacola; and a messenger was despatched to Cuba for supplies to be forwarded to that place.

Early in the spring of 1540, says Mr. Bancroft, "the wanderers renewed their march, with an Indian guide, who promised to lead the way to a country governed, it was said, by a woman, and where gold so abounded that the art of melting and refining it was understood. He described the process so well that the credulous Spaniards took heart. The Indian appears to have pointed towards the gold region of North Carolina. The adventurers, therefore, eagerly hastened to the north-east; they passed the Alatamaha; they admired the fertile valleys of Georgia, rich, productive, and full of good rivers. They crossed a northern tributary of the Alatamaha and a southern branch of the Ogeechee; and at length came upon the Ogeechee itself, which, in April, flowed with a full channel and a strong current. Much of the time the Spaniards were in wild solitudes; they suffered for want of salt and of meat. Their Indian guide affected madness; but 'they said a gospel over him, and the fit left him.' Again he involved them in pathless wilds, and then he would have been torn in pieces by the dogs if he had not still been needed to assist the interpreter. Of four Indian captives, who were questioned, one bluntly answered, he knew no country such as they described; the governor ordered him to be burnt, for what was esteemed his falsehood. The sight of the execution quickened the invention of his companions, and the Spaniards made their way to the small Indian settlement of Cutifa-Chiqui. A dagger and a rosary were found here; the story of the Indians traced them to the expedition of Vasquez de Ayllon; and a two days' journey would reach, it was believed, the harbour of St. Helena. The soldiers thought of home, and desired either to make a settlement on the fruitful soil around them, or to return. The governor was 'a stern man, and of few words.' Willingly hearing the opinion of others, he was inflexible, when he had once declared his own mind; and all his followers, 'condescending to his will,' continued to indulge delusive hopes.

"In May the direction of the march was to the north, to the comparatively sterile country of the Cherokees, and in part through a district in which gold is now found. The inhabitants were poor, but gentle; they offered such presents as their habits of life permitted—deer-skins and wild hens. Soto could hardly have crossed the mountains, so as to enter the basin of the Tennessee River; it seems, rather that he passed from the head-waters of the Savannah or the Chattahoochee to the head-waters of the Coosa. The name of Canasanga, a village at which he halted, is still given to a branch of the latter stream. For several months the Spaniards were in the valleys which send their waters to the Bay of Mobile. Chiaha was an island, distant about one hundred miles from Canasanga. An exploring party which was sent to the north were appalled by the aspect of the Appalachian Chain, and pronounced the mountains impassable. They had looked for mines of copper and gold; and their only plunder was a buffalo robe."

On one occasion during his journeyings, there came to meet the governor an Indian queen, who presented the Spaniards with pearls, telling them there were great quantities to be found in the vicinity. As a sample of De Soto's methods, he retained the queen, or cacica, as a captive, and made slaves and beasts of burden of her subjects; but she managed to make her escape. Her people were the most civilized of any of the Indians yet met with, and wore shoes and clothing made from skins.

The Spaniards reached Coosa in July, and in October they were at Mavilla, or Mobile, a town on the Alabama, above the junction of the Tombigbee, and one hundred miles from Pensacola. The name Mobile is now not only applied to the bay, but to the river, after the union of its numerous tributaries. The Spaniards wished to occupy the cabins of the Indians; and as the latter resisted, there ensued one of the most bloody race battles ever fought in the United States. The town was set on fire, and one witness reported that two thousand five hundred Indians were slain, suffocated, or burnt. Eighteen Christians died, and one hundred and twenty were wounded. Soto's curious collections perished in the flames.

Although De Soto had now lost more than a hundred men, and was within six days of Pensacola, he concealed the latter fact, lest his men should desert him, and determined to push his way towards the north. "A month passed away before he reached winter quarters at Chicaça, a small town in the country of the Chickasaws, in the upper part of the State of Mississippi, probably on the western bank of the Yazoo. The weather was severe, and snow fell; but maize was yet standing in the open fields. The Spaniards were able to gather a supply of food, and the deserted town, with such rude cabins as they added, afforded them shelter through the winter. Yet no mines of Peru were discovered; no ornaments of gold adorned the rude savages; their wealth was the harvest of corn, and wigwams were their only palaces; they were poor and independent; they were hardy and loved freedom. When spring opened, Soto, as he had usually done with other tribes, demanded of the chieftain of the Chickasaws two hundred men to carry the burdens of his company. The Indians hesitated. Human nature is the same in every age and in every climate. Like the inhabitants of Athens in the days of Themistocles, or those of Moscow of a recent day, the Chickasaws, unwilling to see strangers and enemies occupy their homes, in the dead of night, deceiving the sentinels, set fire to their own village, in which the Castilians were encamped. On a sudden, half the houses were in flames; and the loudest notes of the war-whoop rang through the air. The Indians, could they have acted with calm bravery, might have gained an easy and entire victory; but they trembled at their own success, and feared the unequal battle against weapons of steel. Many of the horses had broken loose; these, terrified and without riders, roamed through the forest, of which the burning village illuminated the shades, and seemed to the ignorant natives the gathering of hostile squadrons. Others of the horses perished in the stables; most of the swine were consumed; eleven of the Christians were burnt, or lost their lives in the tumult. The clothes which had been saved from the fires of Mobile were destroyed, and the Spaniards, now as naked as the natives, suffered from the cold. Weapons and equipments were consumed or spoiled. Had the Indians made a resolute onset on this night or the next, the Spaniards would have been unable to resist. But, in a respite of a week, forges were erected, swords newly tempered, and good ashen lances were made, equal to the best of Biscay. When the Indians attacked the camp, they found 'the Christians' prepared."

De Soto's pride was too great to allow him to return and confess that his expedition had been a failure, though none of its objects had yet been accomplished, or seemed likely to be. He therefore still struggled on in quest of the golden regions; and after a painful march through forests and marshes, arrived in April, 1541, at certain Indian settlements in the vicinity of the Mississippi. In the following month the expedition crossed the great river at about the thirty-fifth degree of latitude, or the boundary line between the States of Mississippi and Tennessee.

Progress in ascending the Mississippi was very slow, the Spaniards being sometimes compelled to wade through morasses. But in June they came upon the district of Little Prairie, and the dry and elevated lands extending towards New Madrid. The natives adored the travellers as children of the Sun, and brought their blind to them to receive their sight. The people subsisted on wild fruits. The northernmost point which De Soto reached in his march up the Mississippi was called Pacaha—which cannot now be identified—and here he remained from the 19th of June to the 29th of July. An exploring party sent to the north reported the country to be a desert, and the land still nearer the Missouri to be thinly inhabited. The Indians here were hunters, and the bison abounded, but nothing else.

De Soto now turned to the west and north-west,

and penetrated farther into the interior. With the main body of his men he seems to have got as far as the highlands of the White River, upwards of two hundred miles from the Mississippi, and then to have marched almost southwards through a country well watered, fertile, and thickly inhabited, to the present site of Little Rock, in Arkansas. The expedition came upon the saline springs in Arkansas; and at a town called Antiamque, on the Washita River, it went into winter quarters. The Spaniards cruelly ill-treated the Indians on the very slightest provocation. De Soto and his companions seem to have felt their disappointed hopes most keenly, and this made them still harsher towards the natives. In three years' wanderings the commander had lost two hundred and fifty men and one hundred and fifty horses; and from the time of his first winter at Appalachee Bay, his wife, the Doña Isabella, had received no tidings of him whatever.

The melancholy story of De Soto's tragic end is thus related by the historians:

"With the spring the march was resumed, and the sole object now was to reach the sea. Communication with the Indians had become more difficult, for Ortiz had died in the course of the winter. The Indians, observing the weakness and perplexities of the Spaniards, were more defiant than any of their tribes had hitherto been. A haughty cacique sent word to De Soto that his boast of being the son of the Sun would be accepted when he was seen to dry up the great river; that meanwhile it was not the custom of him who sent this message to visit inferiors; if the stranger wished to see him, he was always at home; if he came in peace, he would find a welcome; if with hostile intentions, the chief was equally ready for him. De Soto was in no condition to punish or resent this defiance. An expedition that was sent down the river to find the sea returned and reported that in eight days' journey they could make but little progress, for the country was full of swamps and dense forests, and that the river with many bends ran far up into the land.

"Worn down with hardships, anxiety, disappointment, and despair, De Soto sank under this accumulation of misfortunes. Conscious of approaching death, he called the principal officers of the expedition about him. He told them he was dying; he thanked them for the fidelity and affection they had always shown him, and regretted that he had not been able to reward them as he had always hoped to do, and according to their deserts; he asked pardon of all who believed they had cause of offence against him, and as a last favour he begged they would in his presence choose a leader to take his place, that he might leave them without fear of dissensions to arise after he was gone. They asked him to appoint his own successor, and he named Luis Moscoso de Alvarado, whom they all swore to obey. The next day, the 21st of May, 1542, he died. It was thought wise to conceal his death from the Indians, for he had assured them not only that he was the son of the Sun, but that Christians could not die. The new governor ordered him to be buried secretly in the gateway of the camp. But the suspicions of the natives, who had seen him sick, were aroused. He was no longer visible, but they saw a new-made grave, and gathering about it looked down with curious eyes and in solemn whispered consultation upon the mysterious heap of earth. Then Moscoso ordered the body to be disinterred with great precaution in the dead of night; and the mantles in which it was wrapped being made heavy with sand, it was dropped silently and in the darkness in the middle of the deep waters of the Mississippi. And when the cacique of Guachoya came to Moscoso and said, 'What has been done with my brother and lord, the governor?' the answer was, 'He has ascended into the skies for a little while, and will soon be back.'

"Either De Soto misunderstood this Luis de Moscoso or history has belied him. It is said that he loved a life of ease and gaiety in a Christian land, rather than one of toil and hardship and self-denial in the discovery and subjection of strange countries. But whether he believed that longer persistence in an enterprise, now in its fourth year, whose sole fruits had been death and disaster, was foolhardiness, or whether he wanted the energy and boldness to pursue it and achieve success, he decided at once to lead his companions back to Cuba, if he could find the way. When this was announced, and a council called to consult as to the best direction to pursue, there were many who were glad that De Soto was quiet in his loaded mantles at the bottom of the great river. With him the enterprise could have ended only with his and their lives, and they rejoiced that he was taken and they left."

Moscoso and his followers endeavoured to search

out their countrymen on the Pacific coast. Out of the wilderness, and from the hunting grounds of the Pawnees and Comanches, they made their way to the Mississippi, reaching it in December at a place called Minoya, a few leagues above the mouth of Red River. Here they rested, and constructed seven brigantines, which were frail barks without decks. Upon these the survivors of the expedition began their voyage down the river on the 2nd of July, 1543. After a passage of seventeen days, they reached the Gulf of Mexico, a distance of nearly five hundred miles. They found the Indians very aggressive; but sailing forth into the gulf, the explorers cruised for fifty days along the coast of Louisiana and Texas, until they reached the Spanish colony of Panuco, their numbers being now reduced to three hundred and eleven men. They were in a most pitiable condition, being half starved and half clothed. But they so rejoiced at finding their countrymen that "on bended knees, with hands raised above them, and their eyes to heaven, they remained untiring in giving thanks to God."

This famous expedition practically achieved nothing, but its members were the first to discover that for some distance from the mouth of the Mississippi the sea is not salt, so vast is the volume of fresh water which the river discharges. Undeterred by the fate of De Soto, and the failures of this first voyage of Europeans to the Mississippi, several other expeditions sailed from Spain to the same quarter, before that of Tristan de Luna, described in the preceding chapter, but they all proved abortive and ended in disaster.

CHAPTER VII.

ENGLISH ADVENTURERS—FROBISHER AND GILBERT.

ENGLISH interest in North American discovery was awakened with the birth of the sixteenth century. Most of the early voyages were undertaken with the view of discovering a short route to India. It is conjectured that two merchants and mariners of Bristol, named Thorne and Eliot, visited Newfoundland in 1502; and certainly in that year savages in their native attire were exhibited to the King of England. Trade privileges had already been granted to an Anglo-Portuguese company, but they chiefly concerned Newfoundland and its fisheries.

In 1527 Robert Thorne, an eminent merchant of London—son of the Thorne mentioned above—urged Henry VIII. to send expeditions to the east by way of the north, believing that there would be found an open sea near the Pole, through which, during the continuous Arctic day, Englishmen might reach the land of spices without travelling half so far as by way of the Cape of Good Hope. Two vessels, the *Mary of Guilford* and the *Samson*—in which Cardinal Wolsey had an interest—sailed from London in the above-named year; but the former accomplished nothing, while the latter was lost.

The tragic voyage of Master Hore, who was "assisted by the King's favour and good countenance," and accompanied by many gentlemen of the Inns of Court and of Chancery, took place in 1536. The party, numbering one hundred and ten persons, sailed from Gravesend in the ships *Trinitie* and *Minion*. They reached Newfoundland in safety, but soon suffered so severely from famine that they murdered each other secretly and fed upon the flesh of the victims. The captain strongly condemned this as a deadly sin before God. Eventually the remnant of the expedition obtained possession of a French ship and returned to England.

The sad fate of Sir Hugh Willoughby is well known. Sailing from London with three ships in May, 1553, with the object of reaching China by doubling the northern promontory of Norway, the admiral got separated from his companions, and was driven in September into a Lapland harbour. His whole company perished from cold; and when search was made in the following spring, Willoughby was found dead in his cabin, a pen between his frozen fingers. His journal, which was lying open on the table before him, showed that he had survived till January.

Sir Martin Frobisher, one of the great Elizabethan seamen, was the next prominent North American navigator. Frobisher was born in Yorkshire in 1535. He was sent to sea as a boy, and soon traded on his own account to Guinea and elsewhere. Like everybody else at this period, he was possessed by the idea of a north-west passage to Cathay, and in this he was strengthened by an ingenious essay written by

Sir Humphrey Gilbert, in which the writer set forth that America was the Atlantis of Plato, Aristotle, and other ancient philosophers, and that it was possible to sail round the north of it to China and East India.

Frobisher was a poor man; but after much solicitation he found a patron in the Earl of Warwick, through whose help he was able to fit out an expedition. "Two small barques of twenty-five and of twenty tons, with a pinnace of ten tons' burden, composed the whole fleet, which was to enter gulfs that none before him had visited. As in June, 1576, they dropped down the Thames, Queen Elizabeth waved her hand in token of favour, and, by an honourable message, transmitted her approbation of an adventure which her own treasures had not contributed to advance. During a storm on the voyage, the pinnace was swallowed up by the sea; the mariners in the *Michael* became terrified, and turned their prow homewards; but Frobisher, in a vessel not much surpassing in tonnage the barge of a man-of-war, made his way, fearless and unattended, to the shores of Labrador, and to a passage or inlet north of the entrance of Hudson's Bay. A strange perversion has transferred the scene of his discoveries to the eastern coast of Greenland; it was among a group of American islands, in the latitude of sixty-three degrees and eight minutes, that he entered what seemed to be a strait. Hope suggested that his object was obtained, that the land on the south was America, on the north was the continent of Asia, and that the strait opened into the Pacific. Great praise is due to Frobisher for penetrating far beyond all former mariners into the bays and among the islands of this Meta Incognita, this unknown goal of discovery. Yet his voyage was a failure. To land upon an island, and perhaps on the main; to gather up stones and rubbish, in token of having taken possession of the country for Elizabeth; to seize one of the natives of the north for exhibition to the gaze of Europe,—these were all the results which he accomplished.

"America and mines were always thought of together. A stone which had been brought from the frozen regions was pronounced by the refiners of London to contain gold. The news excited the wakeful avarice of the city: there were not wanting those who endeavoured to purchase of Elizabeth a lease of the new lands where it had been found. A fleet was immediately fitted out to procure more of the gold, rather than to make further research for the passage into the Pacific; and the Queen, who had contributed nothing to the voyage of discovery, sent a large ship of her own to join the expedition, which was now to conduct to infinite opulence. More men than could be employed volunteered their services; those who were discharged resigned their brilliant hopes with reluctance."

This second expedition embarked in May, 1577, and soon reached the Orkneys. On nearing the American coast, the vessels were steered with difficulty through numberless icebergs. When the explorers landed, they freighted the ships with earth which they believed to contain gold; but it was a delusion, and the whole voyage was a failure, not accomplishing so much as Frobisher had done alone.

A third voyage made by Frobisher in 1578 was

more important than either of those which had preceded it, for it was the first attempt at English colonization in North America. A splendid fleet of fifteen sail was fitted out, partly at the expense of Elizabeth, and the volunteers included sons of many Englishmen of position. One hundred persons were selected to form the colony, which was to secure great wealth for England; and twelve vessels were to return immediately with cargoes of ore, three being ordered to remain and aid the settlement. Alas, for the futility of human hopes! "The entrance to these wealthy islands was rendered difficult by frost; and the fleet of Frobisher, as in midsummer, 1578, it approached the American coast, was bewildered among icebergs, which were so vast that, as they melted, torrents poured from them in sparkling waterfalls. One vessel was crushed and sunk, though the men on board were saved. In the dangerous mists the ships lost their course, and came into the straits which have since been called Hudson's, and which lie south of the imagined gold regions. The admiral believed himself able to sail through to the Pacific, and resolve the doubt respecting the passage. But his duty as a mercantile agent controlled his desire of glory as a navigator. He struggled to regain the harbour where his vessels were to be laden; and after 'getting in at one gap and out at another,' escaping only by miracle from hidden rocks and unknown currents, ice, and a lee shore, which was, at one time, avoided only by a prosperous breath of wind in the very moment of extreme danger, he at last arrived at the haven in the Countess of Warwick's Sound. The zeal of the volunteer colonists had moderated; and the disheartened sailors were ready to mutiny. One ship, laden with provisions for the colony, deserted and returned; and an island was discovered with enough of the black ore 'to suffice all the gold-gluttons of the world.' The plan of the settlement was abandoned. It remained to freight the home-bound ships with a store of minerals. They who engage in a foolish project combine, in case of failure, to conceal their loss; for the truth would be an impeachment of their judgment; so that unfortunate speculations are promptly consigned to oblivion. The adventurers and the historians of the voyage are silent about the disposition which was made of the cargo of the fleet. The knowledge of the seas was not extended; the credulity of avarice met with a rebuke; and the belief in regions of gold among the Esquimaux was dissipated; but there remained a firm conviction that a passage to the Pacific Ocean might yet be threaded among the icebergs and northern islands of America."

The remaining incidents of Frobisher's career are soon told. In 1585 he commanded a vessel in Drake's expedition to the West Indies, and three years later he so distinguished himself in the defeat of the Spanish Armada by his conduct in the *Triumph* that he received the honour of knighthood. He now married a daughter of Lord Wentworth, and settled down as a country gentleman; but the old spirit became too strong in him, and he once more scoured the seas for the treasure-ships of Spain. He was wounded at the Siege of Crozon, near Brest, in November, 1594; and being taken into Plymouth, died there before the end of the same month. We have a permanent reminder of the navigator in **Frobisher Bay**, an inlet opening westward near the mouth of Davis Strait, into the territory called by Frobisher *Meta Incognita*, at the southern end of Baffin Land. It is about two hundred miles long by **twenty** wide, and has rugged, mountainous shores.

Important work was done in Northern America about this time by another **English navigator**, John Davis, whose name is given to the strait above mentioned. Davis was born at Sandridge, near Dartmouth, about 1550; and in 1585 and the two following years he made three voyages to the Arctic Seas in search of a north-west passage. On the third occasion he left his two small vessels on the coast of Cumberland Island to fish, while he went northward in a pinnace, bravely pushing his way through icebergs and fields of ice. He penetrated Baffin Bay as far as the seventy-third degree of latitude, and discovered the strait bearing his name, which connects Baffin Bay with the Atlantic Ocean. Finding on his return that his men had abandoned him, he ventured to cross the Atlantic in his pinnace, and safely reached home. Subsequently he made two ill-fated voyages towards the South Seas, and as pilot of a Dutch vessel bound to the East Indies. In his last voyage as pilot of an English ship of two hundred and forty tons, he was killed in a brush with some Japanese pirates at Bintang, near Singapore, on the 30th of December, 1605.

One of the most touching narratives in Hakluyt is that which relates the adventures of Sir Humphrey Gilbert. This eminent British navigator was born at

Dartmouth in 1539, and was educated at Eton and Oxford. Afterwards abandoning the law for a career of arms, he did such good service against the Irish rebels as earned him knighthood and the government of Munster in 1570. Next he saw five years' campaigning in the Netherlands. In 1576 appeared his *Discourse on a North-west Passage to India*, which was published by George Gascoigne without his knowledge. In 1578 Gilbert secured a charter, extending over six years, with powers to discover "such remote heathen and barbarous lands as were not actually possessed by any Christian prince or people," and to retain them for his own as absolute proprietor. Although the Canadian territory was the best known, Gilbert decided that the lands north of Florida were the best "to be reduced into Christian civility by the English nation."

The various chronicles report that "Sir Walter Raleigh was chief among those who entered into this scheme of his half-brother, who contributed money, influence, and personal effort for its success. When, the year after Gilbert received the charter, he made the first attempt to avail himself of the privileges it bestowed, Raleigh, it is said, sailed with him. The expedition, however, returned within a few days crippled, and with the loss of one ship, probably captured in a fight with the Spaniards at sea. But it encountered many difficulties even before starting. Dissensions had arisen among those who had engaged in it, followed by withdrawals; then Orders of Council came, first that Gilbert should only put to sea under sureties of good behaviour; then that he should abandon the enterprise altogether under pain of the Queen's displeasure. For the watchful Spaniards, jealous of every English vessel that turned her head westward, complained of depredations made or to be made upon Spanish commerce—complaints likely enough to be well founded, for he was no true British sailor in the reign of Elizabeth who did not hate the Spaniard as he hated the enemy of mankind, and did not hold him to be the lawful prey of all Christian men. But in 1583 the start was more successful. Raleigh's influence with Elizabeth removed all obstacles that the Lords of the Council could put in the way, if they were still disposed to listen to Spanish complaints, or the Spaniards to offer them. The Queen wished Gilbert 'as great goodhap and safety to his ship as if herself were there in person,' and desired him to send her his picture as a keepsake. His charter, moreover, expired in a year, and he could afford to delay no longer. He sailed in June in command of five ships, the largest of which, the *Raleigh*, was fitted out by Sir Walter himself at an expense of £2,000, and was two hundred tons' burden. The smallest, the *Squirrel*, was only ten tons' burden; of the other three, the *Golden Hind* and the *Swallow* measured forty tons each; and the admiral's ship, the *Delight*, was one hundred and twenty tons. The *Raleigh* deserted them in a few days, and returned to port, pestilence having broken out, it was said, among her crew; but something else was the matter. 'For,' says Captain Edward Hayes, the owner and captain of the *Golden Hind*, as well as historian of the expedition, 'the reason I could never understand. . . .

Therefore I leave it unto God.' And Gilbert himself wrote to Sir George Peckham, 'The *Ark Raleigh* ran from me in fair and clear weather, having a large wind. I pray you, solicit my brother Raleigh to make them an example to all knaves.'"

The expedition consisted altogether of about two hundred and sixty men, including mechanics, mineral men, and refiners. A band of music, and morris-dancers, etc., were also on board, and many pretty wares wherewith to tempt the savage races. The vessels arrived safely at St. John's, Newfoundland, where Sir Humphrey read to the assembled fishermen and tradesmen his commission from the Queen. He took possession of the place and the neighbouring country, for two hundred leagues in every direction, with proper solemnities, and set up a pillar with the arms of England engraved upon it. His intention was to make his way to the south, but trouble arose among the men. Many were disabled by sickness, others deserted, and some died. A conspiracy was formed to seize the vessels, but this was defeated. Nevertheless, a portion of the crews boarded a fishing vessel, and put out to sea. Gilbert now sent home the *Swallow* with the sick and as many of the discontented and the insubordinate as could be spared. This left him with three vessels only and a small company.

Setting forth at length from St. John's, the expedition doubled Cape Race, sailed along the west coast of Newfoundland as far as Placentia Bay, and then headed for Cape Breton and Sable Island, meaning to land upon the latter. But the vessels were beaten about by contrary winds; and after struggling for more than a week, were driven upon a lee shore on the dangerous coasts of Nova Scotia. The *Delight*, which was the largest ship, struck and went to pieces, and all upon her were drowned, save seventeen men who got away upon a raft, and of whom fifteen reached Newfoundland. The death of Maurice Browne, the captain of the *Delight*, showed the stuff of which these old mariners were made. He refused to leave his ship; but "mounting upon the highest deck, he attended imminent death and unavoidable." Those who perished were the men who had dispossessed the crew of a French fishing vessel and left them to perish, so that this was regarded as God's judgment upon them.

Meanwhile, the *Golden Hind* and the *Squirrel* hauled off the shore and stood out to sea. But the weather was terribly cold and tempestuous, and Gilbert turned his course for England. The last scene in his eventful and fateful history is thus described:

"Notwithstanding the disasters that had attended the expedition, Sir Humphrey was content. At St. John's one of his assayers had brought him an ore which he solemnly affirmed was of silver, and so persuaded of this was Gilbert that he believed he had but to return in the spring to gather great wealth. This vision took possession of him, and was a great comfort in all his trials, though it did not make him forget his wise purpose of colonization on the continent farther south. The specimens of the ore had been left on board the *Delight* by mistake of his servant, and the assayer, who knew most about them, was lost in that vessel.

"But Sir Humphrey knew where to find the mine.

Hitherto he had said little about it, and had enjoined silence upon others; but now that he was far out at sea and returning to England after so many misfortunes, he talked not a little about the great store of silver in his new possessions. The thing he seemed most to regret, next to the loss of his men, was the loss of the lumps of ore; and when long after, on visiting the *Golden Hind* at sea, he met the boy whose fault it was that these precious minerals were left on the *Delight*, he fell upon and beat him 'in great rage.' Good and pious and wise man as he was known to be, he was of a choleric and unforgiving disposition. Years before, when he was putting down the rebellion in Ireland, the castle or fort that did not surrender at his first summons he 'would not afterwards,' he said, 'take it of their gift, but won it perforce—how many lives soever it cost; putting man, woman, and child of them to the sword.' There was good reason why he should be more feared than any other man by the Irish, as Raleigh said he was. Among sailors who were pirates if they had the opportunity, and among Irish outlaws who were no better than half savages, he showed little of the quality of mercy.

"So much did he rely upon his mine of silver, that he was sure the Queen, upon report thereof, would readily advance £10,000 wherewith he would equip two fleets in the spring, one to bring home the ore, the other for a new venture to the south to plant colonies. 'I will set you forth royally next spring,' he said to his companions, 'if God send us safe home.' That hope was not ill-founded; the promise of sudden wealth in the New World was never made to dull ears.

"But it would only have been one more idle tale to be confuted, for there was no mine; the colonies, other hands than his were to plant.

"The vessel Gilbert had last embarked upon was the *Squirrel*, the smallest of the fleet, of only ten tons' burden. He was besought to leave her and find greater safety on board the *Golden Hind*; but his answer was always, 'I will not forsake my little company going homewards, with whom I have passed so many storms and perils.' Severe as he was, he would ask no man to do that which he was himself afraid to do. So small a craft was a poor thing in which to cross the Atlantic in September. The weather was foul, the waves 'terrible, breaking short and high like pyramids. . . . Never men saw more outrageous seas.' On the 9th of the month the *Squirrel* came near foundering, but rode out the storm. The *Golden Hind* approached and hailed; and Sir Humphrey Gilbert, sitting quietly in the stern of the boat with a book in his hand, answered cheerfully, 'We are as near to heaven by sea as by land.' In the darkness of the night that followed they anxiously watched on board the *Hind* for the *Squirrel's* lights; suddenly at midnight, 'as it were in a moment,' they disappeared. The little vessel 'was devoured and swallowed up of the sea.'"

Such was the death of Sir Humphrey Gilbert, and such the sad termination of an expedition upon which great hopes were built. We shall see, however, that Sir Walter Raleigh, undismayed by the failure and death of his kinsman, undertook with great spirit and determination the work of North American colonization.

CHAPTER VIII.

THE EXPEDITIONS OF RALEIGH AND DRAKE.

THERE is no name more typical of the golden age of Elizabeth in all its nobler aspects than that of Sir Walter Raleigh. English history of that glorious period would lose much if his name were dropped out of it, even if we remember all the other names which shed lustre upon it. He was one of the makers of the age, not an offshoot of it, and was as distinguished for his universality as he was for his originality.

Devonshire claimed the honour of his birth, and he was born of a good old family at the manor-house of Hayes, near Budleigh, in the year 1552. His mother, who had been married before, had given birth to the famous Humphrey and Adrian Gilbert. Walter Raleigh was educated at Oriel College, Oxford, and left there in 1569 in order to volunteer for Huguenot service in France. Not much is known of his apprenticeship to arms beyond the fact that he served at Montcontour. He early crossed the Atlantic, and joined in Humphrey Gilbert's disastrous expedition of 1578.

In 1580 we find him in Ireland serving against the Irish rebels, where his boldness and daring soon made him conspicuous. He assisted largely in the drastic policy for stamping out the rebellion, and returned to England in December, 1581. The favourite Leicester took him into his circle, and in February, 1582, he accompanied him to the Netherlands. Soon after his return he became in high favour with the Queen, though the romantic story of his spreading his plush mantle before her in the mud may be apocryphal. Raleigh was a fine, handsome fellow, splendid in dress, witty in conversation, perfect in manners, and with a mind admirably stored with information. But he lacked the weightiness in counsel of a Burghley or a Walsingham, and never in consequence took the first rank of a statesman in the Queen's counsels. Elizabeth, however, lavished wealthy appointments upon him. In 1584 he was knighted, and in the following year he was appointed Lord Warden of the Stannaries, Lieutenant of Cornwall, and Vice-Admiral of Devonshire and Cornwall. The same year he was returned to Parliament as one of the members for Devonshire, and in 1587 he was appointed Captain of the Queen's Guard.

The fact that Raleigh had risked £2,000—then a large sum—in Sir Humphrey Gilbert's last and fatal expedition of 1583, did not deter him, as already stated, from further efforts in American exploration. On the contrary, he at once set to work, and in March, 1584, obtained a new patent from the Queen, with greatly enlarged powers and privileges. It was drawn according to the principles of feudal law, and with strict regard to the Christian faith, as professed in the Church of England. Raleigh was to be a lord proprietary, with almost unlimited powers, holding his territories under homage and at an almost nominal rent; while he possessed jurisdiction over an extensive region, with power to make grants according to his pleasure.

In one month from the date of his patent Raleigh had procured and manned two vessels, which sailed from the Thames on the 27th of April, under the command of Captains Philip Amadas and Arthur Barlow. After voyaging amongst the Canaries and the islands of the West Indies, the expedition sailed for the north, and on the 2nd of July reached the shores of Carolina. The coast was explored for one hundred and twenty miles; and on entering the first convenient harbour, the leaders of the expedition returned thanks to God for their safe arrival, and took possession of the country in the name of the Queen of England.

"The spot on which this ceremony was performed," says Bancroft, "was in the Island of Wocoken, the southernmost of the islands forming Ocracoke Inlet. The shores of North Carolina, at some periods of the year, cannot safely be approached by a fleet, from the hurricanes against which the formation of the coast offers no secure roadsteads and harbours. But in the month of July the air was agitated by none but the gentlest breezes, and the English commanders were in raptures with the beauty of the ocean, seen in the magnificence of repose, gemmed with islands, and expanding in the clearest transparency from cape to cape. The vegetation of that southern latitude struck the beholders with admiration; the trees had not their paragons; luxuriant climbers gracefully festooned the loftiest cedars; wild grapes abounded; and natural arbours formed an impervious shade, that not a ray of the suns of July could penetrate. The forests were filled with birds; and, at the discharge of an arquebuse, whole flocks would arise, uttering a cry, as if an army of men had shouted together.

"The gentleness of the tawny inhabitants appeared in harmony with the loveliness of the scene. The desire of traffic overcame their timidity, and the English received a friendly welcome. On the Island of Roanoke, they were entertained by the wife of Grangamines, father of Wingina, the king, with the refinements of Arcadian hospitality. 'The people were most gentle, loving, and faithful, void of all guile and treason, and such as lived after the manner of the golden age.' They had no cares but to guard against the moderate cold of a short winter, and to gather such food as the earth almost spontaneously produced. And yet it was added, with singular want of comparison, that the wars of these guileless men were cruel and bloody; that domestic dissensions had almost terminated whole tribes; that they employed the basest stratagems against their enemies; and that the practice of inviting men to a feast, to murder them in the hour of confidence, was not exclusively a device of European bigots, but was known to the natives of Secotan. The English, too, were solicited to engage in a similar enterprise, under promise of lucrative booty.

"The adventurers were satisfied with observing the general aspect of the New World; no extensive examination of the coast was undertaken; Pamlico and Albemarle Sound and Roanoke Island were explored, and some information gathered by enquiries from the Indians; the commanders had not the courage or the activity to survey the country with exactness. Having made but a short stay in America, they arrived in September in the West of England, accompanied by Manteo and Wanchese, two natives of the wilderness; and the returning voyagers gave such glowing descriptions of their discoveries as might be expected from men who had done no more than sail over the smooth waters of a summer's sea, among 'the hundred islands' of North Carolina. Elizabeth esteemed her reign signalized by the discovery of the enchanting regions, and, as a memorial of her state of life, named them Virginia."

Raleigh obtained a Bill in Parliament confirming his patent of discovery, and resolved upon honestly pursuing his scheme for the colonization of Virginia. In the ensuing spring a larger expedition, and one with a more definite purpose, was fitted out. It consisted of seven vessels; and the fleet sailed from Plymouth on the 9th of April, 1585, under the command of the celebrated Sir Richard Grenville, who afterwards fought with great valour against the Spaniards. One hundred and eight colonists were to settle in Carolina under Richard Lane as governor. Lane was subsequently knighted. There were likewise attached to the expedition Sir Thomas Cavendish, who soon after circumnavigated the globe; Thomas Hariot, the mathematician and astronomer, and inventor of the system of notation in modern algebra; and John White, artist of the expedition, whose sketches of the appearance and habits of the natives of Virginia were the earliest and most authentic drawn by any European.

Two months after it set sail, the fleet touched the mainland of Florida. It was nearly wrecked on the cape, which now first received the name of Cape Fear; but soon afterwards it came to anchor at Wocoken. The coast being full of shoals, the vessels made their way through Ocracoke Inlet to Roanoke. In July Grenville, accompanied by Lane, Hariot, Cavendish, and others, explored the coast as far as Secotan, being well received by the savages. After their return, Grenville sailed for England.

It is of great interest to read the accounts of the first attempt at an English settlement, made by Lane and his fellow-colonists after the departure of Grenville. "It is the goodliest soil under the cope of heaven," wrote Lane; "the most pleasing territory of the world; the continent is of a huge and unknown greatness, and very well peopled and towned, though savagely. The climate is so wholesome that we have not one sick, since we touched the land. If Virginia had but horses and kine, and were inhabited with English, no realm in Christendom were comparable to it."

Hariot was by far the keenest observer, however, for he was a man of altogether superior parts. As the summary of his own investigations shows, "he carefully examined the productions of the country, those which would furnish commodities for commerce, and those which were in esteem among the natives. He observed the culture of tobacco, accustomed himself to its use, and believed in its healing virtues. The culture and the extraordinary productiveness of maize especially attracted his admiration; and the tuberous roots of the potato, when boiled, were found to be very good food. The natural inhabitants are described as too feeble to inspire terror; clothed in mantles and aprons of deer-skins; having no weapons but wooden swords and bows of witch-hazel with arrows of reeds; no armour but targets of bark and sticks wickered together with thread. Their largest towns contained but thirty dwellings. The walls of the houses were made of bark, fastened to stakes; and sometimes consisted of poles fixed upright, one by another, and at the top bent over and fastened. But the great peculiarity of the Indians consisted in the want of political connection. A single town often constituted a government; a collection of ten or twenty wigwams might be an independent state. The greatest chief in the country could not muster more than seven or eight hundred fighting men. The dialect of each government seemed a language by itself. The country which Hariot explored was on the boundary of the Algonkin race, where the Lenni-Lenape tribes melted into the widely differing nations of the south. Their wars rarely led them to the open battle-field; they were accustomed rather to sudden surprises at daybreak or by moonlight, to ambushes and the subtle devices of cunning falsehood. Destitute of the arts, they yet displayed excellency of wit in all which they attempted. To the credulity of fetishism they joined an undeveloped conception of the unity of the Divine Power, continued existence after death, and retributive justice. The mathematical instruments, the burning-glass, guns, clocks, and the use of letters, seemed the works of gods rather than of men; and the English were reverenced as the pupils and favourites of Heaven.

In every town which Hariot entered, he displayed and explained the Bible; the Indians revered the volume rather than its doctrines; with a fond superstition they embraced the book, kissed it, and held it to their breasts and heads, as an amulet. As the colonists enjoyed uniform health, and had no women with them, there were some among the Indians who imagined the English were not born of women, and therefore not mortal; that they were men of an old generation risen to immortality. The terrors of fire-arms the natives could neither comprehend nor resist; every sickness which now prevailed among them was attributed to wounds from invisible bullets, discharged by unseen agents, with whom the air was supposed to be peopled. They prophesied that 'more of the English generation would come, to kill theirs and take their places'; and some believed that the purpose of extermination was already matured, and its execution begun."

"Was it strange, then," as one of the historians of the period asks, "that the natives desired to be delivered from guests by whom they feared to be supplanted? The colonists were mad for gold; and a wily savage allured them by tales: that the River Roanoke gushed from a rock so near the Pacific that the surge of that ocean sometimes dashed into its fountain; that its banks were inhabited by a nation skilled in the art of refining the rich ore in which the country abounded. The walls of their city were described as glittering with pearls. Lane was so credulous that he attempted to ascend the rapid current of the Roanoke; and his followers would not return until their stores of provisions were exhausted, and they had killed and eaten the very dogs which bore them company. On this attempt to explore the interior, the English hardly advanced higher up the river than some point near the present village of Williamstown.

"The Indians had hoped to destroy the English by thus dividing them; but the prompt return of Lane prevented open hostilities. They next conceived the plan of leaving their lands unplanted, that famine might compel the departure of their too powerful guests. The suggestion was defeated by the moderation of one of their aged chiefs; but the feeling of enmity could not be restrained. The English believed that fear of a foreign enemy was teaching the natives the necessity of union, and that a grand alliance was forming to destroy the strangers by a general massacre. Desiring an audience of Wingina, the most active among the native chiefs, Lane and his attendants were on the first day of June readily admitted to his presence. Immediately, and without any sign of hostile intentions by the Indians, a preconcerted watchword was given, and the Christians, falling upon the unhappy king and his principal followers, put them without mercy to death.

"The discoveries of Lane were inconsiderable: to the south they had extended only to Secotan, in the present county of Craven, between the Pamlico and the Neuse; to the north they reached the River Elizabeth, which joins the Chesapeake Bay at Hampton Roads; in the interior the Chowan had been examined beyond the junction of the Meherrin and the Nottoway; and we have seen that the hope of gold attracted Lane to make a short excursion up the Roanoke. Yet some general results of importance were obtained. The climate was found to be salubrious; during the year not more than four men had died, and of these three brought the seeds of their disease from Europe. The hope of finding better harbours at the north was confirmed; and the Bay of Chesapeake, though so long since discovered by the Spanish, was first made known to the English by this expedition.

"But in the Island of Roanoke the men began to despond; they looked in vain towards the ocean for supplies from England; they were sighing for their native land, when early in June it was rumoured that the sea was white with the sails of three-and-twenty ships, and within three days Sir Francis Drake anchored his fleet outside of Roanoke Inlet, in 'the wild road of their bad harbour.'

"He had come, on his way from the West Indies to England, to visit the domain of his friend, and readily supplied the wants of Lane to the uttermost, giving him a barque of seventy tons, with pinnaces and small boats, and all needed provisions for the colony. Above all, he induced two experienced sea captains to remain and employ themselves in the action of discovery. Everything was furnished to complete the surveys along the coast and the rivers, and in the last resort, if suffering became extreme, to convey the emigrants to England.

"At this time an unwonted storm suddenly arose, and had nearly wrecked the fleet, which lay in a most dangerous position, and which had no security but in weighing anchor and standing away from the shore. When the tempest was over, nothing could be found of the boats and the barque which had been set apart for the colony. The humanity of Drake was not weary; he devised measures for supplying the colony with the means of continuing their discoveries; but Lane shared the despondency of his men; and Drake yielded to their unanimous desire of permission to embark in his ships for England. Thus ended the first actual settlement of the English in America."

It was Hariot who first spoke in his description of the colony of the herb "called by the inhabitants *yppowoc*," which was brought to England and consumed under the name of tobacco. Raleigh himself took kindly to the new luxury, and would enjoy it in pipes of silver, the Queen sitting by him while he smoked.

Soon after Lane and his friends set sail for England, Sir Richard Grenville arrived with three ships and plenty of provisions; but not finding any of the colonists on Roanoke Island, he left fifteen men on the island, well provisioned, to hold possession of it.

Still declining to be discouraged by outward events, in May, 1587, Raleigh sent out three fresh ships under Captain John White, with one hundred and fifty colonists, seventeen of whom were women. Simon Ferdinando was admiral. The two officers were utterly out of harmony with each other, and White accused Ferdinando of wishing to ruin the expedition. The admiral was a violent and passionate man, and greatly addicted to profane swearing. White alleged, moreover, that he left one of the vessels at a port in the West Indies, stealing away in the night in his own ship, and hoping that the captain of the vessel left behind would fail to reach Virginia, or that he would be taken by the

Spaniards. "It was White's intention," observes one writer, "to go up the Chesapeake Bay, in accordance with Sir Walter Raleigh's orders, to find a seat for his colony, after looking on Roanoke Island for the fifteen men whom Grenville had left there the year before. But when Ferdinando had got forty of the colonists on board the pinnace at Hatorask to go to the island, he ordered the sailors not to bring them back again, declaring that the summer was too far gone to admit of time being spent in seeking for the best spot for a settlement. The two men were governed by different motives: one was for delay, the other for speed; the governor wanted time to move with caution and consider consequences; the sailor wanted to reach his port and discharge his cargo, looking forward to some new venture—probably some homeward-bound Spaniard laden with treasure.

"The fifteen men whom Grenville had left at Roanoke were not to be found. The fort was razed to the ground; the huts were standing, but they were overgrown with melon-vines, and the deer roamed through them undisturbed by any fear of human presence. The whitening bones of one man were the only sign of recent habitation. All that White could learn of the fate of his countrymen was that they had been attacked by the Indians, two of them killed, and the rest driven to a little island in the harbour of Hatorask. They could be traced no farther.

"The fleet remained a little more than a month, but before it sailed the enmity between the Englishmen and the Indians was renewed with fresh fury. One of the assistants, Mr. Howe, while searching alone for shell-fish along the beach of Roanoke Island, was killed by some of the tribe of which Pemissippan had been chief. To avenge his death an attack was made before daylight upon an encampment of Indians, who, after one of them was killed, were found to be friends from Croatoan, where Manteo's people lived. The effect upon the Croatoans of this unhappy blunder was probably not favourable to their continued friendship, though they may have been appeased for the moment by the subsequent christening of Manteo, who, by Sir Walter Raleigh's order, was, in reward for his faithfulness to the English, baptized with due ceremony under the name of Lord of Roanoke and Dasamomquepeuk. Before the fleet sailed, also, the daughter of White, the wife of Ananias Dare, one of the assistants, gave birth, on the 18th of August, to a daughter, who was christened Virginia—the first child of English parentage born upon the territory of the present United States."

Being anxious to return to England, White left the colony on the 27th of August, 1587, ostensibly to fetch supplies. Certainly, when he arrived in England, he found it impossible to return at once to Virginia, however anxious he might be to do so, for the country was agitated from end to end over the threatened Spanish invasion. When the Invincible Armada appeared in sight, Raleigh was engaged in superintending the coast defence. His vessels scoured the seas in privateering enterprises, which at once gratified his deep hatred of Spain, and provided the golden sinews of war for his schemes in Virginia. In 1589 we find him in Ireland, deep in his friendship with the poet

Spenser, and planting tobacco on his Youghal estate, as well as the first potatoes that grew on Irish soil.

Matters having at length calmed down in England, White succeeded in 1590 in his efforts to make the return voyage to his colony. Hearing that three vessels had been prevented by an Order in Council from proceeding to the West Indies, White, through the influence of Raleigh, procured their release on condition that they should carry a reasonable number of persons and land them in Virginia. In the end, however, they conveyed only White himself, with whom they arrived at Wocoken on the 9th of August. A few days later the ships anchored in Hatorask harbour; and when White saw smoke arising in the direction of Roanoke Island, he thought to find the colonists there. Neither men nor habitations were, however, discovered. What followed is thus related by the authors of *The Popular History of the United States*:

"A disaster well-nigh put an end to all further attempts to reach Roanoke. The boats were sent ashore at Hatorask for water; the surf was heavy in the inlet; one of the boats was upset, and two of the captains of the ships and five others were drowned. So disheartened were the sailors at this mishap that they refused at first to go on, and this determination was with difficulty overcome by the will and authority of White and the remaining captain. It was night before they reached Roanoke, and approached the spot where White expected to find his friends. Glimmering through the trees they saw the light of a fire, and for a moment their hopes were kindled into enthusiasm. Approaching it along the shore, the notes of a trumpet-call from the boats rang clear and shrill through the silent woods; the sailors sang out in cheering tones the familiar words of English songs, which would have so stirred the blood of any listening Englishmen long exiled from home. But there was no answer. The lights of the distant fire still flickered above the dim line of the forest; but out of the darkness came no friendly shout of men, no woman's glad cry of joy and welcome.

"They landed at daybreak; the fire they had seen was from burning grass and rotting trees, kindled no doubt by the Indians, whose fresh footprints were found in the sand. Pushing through the woods toward the spot where White had left his colony three years before, they saw the letters C. R. O. carved upon the trunk of a tree, upon the brow of a hill. Pausing to consider what this might mean, White remembered that when he left the colony it was proposed that the people should remove to the mainland, and that wherever they went the name of the place should be left behind them here upon trees or doorposts. It was further understood that, should any misfortune have overtaken them, they should carve beneath the name a cross. Here then was the guide, if C. R. O. meant Croatoan, to the place whither the colony had removed, though it was to an outer island rather than to the main. But to the anxious father and governor there was this encouragement—the sign of the cross was wanting.

"Again they pushed on, after a brief consultation upon the 'faire Romane letters curiously carved,' which White had thus explained. It was not far to the deserted post, still surrounded with its palisades.

"Here all doubts were removed: at the entrance, upon one of the largest of the trees from which the bark had been stripped, was carved in capital letters the word Croatoan in full, and still without the cross. Within the palisades the houses were gone, but scattered about were bars of iron and pigs of lead, some large guns with their balls—'fowlers' and 'sacker shot,' they were called—and other things too heavy for a hasty removal, all overgrown with grass and weeds. In a trench not far off were found some chests where they had been buried by the colonists and dug up afterwards by the Indians; among these were three belonging to White, but all had been rifled. Books were torn out of their covers, the frames of pictures and of maps were rotten with dampness, and a suit of armour was almost eaten up with rust. 'Although it much grieved me,' says White, 'to see such spoyle of my goods, yet on the other side I greatly joyed that I had safely found a certaine token of their (the colonists) safe being at Croatoan, which is the place where Manteo was borne, and the savages of the island our friends.'

"It was his only consolation—if he really believed that his friends, among whom was his daughter, had found any such refuge. The boats had hardly regained the ships at Hatorask when a gale of wind with a heavy sea set in, and in attempting to get under way one of the ships lost her anchors and was near going ashore. The water-casks, which had been taken to the land to be filled, could not be brought off; provisions were short, the sailors were despondent and impatient, and it was determined to abandon all attempts to go to Croatoan in further search of the colony, but to sail at once to the West Indies and recruit. White was only a passenger, and could probably do nothing to change this determination, though his friends, if still alive, were not many miles distant. He may, indeed, have been doubtful if they were still alive, for the ships on their arrival on the coast had stopped at Wocoken, had sailed along the shores of Croatoan, and anchored for a night off the north end of the island. Had there been any survivors of the colonists there, they could hardly have failed, on the look-out as they would always have been for succour, to see the passing vessels, and have made their presence known by signals of some sort. But no signs had been seen of living men: no columns of smoke curled up above the trees; no flags of distress were descried; no friendly Indians beckoned them to land; no sound of gun or shout broke the silence of the wilderness. At Roanoke alone, in the one word Croatoan carved upon the trees, and in the crumbling vestiges of the colony, half buried in the rank growth of two or three summers, were there any evidences that Englishmen had ever been there—tokens, also, that they had perished.

"That such was White's conviction—that he believed his daughter and her children, and all the rest whom he had led to this distant land, had fallen victims to the vengeance of the natives—is the most charitable way of accounting for the readiness with which he seems to have acceded to the proposal to sail for the West Indies. It was, indeed, suggested that they should return to Virginia, after taking on board a fresh stock of water and provisions; but this could only have been a pretext; for as Croatoan was directly in their course, a delay of half a day would have sufficed to ascertain whether there were any Englishmen alive upon the island. 'I leave off,' said White, in a letter to Hakluyt, narrating the details of this voyage—'I leave off from prosecuting that whereunto I would to God my health were answerable to my will.' Others did not leave off, no doubt sincerely believing what with White may have been only a desperate hope, that the unhappy planters were not all exterminated. Sir Walter Raleigh seems never to have neglected any chance of finding his lost colony, but excuses were never wanting for not making a thorough search on the part of those whom he engaged to undertake it."

But a great deal happened in England before another attempt could be made to find the lost colony. Raleigh fell into disgrace with his royal mistress over Bessie Throckmorton, one of her maids of honour, and spent four years in the Tower in consequence. On his release he married the fair Bessie. In February, 1595, he explored the coasts of Trinidad and sailed up the Orinoco, but no practical result followed. Some time later he despatched Captain Laurence Keymis to make further explorations, and still later one Captain Berry; but Raleigh failed to rouse any great public interest in England by his splendid dreams of the golden treasures of Guiana. In June, 1596, he had the chief honours in the expedition of Howard and Essex to Cadiz, when the naval strength of Spain was once more shattered. He also was concerned in several other adventures before the century closed, which proved his indomitable spirit and valour.

In 1602 Raleigh again returned to the question of his colony, and bought a vessel, which he manned in order to send out there. The command was given to Samuel Mace, a capable mariner, who had twice already visited Virginia. But Mace, though able enough, was not honest of purpose, and he spent a month on the coast, forty leagues south-west of Hatteras, trafficking with the Indians, and making no attempt to reach Croatoan. This was the last direct effort made by Raleigh to recover his lost colony in Virginia, a scheme which altogether involved him in an expenditure of upwards of £40,000.

The report gained currency that the colonists were all massacred soon after White left in the first instance; but considerable doubt has been thrown upon this. William Strachey, the first secretary of the colony at Jamestown, in his work on Virginia, stated that a chief of the Upper Potomac had preserved seven English settlers alive—namely, four men, two boys, and a young maid. Captain John Smith also, in his references to the Indian emperor Powhatan, would seem to imply that some of the colonists had been spared. Raleigh himself showed by his letters that he believed many of the colonists escaped death. His nephew, Captain Bartholomew Gilbert, went out to Virginia on an exploring expedition, but he and some of his companions were slain by the Indians.

There was something prophetic in Raleigh's faith in the future of Anglo-Saxon America. In a letter to Cecil he used these remarkable words: "I shall yet live to see it an English nation." But although the prophecy was not fulfilled in its exactitude, after a lapse of nearly two centuries the State of North Carolina, in 1792, revived, in its capital, " the city of Raleigh," in grateful commemoration of his name and fame. Raleigh's Virginia patent expired by his attainder, and in 1618 he was sent to the block on a charge of high treason. His execution on insufficient grounds will always remain a dark blot on the character of James I.

Mention must here be made of John Oxenham, a young Devonshire adventurer, who in 1575 undertook a voyage in a single ship to the Isthmus of Darien. He crossed over in a pinnace to Panama and the Pearl Islands, and intended proceeding to the north, when he was seized by the Spaniards, conveyed to Lima, and there executed as a pirate.

Sir Francis Drake, " the first who ploughed a furrow round the world," and who is frequently spoken of as the greatest of the Elizabethan seamen, now demands attention. He was born near Tavistock, of humble parents, about the year 1540. After fulfilling his apprenticeship with the master of a small sailing vessel, he followed the coasting trade for some years. But by 1565 he was voyaging to Guinea and the Spanish Main. In 1567 he commanded the *Judith* in his kinsman John Hawkins's ill-fated expedition to the West Indies. In 1570, and again in 1571, he made voyages to the West Indies, with a view of discovering how he could make good his previous losses sustained at the hands of the Spaniards.

" The great experience he must thus have gained," remarks his biographer Barrow, " would not suffer him to rest in idleness; and in May, 1572, he had provided two small ships, the *Pacha*, of seventy tons, and the *Swan*, of twenty-five tons—the latter commanded by his brother John—all ready for sea, and sailed on the 24th of that month for Nombre de Dios. Here he landed with his handful of men, dismounted the guns on the platform and marched to the market-place, while the alarm-bells were ringing and drums beating. They were attacked, and Drake received a wound, which he concealed, knowing that, 'if the general's heart stoops, the men's will fail.' He ordered one of his trusty followers, Oxenham, and his brother, with sixteen men, to proceed to the king's treasure-house, where vast piles of silver were found, and still more in the governor's house: he then told his people 'that he had brought them to the mouth of the treasury of the world, which, if they did not gain, none but themselves were to be blamed.'

"Here, however, his strength and sight and speech failed him, from loss of blood; his men bound up the wound with his scarf, and by main force (having refused their entreaties) carried him to his pinnace. On recovering, he speedily decided on crossing the Isthmus of Panama; but having lost many of his men by sickness, and among them his brother Joseph, and also the other brother John, who was unfortunately killed in action with a Spanish ship, he removed the whole of the people into his own ship and pinnace, and sank the *Swan*. His object on the isthmus was to intercept a *recoe*, or train of mules, laden with the king's treasure. He met them, attacked and chased the party as far as Vera Cruz, strictly charging all his company on no account to hurt any female or unarmed man. This journey decided the future fate of Drake. He was led to a tree—'a goodlie and great high tree'—and from it had a full view of that sea of which he had heard such golden reports, and with great solemnity 'besought God to give him life and leave once to sail an English ship in those seas.'

"Having so far gratified his curiosity, and intercepted a party of mules laden with treasure, and stripped them of as much as was convenient to carry away, he returned to his ship and made sail for England, where he arrived, at Plymouth, on Sunday, the 9th of August, 1573, during divine service, when all the people in crowds ran out of the church, in the midst of the sermon, 'to witness the blessing of God on the dangerous adventures and enterprises of Captain Drake.'"

His next great enterprise, the voyage round the world, was unexampled for its daring and enterprise. Procuring an audience of the Queen, in 1577, he laid before her his scheme, the first of the kind which any Englishman had thought of, and she gave her sanction to his fitting out an expedition. The squadron, as completed, consisted of the *Pelican*, 100 tons, Drake, commander; the *Elizabeth*, 80 tons, John Winter, commander; the *Marigold*, 30 tons, John Thomas; the *Swan*, fly-boat, 50 tons, John Chester; the *Christopher*, pinnace, 15 tons, Thomas Moone, the whole manned with one hundred and sixty-three stout and able seamen.

The vessels sailed from Plymouth on the 13th of December, 1577. They had not been long at sea before they captured a Portuguese vessel, over which

Drake placed one Thomas Doughty, a volunteer gentleman, as commander. Doughty endeavoured to get the whole expedition into his own hands, and he was accordingly tried and executed at Port St. Julian for his attempts to stir up a mutiny. The squadron, now reduced to three ships by the burning of two, entered the Strait of Magellan—this being the first time any Englishman had done so, or indeed any one else except Magellan himself. Drake changed his own ship's name at this juncture from the *Pelican* to the *Golden Hind*. The passage through the strait occupied sixteen days. Violent tempests followed, when they reached the open sea, and the storms lasted for fifty-two days, during which the *Marigold* foundered with all hands.

"On the 7th of October," says Barrow, "the *Admiral* (which was the vessel captured early from the Portuguese) and the *Elizabeth* under slow sail stood into a bay near the western entrance of the strait, where they hoped to have found shelter from the bad weather; but in a few hours after coming to an anchor, the cable of the *Admiral* parted, and she drove out to sea, and was thus separated from the *Elizabeth*, which remained in the port without making any attempt to follow her. The account given by Cliffe, one of the crew of the *Elizabeth*, is that Winter the next day, after having been in great danger among the rocks, re-entered the strait, and, anchoring in an open bay, made great fires on the shore in the hope that Drake might see them; that he remained there ten days, then went farther, and stayed for three weeks in a sound which he named

'The Port of Health'; and that then, being in despair both as to Drake's existence and as to favourable winds for Peru, he 'gave over the voyage, full sore against the mariners' minds.' Winter arrived safe in England, but he was censured by many for having abandoned his commander.

"The general being now left with only the little pinnace, was driven back once more into the latitude of 55° south, in which he got among some islands, perhaps some of those to the north of Terra del Fuego, where the ship was anchored, and the crew were refreshed with wholesome herbs and good water. After two days, however, they were driven from their anchorage, and the little shallop or pinnace lost sight of the ship, nor did it ever again rejoin her. There were eight men in her, who had provisions only for one day; they, however, reached the shore, procured water and roots, and in the course of a fortnight entered the Strait of Magelhaens. Here they salted and dried penguins, and proceeded to Port Julian, and thence to Rio de la Plata. There six of the party went into the woods to seek for food. A party of Indians met them, wounded them all with their arrows, and took four of them prisoners: the other two escaped to their companions who had remained in the boat. They moved to an island two or three leagues from the shore, where the two wounded men died: the shallop was dashed in pieces against the rocks. The remaining two, Peter Curder and William Pitcher, stayed on this island two months, subsisting on small crabs, eels, and a fruit like an orange; but they had no water. The misery they endured for want of this indispensable necessary of life induced them to endeavour, by means of a plank and a couple of paddles, to reach the mainland. This they accomplished in three days and two nights, and found a rivulet of sweet water—'where,' says Curder, 'Pitcher, my only comfort and companion (although I endeavoured to dissuade him), being pinched with extreme thirst, over-drank himself; and, to my unspeakable grief, died within half an hour, whom I buried as well as I could in the sand.'

"Curder, the only survivor of the party, was kindly treated by some Indians, and at the end of nine years returned to England. The *Golden Hind* was now left completely alone, and with a reduced crew. Another storm arose, and the vessel was driven to the very southern extremity of the American Continent, and thus Drake was the first to discover Cape Horn."

The storm abated on the 30th of October, and Drake then proceeded to the northward, towards the place appointed for the rendezvous of his squadron, 30° south; but no vessels could be found. Coasting along till he came to 38°, he landed on the Island of Macho, where he obtained supplies from the natives, who were apparently friendly. On the second day, however, the Indians mustered in force, and killed and wounded a great many Englishmen, Drake himself being wounded in the face by an arrow, which pierced almost to the brain; and he also received a wound in the head.

On the 30th of November Drake dropped anchor in a bay called St. Philip, and brought away an Indian they had fallen in with. The general obtained plenty of stores, and afterwards seized a Spanish ship, richly laden, and then dismissed the Indian, rewarding him amply for his good services. On the 19th of December Drake entered a bay near a town named Cyppo, where he was greeted by a number of Spaniards and Indians. They were very hostile, and the English retired to their vessel—all except one, who was killed and fearfully mutilated. They next landed at Tarapaca, in about 20° S. lat.

"Coasting along, still in the hope of meeting with his friends, Drake arrived, on the 7th of February, before Arica, where he took two barques, on board of one of which was about eight hundredweight of silver. On the 15th he arrived at Callao, the port of Lima, and entered the harbour without resistance, though about thirty ships were lying there, seventeen of which were prepared for their voyage. Whether these ships were manned and armed, or what was their size, is not stated; but it appears most strange that Drake, with his single ship, should have been able to strike such dismay into the Spaniards that they suffered the plunder of their seventeen loaded ships to be carried on without the least attempt at resistance.

"In one of these ships they found fifteen hundred bars of silver; in another, a large chest of coined money; and valuable lading in the rest, from all of which they leisurely selected what they pleased; and had they been so disposed, they might have set fire to the whole of the ships; but Drake was satisfied in obtaining booty for himself and his crew, in compensation for the former wrongs he had received from the Spanish people. The general, however, in order to secure himself against an immediate pursuit, ordered the cables of the ships to be cut, and let them drive. He had here received intelligence of a very rich ship, that was laden with gold and silver, and had sailed from hence just before his arrival, bound for Panama. Her name was the *Cacafuego*, and she was termed 'the great glory of the South Sea.' As he was in full chase of this vessel he fell in with and boarded a brigantine, out of which he took eighty pounds' weight of gold, a crucifix of the same metal, and some emeralds. In a few days after, near Cape St. Francis, in 1° lat., he got sight of the *Cacafuego*, about one hundred and fifty leagues from Panama. On coming up with her, a shot or two carried away one of her masts, when she was boarded and easily carried. Besides a large quantity of pearls and precious stones, they took out of her eighty pounds' weight of gold, thirteen chests of coined silver, and rough silver enough to ballast a ship. Having transferred all this to the *Golden Hind*, the total amount of which was calculated at three hundred and sixty thousand pieces of eight, or nearly £90,000, they let the *Cacafuego* go. Standing out to the westward to avoid Panama, where probably they considered that they were too well known, they fell in with another ship, from which they obtained some linen, cloth, porcelain, dishes, and silk. The owner of this ship, a Spanish gentleman, was on board her, from whom Drake is said to have received a falcon, wrought in pure gold, with a large emerald set in its breast; but whether by seizure, by purchase, or as a present is not mentioned. After taking out the pilot for his own service, he suffered the ship to proceed on her voyage. He now continued his course; and keeping close to the coast of North America, on the 15th of April came to the port of Aguapulca, in latitude about 15° 30′ N. Having here taken in some bread and other provisions, he prepared to depart northwards; but, as the narrative says, 'not forgetting, before we got a shipboard, to take us also a certain pot (of about a bushell in bignesse) full of ryalls of plate, which we found in the towne, together with a chaine of gold, and some other jewels, which we entreated a gentleman Spaniard to leave behind him, as he was flying out of the towne.'

"At this place the admiral set on shore Nuna de Silva, the Portuguese pilot, whom he had taken from the Cape de Verde Islands, and who, on his arrival at Mexico, gave to the governor a narrative of all the circumstances that had happened on the voyage, which was correct in most particulars; and it was published by Hakluyt."

Drake made a complete refit of his little barque at Aguapulca, and then boldly resolved to try to reach home by way of the north-east. He failed like Cook and many of Cook's successors, and the dream of navigators still remains to be realized. Drake skirted the north-western shores of America, where the people regarded him and his companions as gods. On the 17th of June they entered a convenient harbour in lat. 38° 30′ N., the land being inhabited, and the houses of the natives close to the water's edge. The *Golden Hind* having sprung a leak, she was now put to rights. A great multitude of natives came down from the country, headed by the king. They indulged in singing and dancing, and during the festitives the king placed a feathered cap of network on the general's head and a chain round his neck, and saluted him by the name of *Hioh*—that is, king or chief. Drake took this to mean the submission of themselves and the whole country to the new-comers; and he gave them to understand, in the best way he was able, that he accepted them in the name, and for the use of, the Queen of England.

The natives certainly regarded the English with great favour. Hitherto, this part of the American Continent had been visited by Juan Rodriguez Cabrillo, and by no other European. His intercourse with the natives was of the most friendly kind, and the favourable disposition of the latter towards Europeans Drake strengthened and confirmed by his friendly and humane treatment of them. Before he left, Drake caused a post to be set up on shore, as a monument, and it bore a brass plate, on which was engraved the Queen's name, as well as the assertion of her right and title, and that of her successors, to the new kingdom. Record was also made of "the day and year of our arrival there, and of the free giving up of the province and kingdom, both by the king and people, into her Majesty's hands; together with her Highness's picture and arms in a piece of sixpence, current English money, showing itself by a hole made of purpose through the plate: underneath was likewise engraven the name of our general, etc."

In order to show respect to his native land, and because white cliffs were observed on the coast, Drake gave to all the land he had seen in this part of America the name of New Albion. After remaining thirty-six days in port, Drake and his companions left, to the deep regret of the friendly natives, who expressed a wish for their speedy return. Admiral Burney considered that the port of Drake was that which is now known by the name of Port San Francisco, the latitude of which is 37° 48½' N. "Allowing them to be the same," he continues, " it is remarkable that both the most northern and the most southern ports at which Drake anchored in the course of his voyage should afterwards by the Spaniards—doubtless without any intended reference to the name of *Francis* Drake —be named *San Francisco*." Thus, as it has been observed by another writer, this portion of the west coast of America was discovered, and taken possession of in the usual manner, by an Englishman, in the name of his sovereign, full two hundred years before the United States of America came into existence as such.

The *Golden Hind* left the American coast on the 23rd of July, and Drake resolved to return home by crossing the Pacific. He consequently directed his course towards the Philippine Islands. For the long period of sixty-eight days the expedition was without sight of any land, but " on the 30th of September it fell in with certain islands lying in about 8° to the northward of the Line. The natives came off in their canoes, each hollowed out of a single tree, bringing cocoanuts, fruits, and fish. The first that came appeared to be well disposed, but others acted dishonestly, carrying off whatever articles were once put into their hands. The English therefore would have nothing to do with them in the way of trade. on which, to manifest their resentment, they began to attack the ship with stones, with which they had provided themselves. A gun was fired over their heads, the noise of which frightened them; but none being hurt, they returned, and were more insolent than before. The patience of Drake was now exhausted, and he ordered some muskets to be fired at them; for they could not be got rid of till they were made to feel some smart as well as terror. Drake gave these islands the name of the *Islands of Thieves.* Admiral Burney thinks, from the description of the natives, the time of the passage to them, and the latitude, that they are the islands which in our time have been called the Pelew Islands.

"Leaving these islands, they sailed westerly, from the 3rd to the 16th of October, without seeing any land till they made the Philippine Islands, and coasted them until the 21st, when they anchored and watered the ship at the largest of the group, called Mindanao; and sailing thence about eight leagues, they passed between two islands south of Mindanao, and on the 3rd of November had sight of the Moluccas, and steered for Tidore; but having received information that the Portuguese had been driven out of Ternate, and had taken up their quarters at Tidore, Drake determined to proceed to the former place.

"On anchoring at this city, the capital of the Moluccas, Drake sent a messenger with a velvet cloak to the king, with a request to be supplied with provisions and allowed to purchase various kinds of spices. The king himself came off to the ship, preceded by three large and magnificent canoes, each having eighty rowers, who paddled to the sound of brass cymbals. On each side of these canoes was a row of soldiers, every one having a sword, dagger, and target; and in each there was also a small piece of ordnance mounted on a stock. Drake received the king in great state, himself and all his officers being dressed in their richest clothes, guns firing, and trumpets sounding. The king was a tall, corpulent man, with a good countenance. His attendants showed him great respect, speaking to him only in a kneeling posture.

"On taking leave, he promised to visit the general on the following day, so that the ship should be supplied with provisions. Abundance of rice, fruits, and poultry were sent off, together with a small quantity of cloves. The king, however, instead of visiting them as he had promised, sent his brother with an excuse and an invitation to the general to land. This Drake declined; but some of his officers waited on the king, the brother being detained on board as a pledge for their safety. The king, who was covered with a profusion of gold ornaments and jewels, received them with much parade."

Drake won golden opinions from all with whom he had to deal here; and having duly furnished his ship with provisions, he sailed from the capital of the Moluccas on the 9th of November. The passage home was a lengthy one. He was compelled to make a thorough refit on the south-west coast of Java, after which he held for the Cape of Good Hope, and landed in England on the 26th of September, 1580. For some time he was deprived of his justly earned honours by Spanish protests; but at length, on the 4th of

April, Elizabeth visited his ship at Deptford, and knighted him on its deck.

Four years later, or a little more, Drake sailed with a fleet of twenty-five ships for the Spanish Indies. He harassed Hispaniola, Cartagena, and the coast of Florida; and after terrible losses from illness, brought home the hundred and ninety dispirited colonists whom he found in Virginia, together with cargoes of tobacco and potatoes. This expedition was far inferior, both in interest and profit, to his former enterprises.

Spain and the Azores were the next objects of his exploits—but, indeed, as he said, he was ready to go anywhere "to seek God's enemies and her Majesty's wherever they may be found." In the destruction of the Spanish Armada, Drake's splendid seamanship and his indomitable courage covered him with fresh glory, and made his name one of terror for the Spaniards.

A few peaceful years ensued after this, and then, finally, in August, 1595, Drake sailed on his last voyage to the West Indies. Misfortunes crowded upon him, including the death of Hawkins, his second in command, and at last the gallant Drake himself fell ill of dysentery, and died off Porto Bello on the 28th of January, 1596. The sea received him, for his body was put into a leaden coffin and committed to the deep. But although the element in which he was always so much at home was now his tomb, "the ocean sea was not sufficient room for his fame," as an unknown poet finely wrote.

CHAPTER IX.

OPERATIONS OF THE VIRGINIA COMPANY.

THE history of Virginia is probably more full of romance than that of any other State of the American Union, and it was in this State that the first permanent colony was established by English settlers. It almost lost this distinction, however, owing to the exploits of one Bartholomew Gosnold, whose career we must first glance at, and who nearly secured for New England the honour of being the first lasting English colony.

Gosnold had already made a voyage to Virginia, when he was commissioned to go out to America again by the Earl of Southampton. He sailed from Falmouth on the 25th of March, 1602, in a small vessel called the *Concord*, having as his second in command Bartholomew Gilbert. He had with him thirty-two persons, of whom twenty were to remain and found a colony somewhere on the northern coast of Virginia, as the whole country was then called, from the thirty-fourth to the forty-fifth degree of latitude. Gosnold's idea was to proceed by a direct north-west course, thus avoiding the usual circuitous route by the Canaries and the West India Islands; but he was driven by contrary winds southward to the Azores, and thence he steered almost due west, arriving in seven weeks at Cape Elizabeth, on the coast of Maine. "Following the coast to the southwest, he skirted 'an outpoint of wooded land,' and about noon of the 14th of May he anchored 'near savage rock' to the east of York Harbour. There he met a Biscay shallop, and there he was visited by natives. Not finding his 'purposed place,' he stood to the south, and on the morning of the 15th discovered the promontory which he named Cape Cod. He and four of his men went on shore. Cape Cod was the first spot in New England ever trod by Englishmen, while as yet there was not one European family on the continent from Florida to Hudson's Bay. Doubling the cape, and passing Nantucket, they touched at No Man's Land, passed round the promontory of Gay Head, naming it Dover Cliff, and entered Buzzard's Bay, a stately sound, which they called Gosnold's Hope. The westernmost of the islands was named Elizabeth, from the Queen—a name which has been transferred to the group. Here they beheld the rank vegetation of a virgin soil: noble forests; wild fruits and flowers bursting from the earth; the eglantine, the thorn, and the honeysuckle, the wild pea, the tansy, and young sassafras; strawberries, raspberries, grape-vines,—all in profusion. Within a pond upon the island lies a rocky islet; on this the adventurers built their storehouse and their fort; and the foundations of the first New England colony were laid. The island, the pond, the islet, are yet visible; the shrubs are luxuriant as of old; but the forests are gone, and the ruins of the fort can no longer be discerned.

"A traffic with the natives on the main enabled Gosnold to lade the *Concord* with sassafras root, then esteemed in pharmacy as a sovereign panacea. The band, which was to have nestled on the Elizabeth Islands, finding their friends about to embark for Europe, despaired of supplies of food, and determined not to remain. Fear of the Indians, who had ceased to be friendly, the want of provisions, and jealousy respecting the distribution of the risks and profits defeated the design. The party soon set sail, and bore for England, leaving not so much as one European family between Florida and Labrador. The return voyage lasted but five weeks; and the expedition was completed in less than four months, during which entire health had prevailed."

The favourable reports which Gosnold gave of the regions visited induced the merchants of Bristol—at the instance of Richard Hakluyt, the historian of these discoveries, and with the cordial assent of Raleigh—to pursue the work of exploration. Accordingly, Martin Pring, who was with Gosnold on the *Concord*, was given the command of the *Speedwell*, a ship of fifty tons and thirty men, and the *Discoverer*, a barque of twenty-six tons and thirteen men; and he set sail for America on the 10th of April, 1603. The vessels were well provided with articles to please the natives, and the voyage was successful. The little expedition "reached the American coast among the islands of Penobscot Bay. Coasting towards the west, Pring made a discovery of many of the harbours of Maine; of the Saco, the Kennebunk, and the York Rivers; and the channel of the Piscataqua was examined for three or four leagues. Finding no sassafras, he steered to the south, doubled Cape Ann, and went on shore in Massachusetts; but being still unsuccessful, he again pursued a southerly track, till he anchored in Old Town Harbour, on Martha's Vineyard. Here obtaining a freight, he returned to England, after an absence of about six months, which had been free from disaster or danger.

"The testimony of Pring having confirmed the report of Gosnold, an expedition, promoted by the Earl of Southampton and his brother-in-law Lord Arundel of Wardour, was confided to George Waymouth, a careful and vigilant commander, who, in attempting a north-west passage, had already explored the coast of Labrador. Weighing anchor on Easter Sunday, on the 14th of May, 1605, he came near the whitish, sandy promontory of Cape Cod. To escape the continual shoals in which he found himself embayed, he stood out to sea, then turned to the north, and on the 17th anchored to the north of Monhegan Island, in sight of hills to the north-north-west on the main. On Whit-Sunday he found his way among the St. George's Islands into an excellent harbour, which was accessible by four passages, defended from all winds, and had good mooring upon a clay ooze, and even upon the rocks by the cliff side. The climate was agreeable; the sea yielded fish of many kinds profusely; the tall and great trees on the islands were much observed; and the gum of the silver fir was thought to be as fragrant as frankincense; some trade was carried on with the natives for sables, and skins of deer and otter and beaver; the land was of such pleasantness that many of the company wished themselves settled there.

"Having in the last of May discovered in his pinnace the broad, deep current of the St. George's, on the 11th of June Waymouth passed with a gentle wind up with the ship into that river for about eighteen miles, which were reckoned at six-and-twenty, and 'all consented in joy' to admire its width of a half-mile or a mile; its verdant banks; its gallant and spacious coves; the strength of its tide, which may have risen nine or ten feet, and was set down at eighteen or twenty.

"On the 13th he ascended in a row-boat ten miles farther, and the discoverers were more and more pleased with the beauty of the fertile bordering ground. No token was found that ever any Christian had been there before; and at the point where the river trends westward into the main, he set up a memorial cross, as he had already done on the rocky shore of the St. George's Islands. Well satisfied with his discoveries, on Sunday, the 16th of June, he sailed for England, taking with him five of the natives whom he had decoyed, to be instructed in English, and to serve as guides to some future expedition. At his coming into the harbour of Plymouth, he yielded up three of the natives to Sir Ferdinando Gorges, the governor of that town, whose curiosity was thus directed to the shores of Maine."

It was by voyages like these that the way was paved for the colonization of the United States. The great work of the Virginia Companies was begun in 1606, when James I., delighted at the idea of extending his territories, granted the first patent for a colony to Edward Maria Wingfield, a merchant of the West of England; Robert Hunt, a clergyman of worth and fortitude; John Smith, an adventurer of the first order and the finest qualities; Richard Hakluyt; Sir George Somers; and others who should be joined to them. The patent was dated the 10th of April, 1606.

All the territories on the American coast, between 34° and 45° of north latitude, together with the islands within a hundred miles, were granted to the adventurers. Two companies were to be formed, the first to be called the Southern Colony, and the second the Northern Colony. The jurisdiction of the former company—whose council was chiefly composed of residents of London, and therefore came to be known as the London Company—extended from Cape Fear to the southern limit of Maryland—that is, from 34° to 38°; and the jurisdiction of the other company—whose council was appointed from Plymouth and the vicinity, and therefore came to be known as the Plymouth Company—extended from 41° to 45°. The intermediate district, from 38° to 41°, was open to the competition of both companies.

"Each colony was to be governed by a resident council of thirteen, to be appointed by the King, with power to choose a president, who should not be a clergyman, from their own body, and to fill any vacancies that should occur among themselves from death or resignation. The laws enacted by them were subject to revision either by the King or the Council in England. No part whatever in the government was given to the people; even trial by jury was allowed only in cases of capital crimes, which were 'tumults, rebellion, conspiracy, meetings, and sedition, together with murder, manslaughter, incest, rapes, and adultery.' Lesser crimes and misdemeanours were to be tried before the president and council, and punished according to their will. Real estate was to be held as under the laws of England, but for the first five years all personal property and the fruits of the labours of the colonists were to be held as a common stock, and each member of the community was to be supported from the general store. Religion was to be established in accordance with the rites and doctrines of the Church of England; the people were enjoined, by virtue of such penalties as the president and council should choose to inflict, to 'kindly treat the savage and heathen people in those parts, and use all proper means to draw them to the true service and knowledge of God,' and also to lead them to 'good and sociable traffic.' Such were the essential features of the first constitution of government established within the limits of the present United States. It was especially the work of that pedantic despot James I., who afterwards amused himself with drawing up a code of laws for the administration of a government where, in the last resort, all political power rested in his hands, and the hands of those of his appointment."

The Plymouth Company sent out two ships in the summer of 1606: one in May, commanded by Captain Pring; the other in August, commanded by Henry Chalong. Chalong was captured by the Spaniards, but Pring explored the coast of Maine, and brought home such a favourable report that in the following year Chief Justice Popham sent out an expedition under his brother George Popham and Raleigh Gilbert, a son of Sir Humphrey, to settle a colony at the mouth of the Sagadahoc. As this attempt proved abortive, however, the honour of planting the first permanent colony was destined to accrue to the London Company in Virginia.

This first important band of colonists numbered one hundred and five men, and among these there were only about twenty labourers and mechanics. No women went over. There were forty-eight gentlemen to four carpenters, although they were going to a region where there was not a house standing. The most notable members of the colony included Bartholomew Gosnold, and his companion in the *Concord*, Gabriel Archer; Edward Maria Wingfield, afterwards the first governor; the Rev. Robert Hunt, the chaplain; George Percy, a brother of the Earl of Northumberland, who did excellent service; and the redoubtable Captain John Smith.

As this last-named extraordinary man now comes into great prominence, and as his experiences are amongst the most romantic in the history of colonization, it will be convenient here to refer briefly to his early career. John Smith was born at Willoughby, in Lincolnshire, in 1580, and was educated at the schools of Alford and Louth. He wanted to go to sea on his father's death in 1596, but his guardian bound him apprentice to a merchant of Lynn. Business being obnoxious to him, he accompanied the second son of Lord Willoughby to France, and saw some soldiering at Havre. Afterwards he went into the Low Countries, and thence crossed to Scotland, returning to Willoughby, where he lived in a wood, and studied Machiavelli and Marcus Aurelius, and exercised himself on a good horse with lance and ring. As the Turks were then ravaging Hungary, he decided to join the Christian army, and was plundered on the way thither by four French adventurers. He next joined himself with a piratical merchant, and acquired wealth by the capture of a Venetian argosy, while coasting round Italy and the north of Africa. He next entered the service of Ferdinand, Duke of Austria, under whom he greatly distinguished himself, and had some surprising adventures. Sold as a slave, and marched to Adrianople, he escaped and travelled through Germany, France, Spain, and Morocco. After a sea fight with two Spanish men-of-war, he returned to England in 1604, the richer by a thousand ducats.

The London Company's scheme fell in with Smith's disposition admirably. The fleet sailed from Blackwall on the 19th of December, 1606. It was under the command of Captain Christopher Newport, and consisted of three vessels : the *Sarah Constant,* one hundred tons ; the *God-speed,* forty tons ; and the *Discovery,* pinnace, twenty tons. The instructions of the council were that the ships should seek for a safe port at the entrance of some navigable river ; and if more than one was discovered, that was to be preferred which might have two branches. Should either branch come from the north-west, then that was to be entered, as it might be the passage to the South Sea ; and the hope of finding this passage was never abandoned by the London Council so long as the company was in existence.

During the voyage out dissensions arose among the adventurers, for James I. had foolishly directed that the papers appointing the authorities should not be opened till after the arrival in Virginia. John Smith especially appears to have excited jealousy, probably from his superior abilities, and he was charged with desiring to usurp the government and to assassinate the council. After a stormy passage, the expedition sailed into Chesapeake Bay on the 26th of April, 1607. Cape Henry and Cape Charles were named after the sons of the King.

On the sealed box being opened at Cape Henry, it was ascertained that the council was to consist of Bartholomew Gosnold, John Smith, Edward M. Wingfield, Christopher Newport, John Ratcliffe, John Martin, and George Kendall. Seventeen days were spent in searching for a suitable site for the colony; and at length, on the 13th of May, the council decided upon the present site of Jamestown, so called after the King. It was situate on a peninsula about forty miles from the mouth of the Powhatan, which was called the King's River, and subsequently James River.

The council appointed Wingfield president, and at first excluded Smith from their deliberations. Yet he was the man "without whose aid the vices of the colony would have caused its immediate ruin." Most of the colonists devoted themselves to felling timber and providing freight for the ships, while Captain

Newport and Smith, with twenty others, ascended the James River to the falls. Here they came upon the native chief Powhatan, king of the tribes, whose city of wigwams lay just below the site of Richmond. The two explorers desired to visit the Blue Ridge Mountains; but being dissuaded by Powhatan, they now turned back down the river. On reaching Jamestown, they learned that the Indians had attacked the camp during their absence, wounding several men.

Matters were going very badly in the colony when Newport left it in June to return to England. Before the end of August fifty men had died of sickness and fatigue, including the worthy Bartholomew Gosnold, the projector of the colony. Disunion set in amongst the rest, and the president, Wingfield, was deposed on the ground of appropriating public stores and designing to abandon the colony. His successor, Ratcliffe, proved inefficient, and Smith came to the front by his capable and vigorous management of affairs. Kendall, one of the council, was tried for mutiny, and shot. Ratcliffe and Archer next proposed to abandon the colony to its fate; but the project was suppressed by Smith, and tranquillity was restored before the winter set in.

On the 10th of December Smith left the colony in order to explore the interior. He went up the Chickahominy to trade for corn, and to find the head of that river. On its upper waters two of his men were taken by the Indians and slain, but Smith was saved by an Indian. Smith's own account of what followed is published in his *General History of Virginia*, where he brings in the story of the Princess Pocahontas.

His adventures are thus summarized: "Making his way (with his Indian guide) towards the boat, which he had left in charge of two of his men, he and the guide slipped together into an 'oasie creek,' from which it was impossible to extricate themselves. Half dead with cold, he at length threw away his arms and surrendered, and was taken before Opechankanough, King of Pamunkey. He sought to propitiate the chief by presenting him with 'a round Ivory dowble compass Dyall.' The savages marvelled much at the playing of the needle, which they could see, but, for the glass over it, could not touch. With this 'globelike jewel,' Smith explained to the king and his people the movements of the sun, moon, and stars, the shape of the earth, the extent of land and sea, the difference in the races of men, and 'many other suchlike matters,' at which, it was hardly necessary to add, the savages 'all stood as amazed with admiration.' They nevertheless tied the lecturer to a tree, and were about to shoot him to death with arrows, when Opechankanough, who seemed to have a better appreciation than his followers had of the sciences of astronomy and cosmography, holding up the wonderful compass, stayed the execution. They then released the prisoner, fed him, and used him well. So well, indeed, did they feed him, that he thought they meant to fatten him for a feast; and they received him otherwise with so much honour, that they dressed themselves in their brightest paints, the plumage of the most brilliant birds, the choicest rattlesnake tails, and 'such toys'—adding, perhaps, as Strachey says the Indians sometimes did, 'a dead ratt tyed by the tail, and suchlike conundrums'—and so attired danced before him and the king, 'singing and yelling out with hellish notes and screeches.' They promised him, moreover, life and liberty, land and women, if he would aid them by his advice in an attack upon Jamestown; but from this he dissuaded them by representations of the mines, great guns, and other engines with which such an attack would be repulsed. When he persuaded them to send a letter to the fort, and the messengers brought, as he promised they should, such things as he asked for, the savages were amazed anew, that either the paper itself spoke to those who received it, or that Smith had the power of divination.

"This clothed and bearded white man was a strange spectacle to the Indians, and men, women, and children crowded to see him, as he was led from tribe to tribe. At length he was taken before the great king of all, Powhatan, at a place called Werowocomoco, which signifies king's house, on the north side of the York River, and only fourteen or fifteen miles from Jamestown. When Smith was led into his presence, the emperor received him in state, seated on a throne which was much like a bedstead, clothed in a robe of raccoon skins. On each side of him sat a young girl of sixteen or eighteen years, and beyond them a double row of men and women, their heads and shoulders painted red and adorned with feathers. A queen served the prisoner with water to wash his hands, and a bunch of feathers on which to dry them; a feast was spread before him as if he were an honoured friend and welcome guest, for such was the Indian treatment of those who presently were to be led to die.

"This ceremonious and hospitable reception was followed by a brief consultation between the king and his chief men. Two great stones were then brought in, to which Smith was dragged, and his head laid upon them. The executioners stood ready to beat out his brains with their clubs; but at this critical moment 'Pocahontas, the king's dearest daughter, when no intreaty could prevaile, got his head in her arms, and laid her owne upon his to save him from death; whereat the emperour was contented he should live to make him hatchets, and her bells, beads, and copper.'"

Whatever truth or whatever romance there may be in this account, its main features relating to Smith's capture are probably correct. His captivity resulted in real benefit to the colony; for he not only had opportunity of observing the country between the James and the Potomac, and gaining insight into the habits and character of the natives, but he opened up friendly relations thereby between the English and the tribes of Powhatan.

When Smith reached Jamestown, after an absence of four weeks, he found the colony reduced to forty men, who were planning their escape in the pinnace; but this attempt he sternly suppressed. His own life was placed in jeopardy, but he was saved by the opportune arrival of Captain Newport from England.

Newport had been despatched by the London Council with supplies, and also with one hundred and twenty new emigrants. His arrival was hailed with joy, but the new-comers were consumed by the idea of gold, and Newport himself once more embarked for England with a cargo of worthless earth. Meantime, from July to September, 1608, Smith "surveyed the Bay of the Chesapeake to the Susquehannah, and left only the borders of that remote river to remain for some years longer the fabled dwelling-place of a giant progeny. He was the first to publish to the English the power of the Mohawks, 'who dwelt upon a great water, and had many boats, and many men,' and, as it seemed to the feebler Algonkin tribes, 'made war upon all the world.' In the Chesapeake he encountered a fleet of their canoes. The Patapsco was discovered and explored, and Smith probably entered the harbour of Baltimore. The majestic Potomac especially invited curiosity; and he ascended beyond Mount Vernon and Washington to the falls above Georgetown. Nor did he merely examine the rivers and inlets. He penetrated the territories, and laid the foundation for future beneficial intercourse with the native tribes. The map which he prepared and sent to the company in London delineates correctly the great outlines of nature. The expedition was worthy of the romantic age of American history."

Smith was appointed president of the council on the 10th of September, 1608; and when Newport again returned with supplies, he found a more hopeful feeling in the colony. Seventy new emigrants, including two women, arrived with Newport from England. The two females were Mistress Forrest, and her maid Ann Burras; and we read that Ann was married in the course of a few weeks to one John Laydon.

Newport's new instructions from the London Council were to the effect that he was to bring home a lump of gold, to discover the passage to the South Sea, and to find the survivors of the Roanoke colony. He took out a number of things for Powhatan, including a crown for his coronation. The ceremony was performed; but Newport was no match for the wily savage, and the Indian chief took a high tone afterwards when he referred to his "royal brother of England."

Smith knew Powhatan better, and managed both him and his own fellow-colonists with discretion. But he was sadly handicapped, and he lost in rapid succession Captain Wynne and J. Scrivener, members of the council; Captain Waldo, the commander of the fort in Smith's absence; Anthony Gosnold, a brother of Bartholomew; and eight others. Smith was the only member of the original council left; and in writing to the London authorities, we find him saying, "When you send again, I entreat you rather send but thirty carpenters, husbandmen, gardeners, fishermen, blacksmiths, masons, and diggers up of trees' roots, well provided, than a thousand of such as we have." Meantime, he did his best to enforce industry amongst the surviving colonists.

On the 23rd of May, 1609, the second charter of Virginia was issued under royal authority. It entrusted the colonization of the territory to a very numerous, wealthy, and influential body of adventurers. The list was headed by the name of Robert Cecil, Earl of Salisbury, the enemy and rival of Sir Walter Raleigh, who was now languishing in the

Tower. Among the other names were those of the Earls of Southampton, Lincoln, and Dorset, George Percy, Sir Oliver Cromwell (uncle to the future Protector), Sir Anthony Ashley, Sir Edwin Sandys, Sir Francis Bacon, Captain John Smith, Richard Hakluyt, and George Sandys. Many public companies were represented, as were also the nobility and gentry, the army and the bar, the trade, commerce, and industry of England.

"The territory granted to the company extended two hundred miles to the north, and as many to the south of Old Point Comfort, ' up into the land throughout from sea to sea, west and north-west '; including ' all the islands lying within one hundred miles along the coast of both seas of the precinct.'

" At the request of the corporation, the new charter transferred to the company the powers which had before been reserved to the King. The perpetual supreme council in England was now to be chosen by the shareholders themselves, and, in the exercise of the functions of legislation and government, was independent of the monarch.

"The governor in Virginia, whom the corporation was to appoint, might rule the colonists with uncontrolled authority, according to the tenor of instructions and laws established by the council; or, in want of them, according to his own good discretion, even in cases capital and criminal, not less than civil ; and, in the event of mutiny or rebellion, he might declare martial law, being himself the judge of the necessity of the measure, and the executive officer in its administration. If not one valuable civil privilege was guaranteed to the emigrants, they were at least withdrawn from the power of the King, and the company could at its pleasure endow them with all the rights of Englishmen.

"Lord Delawarre, distinguished for his virtues as well as his rank, received the appointment of governor and captain-general for life, and was surrounded, at least nominally, by stately officers, with titles and charges suited to the dignity of a flourishing empire. The public mind favoured colonization; the adventurers, with cheerful alacrity, contributed free-will offerings; and such swarms of people desired to be transported, that the company could despatch a fleet of nine vessels, containing more than five hundred emigrants."

Sir Thomas Gates was appointed lieutenant-governor of the colony, and Sir George Somers admiral of the expedition; and these, with Captain Newport, the vice-admiral, took passage in the *Sea Adventure*. Among the captains of the fleet were Ratcliffe, Martin, and Archer, whose appointment was somewhat of a reflection upon Smith and his administration, as he had made formal complaints against them. A storm overtook the expedition soon after sailing, but seven of the vessels reached the Chesapeake in August.

One of the two vessels missing was a pinnace, and the other was the admiral's ship conveying Gates, Somers, Newport, and William Strachey. The consequence was that a difficulty was created in Virginia when the other seven ships arrived. "The old charter was abrogated; and there was in the settlement no one who had any authority from the new patentees. The emigrants of the last arrival were dissolute gallants, packed off to escape worse destinies at home, broken tradesmen, gentlemen impoverished in spirit and fortune, rakes and libertines, more fitted to corrupt than to found the new commonwealth. It was not the will of God that these men should 'be the carpenters and workers in this so glorious a building.' Hopeless as the determination appeared, Smith, for more than a year, maintained his authority as president over the unruly herd, and devised new expeditions and new settlements for their occupation and support. When an accidental explosion of gunpowder disabled him by inflicting wounds which the surgical skill of the colony could not relieve, he delegated his office to Percy, and embarked for England, never to see Virginia again. He united the highest spirit of adventure with eminent powers of action. His courage and self-possession accomplished what others esteemed desperate. Fruitful in expedients, he was prompt in execution. He was accustomed to lead, not to send, his men to danger; would suffer want rather than borrow, and starve sooner than not pay. He had a just idea of the public good and his country's honour. To his vigour, industry, and resolution the survival of the colony is due. He clearly discerned that it was the true interest of England not to seek in Virginia for gold and sudden wealth, but to enforce regular industry. 'Nothing,' said he, 'is to be expected thence but by labour.'

"The colonists, no longer controlled by an acknowledged authority, abandoned themselves to improvident idleness. Their ample stock of provisions was rapidly consumed; and further supplies were refused by the

Indians, who began to regard them with a fatal contempt. Stragglers from the town were cut off, parties which begged food in the Indian cabins were murdered, and plans were laid to starve and destroy the whole company. The horrors of famine ensued; while a band of about thirty, seizing on a ship, escaped to become pirates, and to plead desperate necessity as their excuse. Smith had left more than four hundred and ninety persons in the colony: in six months, indolence, vice, and famine reduced the number to sixty; and these were so feeble and dejected, that, if relief had been delayed but ten days longer, they also must have utterly perished."

Sir Thomas Gates and his companions were wrecked on the rocks of the Bermudas, but they all safely reached land. The islands were henceforth known as the Somers Islands (from Sir George Somers) as well as the Bermudas, and the name became corrupted into Summer Islands. There was fortunately abundance of food for Gates and the one hundred and fifty men, women, and children who were with him. During the enforced stay of the colonists there were births, deaths, and a marriage. The wife of one John Rolfe gave birth to a daughter, who was christened Bermuda, and a boy born to another couple was called Bermudas.

The castaways constructed two vessels, in which they embarked for Virginia. When they arrived, on the 24th of May, 1610, instead of finding a prosperous colony, they were shocked at the scene of misery, scarcity, and death which was revealed. The outlook was so hopeless that Gates and the colonists abandoned Jamestown, and in four vessels went down the river in quest of another destination. As they drew near the mouth of the river on the 9th of June, they encountered the long-boat of Lord Delawarre, who had arrived on the coast with supplies and emigrants. All the colonists now returned to Jamestown, and on the 11th Delawarre himself also brought his three ships to anchor opposite the fort, and went ashore. When he landed, the new governor fell upon his knees and engaged in silent prayer.

A procession of colonists met him by the shore; and when his commission as captain-general had been read, Sir Thomas Gates surrendered into his hands the government of the colony. Delawarre at once began to reorganize the colony, combining firmness and urbanity in doing so. In a short time all the old troubles were healed, and the colonists became pacified and industrious. They began the day with prayers in the little church; and after receiving their daily allowance of food, laboured from six in the morning until ten, and from two in the afternoon till four, raising substantial, well-timbered houses, etc.

The governor despatched Sir George Somers and Captain Argall to the Bermudas, to bring off some of the wild swine with which the islands abounded, but the vessels were driven northward by stress of weather. Argall returned to England, but Somers reached the Bermudas, where he soon afterwards, however, died. Argall went on another exploring expedition up the coast, and on the 27th of July he anchored in a very large bay, which he called Delawarre, or Delaware. Forts were built on the James River, and the Indians were brought into peaceable relations.

But while successfully administering the affairs of the colony, Lord Delawarre's health gave way, and he was compelled to return to England, leaving the government in the hands of Percy. This exercised a depressing effect, both upon the colonists and the London Council, and for a time the name of Virginia became a byword in England. Fortunately two fresh expeditions had already sailed for the colony before Delawarre's return. One was under the command of Sir Thomas Gates, and the other under Sir Thomas Dale.

Dale, who was an experienced soldier, arrived in Chesapeake Bay on the 10th of May, 1611. He at once assumed the government, which he soon administered on the basis of martial law. Bancroft, the historian, observes that "the Code—printed and sent to Virginia by the treasurer, Sir Thomas Smith, on his own authority, and without the order or assent of the company—was chiefly a translation from the rules of war of the United Provinces. The Episcopal Church, coeval in Virginia with the settlement of Jamestown, was, like the infant commonwealth, subjected to military power; and though conformity was not strictly enforced, yet court-martial had authority to punish indifference with stripes and infidelity with death. The normal introduction of this arbitrary system, which the charter permitted only in cases of rebellion and mutiny, added new sorrows to the wretchedness of the people, who pined and perished under despotic rule.

"The letters of Dale to the council confessed the small number and weakness and discontent of the colonists, but he kindled hope in the hearts of those constant adventurers who, in the greatest disasters, had never fainted. 'If anything otherwise than well betide me,' said he, 'let me commend unto your carefulness the pursuit and dignity of this business, than which your purses and endeavours will never open nor travel in a more meritorious enterprise. Take four of the best kingdoms in Christendom, and put them all together, they may no way compare with this country, either for commodities or goodness of soil.'

"Lord Delawarre and Sir Thomas Gates confirmed what Dale had written; and, without any delay, Gates, who has the honour, to all posterity, of being the first named in the original patent for Virginia, conducted to the New World six ships, with three hundred emigrants. Long afterwards the gratitude of Virginia to these early emigrants was shown by repeated acts of benevolent legislation. A wise liberality sent also a hundred kine, as well as suitable provisions. It was the most fortunate step which had been taken, and proved the wisdom of Cecil and others, whose firmness had prevailed.

"The promptness of this relief merits admiration. In May Dale had written from Virginia; and the last of August the new recruits, under Gates, were already at Jamestown. So unlooked for was this supply, that, at their approach, they were regarded with fear as a hostile fleet. Who can describe the joy at finding them to be friends? Gates assumed the government amidst the thanksgiving of the colony, and at once endeavoured to employ the sentiment of religious gratitude as a foundation of order and of laws. 'Lord, bless England, our sweet, native country,' was the morning and evening prayer of the grateful emigrants.

"The colony now numbered seven hundred men. Dale, with the consent of Gates, went far up the river to found the new plantation, which, in honour of Prince Henry, a general favourite with the English people, was named Henrico; and there, on the remote frontier, Alexander Whitaker, the self-denying 'apostle of Virginia,' assisted in 'bearing the name of God to the Gentiles.' But the greatest change in the condition of the colonists resulted from the incipient establishment of private property. To each man a few acres of ground were assigned for his orchard and garden, to plant at his pleasure and for his own use. So long as industry had been without its special reward, reluctant labour, wasteful of time, had been followed by want. Henceforward the sanctity of private property was recognized. Yet the rights of the Indians were little respected; nor did the English disdain to appropriate by conquest the soil, the cabins, and the granaries of the tribe of the Appomattocks. It was, moreover, the policy of the government so 'to overmaster the subtile Powhatan' that he would perforce join with the colony in submissive friendship, or, finding 'no room in his country to harbour in,' would 'leave it to their possession.'"

The Spaniards threatened reprisals for the English appropriation of the country on the Chesapeake, but nothing came of their threats, although they made a reconnaissance.

Before the Virginia colony was ten years old,

the London Council began to grant patents of large tracts of land to individuals, and tracts were also given to colonists for meritorious services. The planting of tobacco soon became so profitable that it was necessary to define strictly the proportions of land allowed to corn crops and tobacco culture. In March, 1612, a third patent for Virginia was issued, granting to the adventurers in England the Bermudas and all islands within three hundred leagues of the Virginia shore. These new acquisitions were soon transferred to a separate company. Meetings at least once a week were now ordered to be held by the old company; while all questions affecting government, commerce, and the disposition of lands were reserved for four great general courts, at which all officers were to be elected and all laws established. The character of the corporation was completely changed by transferring power from the council to the company, through whose assemblies the people of Virginia might gain leave to exercise every political power belonging to the people of England. Lotteries were authorized for the benefit of the colony, and these soon produced £29,000 to the company; but as they became a grievance, they were suspended by an Order of Council.

An attempt was made in 1612 to restrain French colonization in North America. Argall made voyages from Virginia up the Potomac, and persuaded an Indian chief to betray the Princess Pocahontas into his hands, to be kept as a hostage at Jamestown for the return of Englishmen held captive by her father Powhatan. In a further expedition Argall destroyed the French settlements on Mount Desert Isle, and expelled the French from the territory. On making his report at Jamestown, he was once more despatched to the north, with authority to remove every landmark of France in the territory south of the forty-sixth degree. He razed the fortifications of De Monts on the Isle of St. Croix, set on fire the deserted settlement of Port Royal, and raised the arms of England on the spot where those of France and De Guercheville had been thrown down. So England asserted her claim to Maine and Acadia—a claim which was ultimately to result in great international strife and bloodshed.

A most interesting incident now took place in the colony of Virginia. The Princess Pocahontas, who had been brought to a knowledge of the truth, and baptized into the Christian faith, married, in April, 1614, one of the settlers, Mr. John Rolfe, who was further distinguished as the first cultivator of tobacco in Virginia. Many eminent Americans trace their descent from this union, and its immediate effects were the pacification of Powhatan and the Chickahominy tribes, and the consolidation of the English settlement.

Pocahontas received the baptismal name of Lady Rebecca. Sir Thomas Dale "took Rolfe and his wife to England, and with them went several other young Indians, men and women, and one Tamocomo, the husband of another of Powhatan's daughters. The young people were under the guardianship of the council, and to be educated as Christians; but Tamocomo was an emissary of his father-in-law, under orders to gather information in regard to the English people. His observations may have been valuable, but he soon gave over an attempt to take a census of the population by notches on a stick. The whole party excited the liveliest curiosity. The Lady Rebecca was received at Court with great favour, though grave doubts were entertained, suggested it was supposed by James, who was never unmindful of the divine right of kings, whether Rolfe had not been guilty of treason in presuming to make an alliance with a royal family. The princess appeared at the theatres and other public places, everywhere attracting great attention as the daughter of the Virginian emperor, and as one to whom the colonists had sometimes been indebted for signal services, and everywhere exciting admiration for her personal graces, and the propriety and good sense with which she always conducted herself. She remained in England for nearly a year, and died as she was about to sail for her native country. Her only child, a son, is claimed as the ancestor of some of the most respectable families of Virginia.

"Alliances by marriage between the whites and Indians were encouraged, and were not infrequent, as it was hoped to establish by such connections more friendly relations with the savages. They had no doubt some influence, the marriage of Pocahontas especially leading to a treaty with Powhatan, which he faithfully observed so long as he lived, and which was renewed after his death, in 1618, by his successor."

With regard to the condition of private property in lands among the Virginian colonists, this "depended in some measure on the circumstances under which they had emigrated. To those who had been sent and maintained at the exclusive cost of the company, and were its servants, one month of their time and three acres of land were set apart for them, besides an allowance of two bushels of corn from the public store; the rest of their labour belonged to their employers. This number gradually decreased; and, in 1617, there were of them all, men, women, and children, but fifty-four. Others, especially the favourite settlement near the mouth of the Appomattox, were tenants paying two and a half barrels of corn as a yearly tribute to the store, and giving to the public service one month's labour, which was to be required neither at seedtime nor harvest. He who came himself, or had sent others at his own expense, had been entitled to a hundred acres of land for each person; now that the colony was well established, the bounty on emigration was fixed at fifty acres, of which the actual occupation and culture gave a right to as many more, to be assigned at leisure. Besides this, lands were granted as rewards of merit; yet not more than two thousand acres could be so appropriated to one person. A payment to the company's treasury of £12 10s. likewise obtained a title to any hundred acres of land not yet granted or possessed, with a reserved claim to as much more. Such were the earliest land laws of Virginia: though imperfect and unequal, they gave the cultivator the means of becoming a proprietor of the soil. These changes were established by Sir Thomas Dale, a magistrate, who, notwithstanding the introduction of martial law, has gained praise for his vigour and industry, his judgment and conduct."

When Dale left the colony, he appointed George Yeardley deputy governor. Captain Argall succeeded for a time in May, 1617; but his administration was so arbitrary and oppressive, that in 1618—after the news had been made public of the death of Lord Delawarre at sea while *en route* to Virginia—he was displaced, and the mild and popular Yeardley was appointed in his stead. Yeardley was granted higher rank and powers, and was knighted. He entered upon his office at Jamestown on the 19th of April, 1619. The colony had fallen into a pitiable condition, not one in twenty of the emigrants remaining alive. "From the moment of Yeardley's arrival dates the real life of Virginia. Bringing with him 'commissions and instructions from the company for the better establishinge of a commonwealth,' he made proclamation 'that those cruell lawes, by which the ancient planters had soe longe been governed, were now abrogated, and that they were to be governed by those free lawes which his Majestie's subjectes lived under in Englande.' Nor were these concessions left dependent on the goodwill of administrative officers. 'That the planters might have a hande in the governing of themselves, yt was graunted that a generall assemblie shoulde be helde yearly once, whereat were to be present the governor and counsell with two burgesses from each plantation, freely to be elected by the inhabitants thereof, this assemblie to have power to make and ordaine whatsoever lawes and orders should by them be thought good and profitable for their subsistence.'

"In conformity with these instructions, Sir George Yeardley 'sente his summons all over the country, as well to invite those of the counsell of estate that were absente, as also for the election of burgesses.'"

Beneficial changes were likewise effected in the London Company. Sir Thomas Smith was dismissed, and Sir Edwin Sandys was elected by a great majority governor and treasurer. John Ferrar was elected deputy, and his brother Nicholas, one of the purest and most unselfish of men, was appointed counsel to the corporation. The conduct of business gradually fell into the hands of Nicholas Ferrar, who combined a reverence for monarchy with a true regard for English liberties, and the effect of his action was most beneficial upon the future of the Virginia Company.

The 30th of July, 1619, was a day memorable in the history of the colony, for on that date the first legislative assembly from the eleven plantations of Virginia met at James City. It consisted of twenty-two representatives and the governor and council. "The inauguration of legislative power in the Ancient Dominion," says Bancroft, "preceded the introduction of negro slavery. The governor and council sat with the burgesses, and took part in motions and debates. John Pory, a councillor and secretary of the colony, though not a burgess, was chosen speaker. Legislation was opened with prayer. The assembly exercised fully the right of judging of the proper election of its members; and they would not suffer any patent, conceding manorial jurisdiction, to bar the obligation of obedience to their decisions. They wished every grant of land to be made with equal favour, that all complaint of partiality might be avoided, and the uniformity of laws and orders never be impeached. The commission of privileges sent by Sir George Yeardley was their 'great charter' or organic act, which they claimed no right 'to correct or control'; yet they kept the way open for seeking redress, 'in case they should find ought not perfectly squaring with the state of the colony.'

"Leave to propose laws was given to any burgess, or by way of petition to any member of the colony; but, for expedition's sake, the main business of the session was distributed between two committees; while a third body, composed of the governor and such burgesses as were not on those committees, examined which of former instructions 'might conveniently put on the habit of laws.' The legislature acted also as a criminal court.

"The Church of England was confirmed as the Church of Virginia; it was intended that the first four ministers should each receive £200 a year; all persons whatsoever, upon the Sabbath days, were to frequent divine service and sermons both forenoon and afternoon; and all such as bore arms, to bring their pieces or swords. Grants of land were asked not for planters only, but for their wives, 'because, in a new plantation, it is not known whether man or woman be the most necessary.' Measures were adopted 'towards the erecting of a university and college.' It was also enacted that, of the children of the Indians, 'the most towardly boys in wit and graces of nature should be brought up in the first elements of literature, and sent from the college to the work of conversion' of the natives to the Christian religion. Penalties were appointed for idleness, gaming with dice or cards, and drunkenness. Excess in apparel was taxed in the Church for all public contributions. The business of planting corn, mulberry trees, hemp, and vines was encouraged. The price of tobacco was fixed at three shillings a pound for the best, and half as much 'for the second sort.'

"When the question was taken on accepting 'the great charter,' 'it had the general assent and the applause of the whole assembly,' with thanks to it for Almighty God and to those from whom it had issued, in the names of the burgesses and of the whole colony whom they represented: the more so, as they were promised the power to allow or disallow the orders of court of the London Company."

The laws made by this first elective body were pronounced by Sir Edwin Sandys to be on the whole "very well and judiciously formed." They were instantly put in force, former griefs were forgotten, and the colony began an era of prosperity. Although, in the twelve years before Sandys assumed office, the company had spent £80,000, with the result that there were only six hundred men, women, and children in the colony, in one year after Sandys took up the governorship the company and private adventurers made provision for sending over twelve hundred and sixty-one persons. Great interest in Virginia was kindled throughout England, and gifts and bequests flowed in for founding a colonial college and building up the colonial Church. George Herbert, the poet, and the bosom friend of Nicholas Ferrar, voiced the feeling of the mother country in his verse; while another poet, George Sandys, son of the Archbishop of York, went out to Virginia as the resident treasurer of the colony of the London Company.

On the 17th of May, 1620, the quarter session was attended by nearly five hundred persons, among whom were twenty peers of the realm, about one hundred knights, an equal number of officers of the army and renowned lawyers, and numerous merchants and men of business. It was the general desire that Sir Edwin Sandys should be continued in the office of governor, but the meeting was postponed in consequence of an effort by the King to nominate another treasurer and governor. At the next quarter session in June, however, Sir Edwin Sandys withdrew his claim in consequence of the ill-will of the sovereign. Thereupon the whole court, "with much joy and applause," nominated the Earl of Southampton, and he was elected by a universal show of hands, without having recourse to the ballot-box.

But Southampton stipulated for the assistance of his friend Sir Edwin Sandys; and these two, with the further co-operation of Nicholas Ferrar, now for a time managed "the great work of redeeming the noble plantation of Virginia from the ruins that seemed to hang over it." All three were men of high character and ability, the friends of liberty, and thorough Protestants. Under their auspices, more than eleven hundred persons now made their way annually to Virginia. Among the emigrants were ninety young women, agreeable in person and respectable in character, who were sent out at the expense of the company, and were speedily married to enterprising colonists, who repaid the cost of their passage out. In 1621 sixty more were despatched, maids of virtuous education, young, handsome, and well recommended. The price rose from one hundred and twenty to one hundred and fifty pounds of tobacco, and the debt for a wife was regarded as a debt of honour, which took precedence over any other. In conferring employments, the company gave the preference to married men, and in the course of three years fifty patents for land were granted, the colony thus being placed on a stable foundation. Wrongs were redressed, and the right of the colonists to trial by jury confirmed. The freedom of the northern fisheries was soon equally asserted, and the monopoly of a rival corporation successfully opposed.

By an important ordinance of the 24th of July, 1621, a written constitution was granted to the colony. It was taken out by Sir Francis Wyatt, who succeeded Yeardley in the governorship. The form of government was to be analogous to the English Constitution, and it was to a large extent the model for later settlements and colonies. The terms of the Virginia Constitution were few and simple: " a governor, to be appointed by the company; a permanent council, likewise to be appointed by the company; a general assembly, to be convened yearly, and to consist of the members of the council, and of two burgesses to be chosen from each of the several plantations by the respective inhabitants. The assembly might exercise full legislative authority, a negative voice being reserved to the governor ; but no law or ordinance would be valid, unless ratified by the company in England. It was further agreed that, after the government of the colony should have once been framed, no orders of the court in London should bind the colony, unless they should in like manner be ratified by the general assembly. The courts of justice were required to conform to the laws and manner of trial used in the realm of England."

Representative government and trial by jury were thus conceded as a right; and "on this ordinance Virginia erected the superstructure of her liberties. Its influences were wide and enduring, and can be traced through all her history. It constituted the plantation, in its infancy, a nursery of freemen; and succeeding generations learned to cherish institutions which were as old as the first period of the prosperity of their fathers. The privileges then conceded could never be wrested from the Virginians; and as new colonies arose at the south, their proprietaries could hope to win emigrants only by bestowing franchises as large as those enjoyed by their elder rival. The London Company merits the praise of having auspicated liberty in America. It may be doubted whether any public act during the reign of King James was of more permanent or pervading influence; and it reflects honour on Sir Edwin Sandys, the Earl of Southampton, Nicholas Ferrar, and the patriot royalists of England, that, though they were unable to establish guarantees of a liberal administration at home, they were careful to connect popular freedom inseparably with the life, prosperity, and state of society of Virginia."

The question of slavery in Virginia now calls for notice. Slavery was prevalent both in the earlier ages of the world and in mediæval times. The Egyptians, the Hebrews, the Moors, and the Christians were all guilty of the practice, and we have already seen that the first discoverer of America enslaved the native Indians. The practice was continued wherever colonization went on, and Virginia and other colonies were corrupted by it, New England also falling into the custom of importing negro slaves.

A form of slavery known as conditional servitude, under indentures or covenants, existed from the first in Virginia. Men sent over from England were obliged to discharge the costs of their emigration, and oppression by the masters speedily ensued. White servants or slaves were sold at prices ranging from £40 to £80, and came to be regarded as customary articles of traffic. Negroes were valued at £20 or £25. In the year 1619 a Dutch man-of-war entered James River, and landed twenty African negroes for sale, and this formed the epoch of the introduction of negro slaves into the English colonies. By-and-by there was a regular slave trade in the markets of Virginia, and the antipathy between the white and the black races became every year more strongly pronounced.

The first session under the new constitution was held in November and December, 1621, and the subjects discussed related chiefly to the encouragement of domestic industry. From this period dates the first planting of cotton, also the sending of beehives to Virginia, and the exportation of skilful workmen to extract iron from the ore. Five-and-twenty shipwrights likewise landed in 1622. Education and religious worship received attention, and the Bishop of London collected and sent over £1,000 towards the erection of a university, which was afterwards liberally endowed with lands.

Wyatt adopted a policy of conciliation towards the natives; and the latter, gradually losing their fears of the British, were employed as fowlers and huntsmen. The English plantations were widely extended along the James River and towards the Potomac, and the great chief Powhatan remained the friend of the colonists. Everything seemed peaceable and prosperous, when suddenly a great act of treachery was perpetrated by the Indians on the 22nd of March, 1622. At midday they fell upon a scattered and unsuspecting population occupying an area of one hundred and forty miles on both sides of the river. In one hour no fewer than three hundred and forty-seven persons were slaughtered, including women and children and missionaries. Jamestown was saved by being warned, and placed in a state of resistance; but whereas before the massacres the emigrants in the colony exceeded four thousand, a year afterwards there only remained two thousand five hundred men.

The immediate consequences of the Indian rising were disastrous. Public works were abandoned, and the settlements reduced from eighty plantations to eight; many colonists returned to England; while numbers of those remaining were ill and dispirited. In England the news excited angry feelings, but the London Company redoubled its energies in strengthening the colony and sending out further detachments of emigrants. Meanwhile, expeditions against the Indians were undertaken by George Sandys, the colonial treasurer, Yeardley, the ex-governor, and

Captain Madison; and stern reprisals were the order of the day for several years.

In 1623 another difficulty arose, which seriously affected the status of the London Company. The Earl of Southampton and his friends were true to the interests of the colony; but the adherents of the former treasurer—conspicuous amongst whom were Argall and his patron the Earl of Warwick—misrepresented matters to the King. Then, as James was contemplating the Spanish marriage with his son, he was further influenced by Gondomar, the Spanish envoy in London, who described the Virginia courts as "but a seminary to a seditious parliament." The company fully answered all allegations against it; but the King was resolved to recover his authority, which he had signed away in the charter.

Accordingly, on the 9th of May, 1623, commissioners were appointed to engage in a general investigation of the concerns of the corporation; the records were seized, the deputy treasurer imprisoned, and private letters from Virginia intercepted. A long examination of Smith seemed to favour the cancelling of the charter as an act of benevolence to the colony. After a preliminary order to the Virginia court in June to delay the election of officers—which was disobeyed on grounds furnished by the charter itself—the King, in October, by an Order in Council, made known to the company that the disasters in Virginia were a consequence of their ill government; that he had resolved by a new charter to reserve to himself the appointment of the officers in England, a negative on appointments in Virginia, and the supreme control of all colonial affairs.

The Virginia Company took this order into consideration on the 20th of October, and by a majority of sixty votes to nine refused to surrender its charter into the King's hands. Nevertheless, on the 24th, James appointed commissioners to proceed to Virginia, to enquire into the state of the plantation; and among these commissioners were John **Harvey** and Samuel Matthews, men whose names assumed great prominence in the later annals of Virginia. When the commission arrived in the colony, the general assembly was at once convened, and it was decided to send an agent to England representing the true state of affairs, and entreating the King not to give credence to the statements in favour of Sir Thomas Smith's miserable rule, and repelling the imputations on the administration of Southampton and Ferrar.

But the King was exasperated because the colonists would not voluntarily surrender their charter. The aid of the Privy Council was again invoked, whereupon the company appealed to the House of Commons for protection. James sent a message to the effect that the Virginia matter was in his hands, and "he would make it one of his masterpieces"; so they must let it alone. Parliament grudgingly acquiesced; and the next step was that the case was taken to the Court of King's Bench, where, on the 16th of June, 1624, the patent was declared by the Chief Justice to be null and void.

Thus was brought about the dissolution of the London Company, but not until it had done noble work in completing the colonization of Virginia, and securing a liberal form of government for the English colonists in America. James partially compromised matters by putting the new administration into the hands of a commission, at the head of which, however, he placed Sir Thomas Smith. But the King was prevented by the hand of death from fulfilling his intention to prepare a new code of laws for his colony of Virginia, so that posterity was spared one of his juridical masterpieces.

CHAPTER X.

SKETCH OF THE PLYMOUTH COMPANY.

THE efforts at colonization made by the Northern Company—or the Plymouth Company, as it is frequently called—were of no less interest than those of the Southern Company.

Even before the incorporation of the two companies, Sir John Popham, Chief Justice of England, and Sir Ferdinando Gorges, Governor of Plymouth, had agreed to send out a ship each to begin a plantation in the northern region which Captain Waymouth had explored in 1605. Popham had already had experience in colonization, for he was concerned in the project for the plantation of Munster; while Gorges had for some time indulged the hope of acquiring domains and fortune in America.

On the last day of May, 1607—that is, not many months after the first southern expedition sailed—a small expedition fitted out by the Northern Company set forth from Plymouth. It consisted of the *Mary and John*, commanded by Raleigh Gilbert, a younger son of Sir Humphrey; and the *Gift of God*, commanded by Sir George Popham, brother of the Chief Justice, who was " well stricken in years and infirm, yet willing to die in acting something that might be serviceable to God and honourable to his country." On board the former vessel were one hundred and twenty persons, most of whom were well adapted to the work of planting. They had for guide an Indian named Skitwarroes, who had been captured by Waymouth. In exactly two months the vessels came to anchor on the American coast, off Monhegan Island.

The emigrants were received in a friendly way by an Indian chief, Nahanada, and they forthwith proceeded to explore the coast and islands, both ships entering the Kennebec on the 16th of August. Three days later they went ashore, and chose the Sabino Peninsula, near the mouth of the River Sagadahoc, for their colony and fort. They "had a sermon delivered unto them by their preacher," the chaplain Richard Seymour, after which Popham's commission was read, as well as the laws appointed by King James. "Without delay, most of the men, under the oversight of the president, laboured hard on a fort which they named St. George, a storehouse, fifty rude cabins for their own shelter, and a church. The carpenters set about the building of a small pinnace, the chief shipwright being one Digby, the first constructor of sea-going craft in New England. Meanwhile, Gilbert coasted toward the west, judged it to be exceeding fertile from the goodly and great trees with which it was covered, and brought back news of the beauty of Casco Bay with its hundreds of isles. When, following the invitation of the mighty Indian chief who ruled on the Penobscot, Gilbert would have visited that river, he was driven back by foul weather and cross winds. But he remained faithfully in the colony; and, in December, despatched his ships under another commander, who bore letters announcing to the Chief Justice the forwardness of the plantation, and importuning supplies for the coming year. A letter from President Popham to King James informed that monarch that his justice and constancy, his praises and virtues, had been proclaimed to the natives; and that the country produced fruits resembling spices, as well as timber of pine, and lay hard by the great highway to China over the southern ocean. The winter proved to be intensely cold; no mines were discovered; the natives, at first most friendly, grew restless; the storehouse caught fire, and a part of the provisions of the colony was consumed; the emigrants had brought discontent with them; their president found his grave on American soil, 'the only one of the company that died there'; to the discomfort and despair of the poor planters, the ships which revisited the settlement with supplies brought news of the death of the Chief Justice, who had been the stay of the enterprise; and Gilbert, who had shown rare ability, and had succeeded to the command at St. George, had, by the decease of his brother, become heir to an estate in England which required his presence. So, notwithstanding all things were in good forwardness, the fur trade with the Indians prosperous, and a store of sarsaparilla gathered, 'all former hopes were frozen to death,' and nothing was thought of but to quit the place. Wherefore, they all embarked in the newly arrived ships, and in the new pinnace the *Virginia*, and set sail for England. Here was the end of that northern colony upon the River Sagadahoc. The returning colonists 'did coyne many excuses' to conceal their want of spirit; but the Plymouth Company was dissatisfied; Gorges esteemed it a weakness to be frightened at a blast. Three years had elapsed since the French had hutted themselves at Port Royal; and the ships which carried the English from the Kennebec were on the ocean at the same time with the squadron of those who built Quebec during the summer in which Maine was deserted."

The collapse of the Popham colony did not deter Sir Francis Popham, son of the Chief Justice, from sending several later expeditions to the coast of Maine, at his own cost. But no settlement was effected, and the Northern Virginia Company remained for a time quiescent. In 1614, however, a number of London merchants sent out Captain John Smith with two vessels to Maine. It was a prosperous venture, and much business was done with the fishermen. Smith explored the coast from Penobscot to Cape Cod, prepared a map, and named the country New England, which title Prince Charles confirmed. After Smith left for England, Captain Thomas Hunt, master of the second ship, kidnapped a considerable number of Indians, and sold them as slaves to the Spaniards. One of these escaped, made his way to London, and was restored to his native land to be an interpreter for English emigrants.

In 1615 Smith was despatched by Gorges and other leading members of the Plymouth Company to found a colony in New England. The effort proved abortive, for Smith was compelled by violent storms to return to England. During this same year Richard Hawkins, president of the Plymouth Company, sailed to the coast of New England; but finding a desperate war going on between the savages, he returned to England. Gorges next sent out, at his own expense, Richard Vines, who was a physician, to found a settlement. Vines spent the winter of 1616-17 at Winter Harbour in Saco Bay. There was a severe pestilence amongst the natives, and Vines nursed them with such skill and assiduity that he was soon held in veneration and affectionate esteem by the natives. Vines traded with the Indians, and also did a great deal of exploring work entirely alone and unaided. In a little canoe he traced the Saco River to its course at Crawford's Notch, a place afterwards painfully associated with the captivity of white men. Vines first described the White Mountains. He restrained the trafficking in rum with the Indians, and thus "favoured a kind of Maine Law before Maine existed."

In 1619 Gorges fitted out an expedition under Captain Rocroft, who had before been in Virginia; but he was killed by his men in a quarrel, and the vessel was lost. Gorges next tried a Captain Dermer, who had once sailed on a voyage with Smith. He left Plymouth in a ship fully commissioned; and after reaching the Island of Monhegan, he explored the coast from Maine to Virginia in an open pinnace. Next he sailed through Long Island Sound, being the first Englishman to discover the passage. He acquired from the Indians the knowledge, as he thought, of a passage to the South Sea; but this may have referred to the Hudson River. Proceeding to Virginia again, he soon afterwards died there.

The Plymouth Company had always been dissatisfied with the joint charter with the Southern Company, under which the rights of both were specifically defined. So after nearly two years of agitation, they succeeded in obtaining from King James, in November, 1620, a new and comprehensive charter for themselves. It was strongly opposed by the Virginia Company; but Gorges laboured strenuously for it, and succeeded, after ably arguing for the charter before a committee of the House of Commons. The charter was granted to forty persons, some of them members of the King's household and government. The adventurers and their successors were incorporated as "The Council established at Plymouth, in the County of Devon, for the planting, ruling, ordering, and governing New England, in America." Their territory was defined as that land from the fortieth to the forty-eighth degree of latitude; so that "nearly all the inhabited British possessions to the north of the United States, all New England, New York, half of New Jersey, very nearly all Pennsylvania, and the whole of the country to the west of these States, comprising, and at the time believed to comprise, much more than a million of square miles, and capable of sustaining far more than two hundred millions of inhabitants, were, by a stroke of the pen of King James, given away to a corporation within the realm, composed of but forty individuals. The grant was absolute and exclusive: it conceded the land and islands, the rivers and the harbours, the mines and the fisheries. Without the leave of the council of Plymouth, not a ship might sail into a harbour from Newfoundland to the latitude of Philadelphia, not a skin might be purchased in the interior, not a fish might be caught on the coast, not an emigrant might tread the soil. Those who should become inhabitants of the colony were to be ruled, without their own consent, by the corporation in England. A royal proclamation was soon issued, enforcing these provisions; and a revenue was considered certain from an onerous duty on all tonnage employed in the American fisheries."

"The results which grew out of the concession of this charter," says Bancroft, "form a new proof, if any were wanting, of that mysterious connection of events by which Providence leads to ends that human councils had not conceived. The patent left the emigrants at the mercy of the unrestrained power of the corporation; and it was under grants from that plenary power, confirmed, indeed, by the English monarch, that institutions the most favourable to colonial liberty were established. The patent yielded everything to the avarice of the corporation; the very extent of the concession rendered it of little value to them. The English nation, incensed at the erection of vast monopolies by the royal prerogative, prompted the House of Commons to question the validity of the gift; and the French, whose traders had been annually sending home rich freights of furs, derided the tardy action of the British monarch in bestowing lands and privileges which their own sovereign, seventeen years before, had appropriated. The patent was designed to hasten plantations, in the belief that men would eagerly throng to the coast, under the protection of the council; and, in fact, adventurers were delayed through fear of infringing the rights of a powerful company. While the English monopolists were wrangling about their exclusive possessions, the first permanent colony on the soil of New England was established without the knowledge of the corporation and without the aid of King James."

The Plymouth Company, on finding itself firmly established, made a grant of Nova Scotia, in 1621, to Sir William Alexander, afterwards Earl of Stirling. His rights extended from Cape Sable to the St. Lawrence, including Cape Breton and all the islands within six leagues. This grant encroached upon the disputed territory lying between the French and English settlements. Alexander seems to have desired to set up Scotch Presbyterianism against the growing bands of French Catholic emigrants.

But the sea-coast of Maine, New Hampshire, and Massachusetts, and the lands extending to the little Plymouth colony just founded, were still unappropriated. Therefore Gorges, in conjunction with John Mason, also a member of the Plymouth Company, obtained for himself and co-adventurer a grant of the region between the Merrimac and the Kennebec, stretching back to Canada and the Great Lakes. The owners called their territory Laconia; and their grant being confirmed in 1623, they despatched from England a ship-load of emigrants, consisting of planters and fishermen, to effect a permanent settlement. When these new settlers arrived off the mouth of the Piscataqua, they divided into two parties, one of which chose the site of the old town of Portsmouth, New Hampshire, while the other went up the river a few miles and began the settlement of Dover. These were two of the oldest towns in New England. Shortly afterwards Christopher Lovett made an attempt to colonize the county and city of York.

In the above year, 1623, Robert Gorges, a son of Ferdinando, was appointed governor-general of the whole of the domains belonging to the Plymouth Company, with authority to establish laws and principles of government similar to those of England. An extensive tract of land on Massachusetts Bay, three hundred square miles in extent, was given him by the company. Under him were Captain West and Captain Lovett, and the governor of the New Plymouth colony recently established. Gorges' wife was a daughter of the Earl of Lincoln, who was interested in Puritan emigration. Not liking the country, however, Gorges returned to England in 1624. His rights were made over to his brother, John Gorges, who subsequently surrendered them to William Brereton, who settled several families upon the lands.

As yet no permanent settlement had been made on the coast of Maine; but in 1625 two Bristol merchants, Aldworth and Eldridge, bought Moneghan Island, and established an agent there. Later, they acquired the Point of Pemaquid, where they founded a flourishing colony, which by 1630 numbered eighty-four families. Richard Vines and John Oldham were also granted a tract of land each by the council on the Saco River. These lands had a breadth of four miles each on the sea, and extended inland for eight miles. The two proprietors founded the towns of Bideford and Saco, which were opposite each other on the banks of the river. Thus began the settlements in Maine; but unfortunately they were of a straggling character, and the colony made but slow progress. In 1631 Mason and Gorges agreed to divide their grant, the former taking all west of the Piscataqua, and calling it New Hampshire, after his own English county, while Gorges took all land east of that stream to the River Sagadahoc, which he named New Somersetshire, after his own native county. Gorges' settlers planted the town of York, on which an emigrant named Edward Godfrey became the first settler. Gorges set aside twelve thousand acres as a kind of future provisional interest for his family.

In 1635, however, the reign of the Plymouth Company itself came to an end. In detailing the reasons for this, the historians Bryant and Gay remark:

"Already bitter complaints were made in England, that discontented spirits, full of disaffection to the King, and hostile to the government of the Established Church, were settling on the grants made by the Plymouth Company. Gorges, in New England, was looked upon with jealousy and dislike by many of the Puritans, because of his large territorial claims in their vicinity, as well as on account of his opinions as a loyalist and member of the English Church; on the other hand, he was attacked in England as an upholder and author of the reputed licence of laws and opinions among the new colonies in Massachusetts. He seems to have been deeply hurt at this, after his long and arduous work in forwarding the plantation of English colonies in New England, and he 'therefore was moved to desire the rest of the lords, that were the principal actors in this business, that we should resign our grand patent to the King, and pass particular patents to ourselves, of such parts of the country about the sea-coast as might be sufficient to our own uses, and such of our private friends as had affections to works of that nature.' This was done in 1635, and the lands of the company lying between the forty-eighth and thirty-sixth degree of latitude were parcelled out among its members.

"This new division confirmed the right of Gorges to the tract lying between the Piscataqua and the Kennebec, with a sea-coast of sixty miles, and an extent of one hundred and twenty miles inland. And now for the first time he called this his province of Maine, and he drew up for it a code of laws, dividing the land first into counties, subdividing these into hundreds, and again into parishes or tithings, as fast as population flowed in to fill up the vacant places. He offered also to transport planters to his domain, promising to assign them a certain portion of land at the low rate of two or three shillings for a hundred acres; and if any would found a town or city, he would endow it with such liberties and immunities as they would have in England. Others of poorer condition, who would go as labourers, should have as much land as they could till, at the rent of four or six pence an acre, according to the situation."

King Charles granted a commission to Gorges in April, 1639, constituting him governor of New England, in order to recompense him for past labours and losses.

Gorges had never seen America, but now in his old age he made preparations to go out to Maine to assume the duties of his important office. He was anxious to found cities, draw up laws, and propound a scheme of colonial government. He never lived to carry out his ideas, however, but was content to send over, in 1640, his kinsman Thomas Gorges instead. But Ferdinando Gorges rendered very serviceable work in the early settlement of New England, and he was a real friend to colonization, working unselfishly with this view.

Here we pause in our survey of the New England colonies, which, after the close of the operations of the two Virginia Companies, enter upon a new stage of existence.

CHAPTER XI.

COLONIZATION OF MARYLAND.

THE foundation of Maryland forms an interesting chapter in the history of North American colonization. It is inseparably interwoven with the name of Sir George Calvert, first Lord Baltimore, and with those of his son and grandson, Cecil and Charles Calvert, who ruled the colony for upwards of fifty years.

Originally, the land which forms the State of Maryland was included in the second charter of the Virginia Company; but before Virginia could occupy the territory north of the Potomac, it was promised to George Calvert for his separate government. Calvert was a Yorkshireman, and was born at Kipling about the year 1582. He graduated at Oxford in 1597, and became secretary to Sir Robert Cecil, who obtained for him a clerkship of the Privy Council. He was knighted by King James in 1617, and made a Secretary of State, but resigned the office in 1624, as he had become a Roman Catholic. In 1625, however, he was made a peer of Ireland, with the title of Lord Baltimore.

At a very early stage in his career Calvert was

interested in the work of colonization. He was a member of the Virginia Company, and in 1621 obtained a patent from the King for the southern promontory of Newfoundland, which he named Avalon. Here he expended money lavishly in building warehouses and a splendid mansion. Soon after the death of his royal patron he visited his colony, and again in 1629, when he captured some French ships which had been harassing the colonists. But Calvert found the climate too severe, and wrote to Charles I. requesting another grant farther south. He visited Virginia and explored Chesapeake Bay, but his religion made him unpopular with the settlers. The King endeavoured to dissuade him from founding another colony; but Calvert was so persistent, and was so delighted with the country, that he overcame the King's scruples.

Accordingly, early in 1632, Charles promised Baltimore a new patent, granting him all that part of the country now included in the States of Maryland and Delaware. As Baltimore died in April, 1632, however, the patent was continued to, and made out in the name of, his son Cecilius, or Cecil, Baron Baltimore. The limits of the territory were defined as the ocean, the fortieth parallel of latitude, the meridian of the western fountain of the Potomac, the river itself from its source to its mouth, and a line drawn due east from Watkin's Point to the Atlantic. The name of Maryland was given to the province, after Charles's wife, Queen Henrietta Maria. The land was given to Lord Baltimore and his heirs and assigns for ever, as true and absolute lords and proprietaries. They held by the tenure of fealty only, paying a yearly rent of two Indian arrows, and a fifth of all gold and silver ore which might be found.

But the authority of the governor of Maryland was absolute rather as regarded the Crown than the colonists. "The charter, like the constitution of Virginia of July, 1621, provided for a resident council of state; and like Calvert's patent, which in April, 1621, had passed the Great Seal for Avalon, secured to the emigrants themselves an independent share in the legislation of the province, of which the statutes were to be established with the advice and approbation of the majority of the freemen or their deputies. Authority was entrusted to the proprietary, from time to time, to constitute fit and wholesome ordinances, provided they were consonant to reason and the laws of England, and did not extend to the life, freehold, or estate of any emigrant. For the benefit of the colony, the statutes restraining emigration were dispensed with; and all present and future liege people of the English King, except such as should be expressly forbidden, might transport themselves and their families to Maryland. Christianity as professed by the Church of England was protected; but the patronage and advowsons of churches were vested in the proprietary; and as there was not an English statute on religion in which America was specially named, silence left room for the settlement of religious affairs by the colony. Nor was Baltimore obliged to obtain the royal assent to his appointments of officers, nor to the legislation of his province, nor even to make a communication of the one or the other. Moreover, the English monarch, by an express stipulation, covenanted that neither he, nor his heirs, nor his successors should ever, at any time thereafter, set any imposition, custom, or tax whatsoever upon the inhabitants of the province. To the proprietary was given the power of creating manors and courts baron, and of establishing a colonial aristocracy on the system of sub-infeudation. But feudal institutions could not be perpetuated in the lands of their origin, far less renew their youth in America. Sooner might the oldest oaks in Windsor forest be transplanted across the Atlantic than the social forms which Europe was beginning to reject as antiquated. But the seeds of popular liberty, contained in the charter, would find in the New World the soil best suited to quicken them."

Athough the first Lord Baltimore was a strong supporter of royal prerogative in England, he favonred popular institutions and liberty of conscience in the colonies. Many of the provisions of the Maryland charter were supposed to be due to him, and it was even thought that he might have drawn up the entire paper. His design was to found a colony where there should be, on the one hand, a hereditary landed aristocracy and many features of the feudal system, and, on the other hand, an assembly of freemen whose consent should be necessary to all laws.

In November, 1633, Cecil Calvert, the new Lord Baltimore, sent out an expedition under his brother Leonard to his new domain. The bulk of the emigrants were labourers, but there were some twenty gentlemen of influence and wealth. Accompanying the expedition, which was under Roman Catholic leadership, were Father Andrew White and Father

John Altham, men of pious and self-sacrificing lives. The former wrote a narrative of the expedition in Latin. The emigrants sailed from Cowes, in the Isle of Wight, in two vessels, the *Ark* and the *Dove*, and they arrived at Point Comfort, in Virginia, on the 24th of February, 1634, when they received a warm welcome from the governor, Harvey.

On the 3rd of March the adventurers resumed their journey, and entered the Potomac. The *Ark* came to an anchor under an island, but Calvert, with the *Dove* and another pinnace, ascended the stream. About one hundred and fifty miles from the mouth of the river, Calvert landed at the Indian settlement of Piscataqua, nearly opposite Mount Vernon, where he met with an Englishman who traded amongst the Indians. With the aid of this interpreter, who was a Captain Henry Fleet, the settlers parleyed with the Indians, who neither opposed nor welcomed their arrival. Not deeming it wise to plant so far from the sea, Calvert went down the river, examining the creeks and estuaries nearer the Chesapeake. One stream which flowed into the Potomac he named the St. George, and one of the two harbours which formed its mouth he called St. Mary's, which has since become the name of the whole river. About four leagues from the junction of the river with the Potomac, he anchored at the Indian town of Yoacomoco. As the Indians were already quitting the town for a place of more security against the Susquehannah tribes, they readily came to an understanding with the English, whom they permitted to take possession of the site.

On the 25th of March, the day of the Annunciation,

the emigrants took possession of the country with solemn ceremonies. Mass was celebrated on the beach —this being the first time in that region—and then, on the highest part of the island, a great cross of wood was erected, round which the emigrants knelt while the Litany was read. Leonard Calvert next proclaimed the English right to the territory, which was taken possession of "for our Saviour and for our Sovereigne Lord and King of England." The governor named the first village of Maryland St. Mary's, and the work of building and planting was at once begun. A Roman Catholic church was erected, and two fragments of its rude altar-piece are still preserved in the Roman Catholic College at Georgetown.

The colonists, more fortunate than many others, endured no sufferings; "no fears of want arose, the foundation of the colony of Maryland was peacefully and happily laid, and in six months it advanced more than Virginia in as many years. The proprietary continued with great liberality to provide everything needed for its comfort and protection, expending £20,000 sterling, and his associates as many more. But far more memorable was the character of the Maryland institutions. One of the largest wigwams was allotted to the Jesuit missionaries, who relate that the first chapel in Maryland was built by the Indians. Of the Protestants, though they seem as yet to have been without a minister, the religious rights were not abridged. This enjoyment of liberty of conscience did not spring from any act of colonial legislation, nor from any formal and general edict of the governor, nor from any oath as yet imposed by instructions of the proprietary. English statutes were not held to bind the colonies, unless they especially named them; the clause which, in the charter for Virginia, excluded from that colony 'all persons suspected to affect the superstitions of the Church of Rome' found no place in the charter for Maryland; and while allegiance was held to be due, there was no requirement of the oath of supremacy. Toleration grew up in the province silently, as a custom of the land. Through the benignity of the administration, no person professing to believe in the divinity of Jesus Christ was permitted to be molested on account of religion. Roman Catholics, who were oppressed by the laws of England, were sure to find a peaceful asylum on the north bank of the Potomac; and there, too, Protestants were sheltered against Protestant intolerance. From the first, men of foreign birth were encouraged to plant, and enjoyed equal advantages with those of the English and Irish nations."

Grave difficulties arose, however, in connection with the proceedings of an adventurer named William Clayborne, who was protected by the Virginians, and who had purchased from the Indians the right to the soil of the Isle of Kent. The allegiance of Clayborne's settlement was claimed under the patent of Maryland; but the governor of Virginia told Clayborne that this question was as yet undetermined in England, so the latter went on trading with the natives. Lord Baltimore gave orders to seize him if he did not submit, and the English Secretary of State directed Sir John Harvey to assist in suppressing Clayborne's malicious practices.

So matters stood when the colony of Maryland was first convened for legislation in February, 1635. Unfortunately, no account of the proceedings has come down to us, so it is impossible to say what was done to vindicate the authority of the province. But in April of the above year there was an armed conflict between Clayborne's vessel, the *Long Tail*—while on a trading voyage—and two pinnaces commissioned by the Marylanders, and commanded by one Cornwallis. The *Long Tail* was captured; and when Clayborne sent an armed boat under Ratcliff Warren to recapture her or seize any Maryland vessels he might encounter, Cornwallis, on the 10th of May, slew Ratcliff and two others of the Virginians, taking the rest prisoners.

As matters now became serious, and the Marylanders demanded the surrender of Clayborne on the charge of felony, the latter proceeded to England to lay his case before the King. There was great excitement at Jamestown, but while Clayborne was away the government of Maryland was established on the Isle of Kent. In January, 1638, a new assembly was convened, in which the Isle of Kent was represented. An act o attainder was carried against Clayborne, and his officer, Thomas Smith, was brought to trial, condemned, and executed. Meanwhile, the General Assembly of Virginia, equally excited and angry with its governor for not taking strong measures to protect Clayborne and his rights, deposed Harvey and sent him to England for trial, and elected John West as governor in his stead.

In England Clayborne procured a favourable hearing from Charles; but when his case was finally referred to the commissioners for the plantations, it was decided that Clayborne had no rights as against the charter of Maryland, and that the Isle of Kent belonged to Lord Baltimore, who alone could permit plantations to be established, or commerce with the Indians to be conducted, within his territory.

The colonists of Maryland were very jealous of their liberties; and while the first assembly vindicated the jurisdiction of the colony, and the second asserted its claims to original legislation, the third framed a declaration of rights, asserting the liberties which Englishmen enjoyed at home, establishing a system of representative government, and asserting such powers as were exercised by the Commons of England. As negro slavery already prevailed, however, native or foreign slaves were debarred from the rights enjoyed by the settlers. "In October, 1640, the Legislative Assembly of Maryland, in the grateful enjoyment of happiness, seasonably guarded the tranquillity of the province against the perplexities of an 'interim,' by providing for the security of the government in case of the death of the deputy governor. Commerce was fostered, and tobacco, the staple of the colony, subjected to inspection. The act which established Church liberties declares that 'Holy Church, within this province, shall have and enjoy all her rights, liberties, and franchises, wholly and without blemish.' This enactment of a clause in Magna Charta, cited in the preceding century by some of the separatists, as a guarantee of their religious liberty, was practically interpreted as in harmony with that toleration of all believers in the divinity of Jesus Christ which was the recognized usage of the land. Nor was it long before the inhabitants acknowledged Lord Baltimore's great charge and solicitude in maintaining the government and protecting them in their persons, rights, and liberties; and therefore, 'out of desire to return some testimony of gratitude,' they granted 'such a subsidy as the young and poor estate of the colony could bear.' Ever intent on advancing the interests of his colony, the proprietary invited the Puritans of Massachusetts to emigrate to Maryland, offering them lands and privileges, and 'free liberty of religion'; but Gibbons, to whom he had forwarded a commission, was 'so wholly tutored in the New England discipline' that he would not advance the wishes of the Irish peer, and the people were not tempted to desert the Bay of Massachusetts for the Chesapeake.

"The aborigines, alarmed at the rapid increase of the Europeans, and vexed at being frequently overreached by their cupidity, commenced hostilities; for the Indians, ignorant of the remedy of redress, always plan retaliation. After a war of frontier aggressions, marked by no decisive events, peace was re-established with them on the usual terms of submission and promises of friendship, and rendered durable by the prudent legislation of the assembly and the humanity of the government. Kidnapping them was made a capital offence; the sale of arms to them prohibited as a felony; and the pre-emption of the soil reserved to the proprietary. To this right of pre-emption Lord Baltimore would suffer no exception. The Jesuits had obtained a grant of land from an Indian chief; the proprietary, 'intent upon his own affairs, and not fearing to violate the immunities of the Church,' would not allow that it was valid, and persisted in enforcing against Catholic priests the necessity of obtaining his consent before they could acquire real estate in his province in any wise, even by gift."

In April, 1642, Clayborne was compensated for the loss of his alleged rights by being appointed by the King treasurer of Virginia for life. Meanwhile, Maryland, which was very largely Protestant, though governed by Roman Catholics, was greatly disturbed by the events in England, where Charles and his Parliament were in conflict. Leonard Calvert, Baltimore's deputy, consequently went to England for advice; and during his absence, Brent, the acting governor, seized a London ship which anchored at St. Mary's, and under a general authority from the King tendered to its crew an oath against the Parliament. But Richard Ingle, the commander, escaped in January, 1644, and it was sought to recapture him and convict him of treason. Calvert returned to find the colony rent by discord, and Clayborne reasserting his claims. Ingle, who had been to England, now returned, and overran the colony. He raised the standard of Parliament, destroyed the records and the Grand Seal, and compelled the governor and secretary, with a few of their adherents, to fly to Virginia. Father White and the other Jesuit missionaries were sent to England, but Ingle tried in vain to impose an oath of submission upon the colonists.

Calvert appealed to the Virginians for aid, but they only offered to arbitrate, at the same time inviting Clayborne to cease from intermeddling on Kent

Island. At length, towards the close of 1646, Calvert organized a considerable force, with which he swept down upon St. Mary's and recovered the province. He next reduced Kent Island, and appointed Robert Vaughan, a Protestant, as its commander. Calvert had begun anew a wise and clement rule, when he somewhat suddenly died on the 9th of June, 1647. He appointed Thomas Greene, one of his council, to be his successor, but times of turmoil and difficulty for the colony ensued.

The English Parliament was petitioned to remove Lord Baltimore and his deputy, and to settle the government of Maryland in the hands of Protestants. But the matter dragged on for three years without result, which gave Baltimore time to set his own house in order. In August, 1648, he removed Greene, who was a Roman Catholic, and appointed in his place a Protestant named William Stone, who had promised to take out a large number of emigrants to the colony. Stone was bound by an oath to maintain the rights of his lord, but there was to be no persecution of the Roman Catholics. A general amnesty was proclaimed; and at the instance of Stone, his council of six was constituted with three Protestants and three Catholics. These, with the representatives of the people of Maryland—of whom five were Catholics—met in a general session of the assembly, held in April, 1649. There was then placed upon the statute-book an Act securing religious freedom for all in the colony. This noble declaration appeared in the Act: "And whereas the enforcing of the conscience in matters of religion hath frequently fallen out to be of dangerous consequence in those commonwealths where it has been practised, and for the more quiet and peaceable government of this province, and the better to preserve mutual love and amity among the inhabitants, no person within this province, professing to believe in Jesus Christ, shall be in anyways troubled, molested, or discountenanced, for his or her religion, or in the free exercise thereof." But this clause was introduced by a proviso couched in a very severe spirit, to the effect that "whatsoever person shall blaspheme God, or shall deny or reproach the Holy Trinity, or any of the three Persons thereof, shall be punished with death."

Still, freedom of conscience was the cardinal principle of the Act, and Maryland soon became a refuge for oppressed colonists from Virginia. One band of Puritans or Independents who had been banished for Nonconformity by Sir William Berkeley, the governor of Virginia, were granted lands on the banks of the Severn by the Marylanders; and their place of refuge, to which they gave the name of Providence, is now known as Annapolis.

By an Act passed in 1650, the Maryland house of representatives was separated from the council, and the right of veto was thus secured to the people. The employment of martial law was limited to the precincts of the camp and the garrison; and a perpetual Act declared that no tax should be levied upon the freemen of the province, except by the vote of their deputies in a general assembly. Acknowledgment was made of the efforts of the proprietor to secure the peace and happiness of the colony. But after the overthrow of the monarchy and the peerage in England, difficulties supervened in Maryland; Virginia tried to revive its rights beyond the Potomac; Stone was active as Lord Baltimore's deputy; the Long Parliament threatened to intervene; and, finally, Charles II. issued a commission to Sir William Davenant as governor.

Owing to some unexplained reason, in the last draft of the instructions to the Parliamentary Commissioners, in 1651, authority was given to reduce "all the plantations within the Bay of the Chesapeake," which included Maryland. Acting upon this, Bennett and Clayborne entered the province in March, 1652. They seized the commissions of Stone and his council, declared them to be null and void, and appointed an executive council to direct the affairs of the colony. An assembly was summoned of burgesses elected only by those freemen who had taken the oath to the Commonwealth of England. But in April the assembly of Virginia, acting in conformity to the manifest desire of the inhabitants of Maryland, reinstated Stone as governor, with a council of which three at least were friends of Lord Baltimore.

In England, Baltimore was working for the independence of his own colony, and against its union with Virginia. But the dissolution of the Long Parliament brought fresh difficulties. Although, in May, 1654, Stone proclaimed Cromwell as Lord Protector, Bennett and Clayborne—then governor and secretary of Virginia—entered Maryland, and raised troops. Stone was prevailed upon by his Roman Catholic friends to surrender his commission, and

Bennett and Clayborne appointed Captain William Fuller and nine others commissioners for governing Maryland. An assembly was summoned, but all Roman Catholics, and persons who had borne arms against the Parliament, were disqualified from being either electors or representatives.

Religious feuds arose; and when the assembly met in October, 1654, at Patuxent, the authority of Cromwell was recognized, and the whole Romish party were formally disfranchised. Baltimore, who described these proceedings, when he heard of them, as "illegal, mutinous, and usurped," took steps through his officers to vindicate his supremacy. Stone resumed his authority, stating that his resignation had been extorted by force, and Papists and friendly Protestants were empowered to levy men. The leaders regained possession of the provincial records. But in a conflict with his opponents Stone was defeated, and yielded himself and his company as prisoners. A council of war condemned the governor and his councillors, with some others, to be shot; but although three Roman Catholics and one Protestant were executed, Stone and five others were spared.

Cromwell was appealed to in order to effect a settlement in Maryland, but he left the jurisdiction an open question. In July, 1656, consequently, Baltimore commissioned Josiah Fendall as his lieutenant, and sent over his brother Philip Calvert as councillor and principal secretary of the province. But Fendall was seized by those who had usurped authority, and he was only released on promising to return to England, there to await a final decision. "To England, therefore, he sailed the next year, that he might consult with Baltimore, leaving Barber, a former member of Cromwell's household, as his deputy. Still the Protector, by reason 'of his great affairs,' had not leisure to consider the report of the commissioners for trade on the affairs of Maryland.

"At last, in November, 1657, Lord Baltimore, by 'the friendly endeavours of Edward Digges,' negotiated with Bennett and Matthews, all being then in England, an agreement for the recovery of his province. The proprietary covenanted so far to waive his right of jurisdiction as to leave the settlement of past offences and differences to the disposal of the Protector and his Council; to grant the land claims of 'the people in opposition,' without requiring of them an oath of fidelity, but only some engagement for his support; and, lastly, he promised for himself never to consent to a repeal 'of the law whereby all persons professing to believe in Jesus Christ have freedom of conscience there.'

"Returning to his government with instructions, Fendall, in the following March, held an interview with Fuller, Preston, and the other commissioners at St. Leonards, when the agreement was carried into effect. The Puritans were further permitted to retain their arms, and were assured of indemnity for their actions. The proceedings of the assemblies and the courts of justice, since the year 1652, in so far as they related to questions of property, were confirmed."

After the death of Cromwell, further action on the part of the colony of Maryland became necessary. Consequently, on the 12th of March, 1660, its representatives—meeting in the house of one Robert Slye —voted themselves a lawful assembly, without dependence on any other power in the province. The burgesses refused to acknowledge the rights of the body claiming to be an upper house, and Governor Fendall yielded to the popular will. The representatives having settled the government, irrespective of Baltimore and his deputy and council, further passed an Act making it felony to disturb the new order of things.

Maryland, in the year of the Restoration of the Stuarts, was thus in possession of its liberties, asserted and defined by representatives elected by the popular vote.

CHAPTER XII.

SETTLEMENT OF NEW AMSTERDAM.

IT was naturally to be expected that the Dutch, who were a race of navigators, would early turn their attention to North American exploration.

Consequently, we find that William Barentz, a pilot of Amsterdam, sailed with several expeditions from Holland, in search of a north-east passage, towards the close of the sixteenth century. The first vessel, which was fitted out by the city of Amsterdam, left Holland on the 5th of June, 1594, reached the north-east extremity of Nova Zembla, and returned. A second expedition of seven vessels was despatched in 1595, but too late to be successful; a third, however, consisting of two ships, which left in May, 1596, reached Spitzbergen. The two vessels parted, and Barentz's vessel, encountering ice to the north-east of Nova Zembla, turned southwards. Barentz and his crew were frozen up in Ice Haven, where they spent a terrible winter. In June, 1597, they were able to leave in two boats, and Barentz died shortly afterwards. The Barentz Sea, between the European mainland and Nova Zembla, Spitzbergen, and Franz Josef Land, still preserves the name of this adventurous mariner.

The next explorer in these regions was the distinguished English navigator **Henry Hudson**, of whom little is known until 1607, when he commanded the last expedition under the Muscovy Company. He was instructed to proceed directly across the Pole, but he was stopped by the ice. On a second expedition he penetrated as far as Nova Zembla, but was again blocked by the ice and compelled to return. Being invited to the Netherlands, Hudson undertook a third voyage in 1609 from Amsterdam, at the expense of the Dutch East India Company. Abandoning all hope of finding a north-east passage, he sailed for Davis Strait, then steered southwards, and discovered the mouth of the river which now bears his name, sailing up its waters for one hundred and fifty miles. Hudson's last voyage was undertaken in 1610, when, in the *Discoverie*, of seventy tons, he reached Greenland in June. Turning towards the west, he discovered the strait now known as Hudson Strait, passed through it, and entered the great bay now known as Hudson Bay. Here he resolved to winter, but food fell short, and the men mutinied. Hudson was cast adrift, with eight others, on Midsummer Day, 1611. The leading mutineers perished miserably in a scuffle with savages, and the survivors, after great suffering, landed safely on English shores.

Although Hudson's discoveries were of great importance, they were regarded with comparative indifference by the Netherlanders as a whole. The States-General placed commercial results before any others. When enquiries from various Dutch cities reached them, they simply gave information about the situation of the new river and the best route to reach it. So also the East India Company by no means regarded the discovery by Hudson of the Great River of the Mountains as a set-off for his failure to find the north-east passage. But when Hudson's vessel, the *Half-moon*—which he used in the expedition of 1609 —reached Amsterdam, after being detained in England, the Company engaged part of her crew to go out to the great bay and river in a vessel of their own, and trade with the natives for furs, etc. The experiment proved a very profitable one, and a brisk trade began to spring up, which ultimately grew into an important branch of commerce.

Little round-prowed Dutch vessels soon became familiar objects to the Indians, as the explorers sailed up the Hudson in quest of trade. In the course of a few years, Manhattan Island formed the principal station for the collection of peltries, etc., and their shipment to home ports. Unsuccessful efforts were made to raise European goats on the island, which boasted of a fort and several small buildings. The Dutch began to call the river the Mauritius, after the Stadtholder Maurice of Orange. In addition to trading on the river, the Netherlanders included in their operations the bays of what is now New Jersey, as well as the coast as far south as Delaware Bay, besides opening up fresh stations.

"Foremost in these enterprises," observes one historian, "were Hendrick Christaensen, Adriaen Block, and Cornelis Jacobsen May, three Dutch captains, who, by the end of the four years following Hudson's voyage, had grown most familiar with the new region, and had engaged their ships most successfully in its trade. Christaensen, who by that time had made ten voyages to the river, built the first great trading post upon it, in 1614—Fort Nassau, on Castle Island, close by Albany—and was appointed its commander.

"Block spent the winter of 1613-14 on Manhattan Island in building a yacht of sixteen tons, the *Onrust* (*Restless*), to take the place of his ship, the *Tiger*, which had accidentally been burned. In the spring he sailed eastward, passing through the rapids of Hell-Gate in the East River, explored Long Island Sound from end to end, discovered and entered the Quonehtacut or Connecticut River, and made his way up the New England coast as far as what he called Pye Bay—now the Bay of Nahant—which he called 'the limit of New Netherland.' He visited the shores of Narragansett Bay, and saw within it that 'Roode' or 'Red' Island from which the modern State of Rhode Island derives its name. Martha's Vineyard and Nantucket the Dutch named Texel and Vieland; the waters surrounding them the Zuyder Zee; the island which still bears Block's name, north-east of Montauk Point, they called 'Visscher's Hoeck.' Meeting Hendrick Christaensen's ship, the *Fortune*, which had been sent to Cape Cod Bay, perhaps to take him on board, Block transferred the *Restless* to another skipper, Cornelis Hendricksen, and sailed in the other vessel to Holland, adding his report to the list of explorations which revealed the extent and wealth of the new country.

"May had seen 'Visscher's Hoeck' even before Block, and had visited the coast of Martha's Vineyard.

But his name is perpetuated farther south, in the Cape May of Southern New Jersey; though New York Bay was for many years called, in his honour, Port May."

On the 20th of March, 1614, the traders secured from the States-General a decree, in general terms, by which any discoverers of "new passages, havens, lands, or places" should have "the exclusive right of navigating to the same for four voyages," provided they reported their discoveries within fourteen days after their return to Holland. Some months later, they appeared before the Assembly of the States, and asked for a more extended protection and a special charter, pointing out the expense and the dangers attending their labours. A charter was consequently granted on the 11th of October, in which the name "New Netherland" was first officially applied to the American region "between New France and Virginia, being the sea-coasts between 40° and 45°." A company was formed called the New Netherland Company, and to it was granted the monopoly of the trade for three years, from the 1st of January, 1615. No other Dutch citizens were permitted to frequent or navigate the newly discovered lands, havens, or places, "on penalty of the confiscation of the vessel and cargo, besides a fine of fifty thousand Netherlands ducats."

The company cared little for exploration, but made the most of the commercial advantages allotted to them for the brief period of their charter. Friendly relations were maintained with the Indians, though the traders promptly executed a native who was guilty of the murder of Hendrick Christaensen. All went well, and trade increased, while the interest of Holland was naturally kept alive in the company's operations. A trading house and defences were erected at Fort Nassau, and from this place the director, Jacob Eelkens, despatched ever-increasing stores of furs down the river to Manhattan. His assistants made frequent expeditions into the great western forests to trade for skins with new Indian tribes. One party, consisting of three men, reached the upper waters of the Delaware; but on descending the stream to the mouth of the Schuylkill, were seized by the Indians and held as prisoners. They were not slain or injured, however.

As soon as the Manhattan traders heard of their detention, they sent Cornelis Hendricksen in the yacht *Restless* to go and ransom them. Hendricksen explored the shores of Delaware Bay and River, rescued the captives, and returned with glowing accounts that the river banks were covered with grape-vines and abounded in game. He reported, too, that he had opened up a trade with the natives for seal-skins. Hendricksen's discoveries completed the survey of the whole coast belonging to the New Netherland Company; and on the strength of his discoveries the company applied for a new special charter, but the States-General were too reluctant to encroach upon the territories of Virginia to grant it.

In 1617 Jacob Eelkens concluded the first formal treaty with the Indians; but on the 1st of January, 1618, the New Netherland Company's charter expired, and all efforts to renew it failed. Traders, however, still continued to use their old privileges without molestation or competition. But Holland was now fully awake to the value of the territories in North America, especially for extending Dutch commercial relations abroad. The result was that, in 1621, the great West India Company was incorporated, and chartered by the States-General with powers almost equal to those of the Eastern Company. The patent of the West India Company, "with that assumption of authority which belonged to the great monopolies of the time, forbade any and all inhabitants of the United Netherlands, for twenty-two years after the 1st of July, 1621, to sail to the coast of Africa between the tropic of Cancer and the Cape of Good Hope, or to those of America between the Banks of Newfoundland and the Straits of Magellan, except in the service of the West India Company. In the Dutch territory in America its power was practically absolute. It could make treaties, appoint governing officers from the highest to the lowest, build and garrison forts, administer justice, exercise, in fact, all the functions of a government, and was only responsible to the States-General for its acts as shown through its own reports. Its central board of nineteen delegates, drawn from its five chambers of directors in Amsterdam, Middleburg, Dordrecht, North Holland, Friesland and Groningen, together with a representative of the States-General, sat at their council-board at home, and ruled a territory immeasurably greater than their little state built upon the marshes; a small army of officials and a considerable merchant fleet carried out their orders; thirty-two vessels of war and eighteen armed yachts were at their service in case they needed defence.

"It was to the Amsterdam chamber of this powerful corporation that the affairs of all the region of New Netherland were given in charge; and by the authority of their patent the West India Company formally 'took possession' of the country in the spring of 1622. The enterprise of private traders had not been discontinued in the meantime; for the fur trade had been so vigorously prosecuted along the coasts to the south and east of Manhattan, and even in the bays near which the New English colony of Plymouth had been founded, that Sir Dudley Carleton, King James's ambassador at The Hague, had entered a protest against the encroachment. But this remonstrance went through a process which would now be called 'stifled in committee'; for it was referred first to one branch of the Netherlands Government and then to another, each professing ignorance of any actual Dutch establishment in America, until at last the subject was fairly forgotten. At all events, it was not permitted to interfere with the West India Company's plans; these went steadily on, and now took such shape as for the first time promised the new territory a permanent population, and began to change it from being the resort of transient traders to the site of settled and lasting colonies."

In March, 1623, the ship *New Netherland* left Amsterdam with the first colonists. These were chiefly Walloons, Netherlanders of French origin, who had been driven from their homes in the southern provinces by the fierce religious persecution of the Spaniards. They now went out to their new home under the command of Captain Cornelis Jacobsen

May. They were landed on the west bank of the Mauritius or North River, as far north as where the fort had been on Castle Island. This was the actual site of Albany, now the capital of the State. Here they set to work with a will, erecting huts, raising corn, and carrying on an amicable trade with the Indians. This new and permanent settlement was named New Amsterdam. A fort was thrown up called Fort Orange.

A few settlers were sent from Manhattan to the South Delaware River, and a number of others to the north of the Connecticut or Fresh River, and to the western end of Long Island at Walloons Bay, or Wallabout, as the English corrupted the name. Eight men were also appointed to form a trading establishment for the company at Manhattan Island. The settlers on the South River built a fort, and they were soon trading northward and eastward all along the coast to Narragansett Bay. By December, 1624, all was going on peaceably and profitably in the settlements.

May, who was the first governor of New Amsterdam, was appointed in 1624; William Verhult, the second, was commissioned in 1625; and Peter Minuit, the third, was appointed in 1626. Minuit seems to have been an able and enterprising man, and it was he who made Manhattan what it came to be politically. He bought the whole island for sixty guilders, or about £5 of English money; but a thousand millions would not now buy the island on which New York stands. Danger of disturbances having arisen at Fort Orange, the plans of Minuit for Manhattan were assisted by his withdrawal of the colonists from the fort, leaving only a small garrison. Concentration was further assisted by the migration of the settlers on the South River to the main colony. In a short time a large quadrangular stone fort was constructed, which was called Fort Amsterdam.

The West India Company soon began to convey valuable cargoes to Holland, and to bring back other goods and fresh settlers. The governor of New Amsterdam sent his secretary as a formal ambassador to Bradford, the Puritan governor of New England; and although the latter looked askance at the new settlers, and at first questioned their rights, eventually an excellent trade sprang up in various native commodities between Manhattan and Plymouth.

By the year 1628 the Island of Manhattan had a population of two hundred and seventy, and the profits of the West India Company's fur trade had more than doubled. The colony went on prospering, and mills and factories began to be erected. The early settlers had many trials and struggles, as was the case indeed with all the American colonies; and they were frequently engaged in conflict with the Indians. In August, 1664, the English, under Colonel Nichols, dispossessed the Dutch and the Swedes, and changed the name of the colony to New York, Charles II. having given the territory to his brother the Duke of York. The city was confirmed to England by the Peace of Breda, the 24th of August, 1667; but in 1673 it was retaken by the Dutch, and named New Orange. In 1674, however, the English once more captured the city, and it remained henceforward in their possession until the War of the Revolution.

CHAPTER XIII.

THE PURITANS—LANDING OF THE PILGRIM FATHERS.

IN order to understand the circumstances which led a number of the English Puritans to leave their native land and establish themselves as settlers in New England, a brief sketch of the Puritan movement is necessary.

It was a movement which sprang up within the Church of England itself. According to Fuller and Strype, the name of Puritan was first given—between 1560 and 1570—to those clergymen who refused to conform to the English liturgy, ceremonies, and discipline as arranged by Archbishop Parker and his coadjutors. Fuller fixes 1564 and Strype 1569 as the date of the first use of the word. The Puritan clergy believed that the Church did not separate itself decisively enough from Roman Catholicism, and that it needed further reformation. These principles gradually spread among the serious portion of the laity, who likewise came to be distinguished by the title of Puritans. Ultimately the word came to be used by the Elizabethan dramatists and others to mean all persons who gave up the pleasures of the world, and assumed a grave and strict habit of life.

As regards the Puritans in the Church, some would have accepted a moderate reform in the rights, discipline, and liturgy ; others, like Cartwright, desired to abolish Episcopacy altogether, and to substitute Presbyterianism ; while a third party, the Brownists, were uncompromising dissenters, opposed both to Presbyterianism and Episcopacy. The historian Hume, who certainly cannot be accused of undue partiality for the Puritans, was constrained to acknowledge that they were the preservers of civil and religious liberty in England.

The first secession from the Church took place in 1563, but the leading foreign Reformers deplored it, as they wished for an adjustment. Nevertheless, Puritan principles spread rapidly. Robert Browne, the founder of the Brownists, was born about 1550 at Tolethorpe, in Rutlandshire. He graduated at Cambridge in 1572, and became a schoolmaster and an open-air preacher in London. In 1580 he began his campaign against the order and discipline of the Established Church, and soon afterwards formed a distinct Church on apostolic and congregational principles at Norwich. He was imprisoned by Bishop Freake, but released through the influence of his kinsman Lord Burghley. In 1581, however, he was compelled to take refuge with his followers at Middleburg, in Holland. Browne returned to England in 1584 ; and reconciling himself to the Established Church, was appointed master of Stamford Grammar School in 1586, and rector of a Northamptonshire church in 1591. Being of a very violent temper, when upwards of eighty years of age he was sent to Northampton Jail for an assault on a constable, and died in jail about 1633.

But although Browne early abandoned the distinctive principles associated with his name, those principles made great headway, and they may be said to have given birth to the Independents and Congregationalists. As an example of the religious persecution which the Puritans had to undergo in Elizabeth's reign, we may cite the case of John Udall, a Brownist minister, who was tried in the year 1591 for having published a defence of the doctrines of the Brownists. This work was entitled, *A Demonstration of the Discipline which Christ hath prescribed in His Word for the Government of the Church in all Times and Places until the World's End.* An attack on the Established Church Elizabeth regarded as an attack upon herself, so Udall was arrested for a political libel, and arraigned on a capital charge of felony. According to the barbarous usages of the time, the witnesses were not confronted with the prisoner, and he was not allowed to call exculpatory evidence. As he declined to swear that he was not the author of the book, his refusal was treated as a confession of guilt. When he was told by one of the judges that "a book replete with sentiments so inconsistent with the established institutions tended to the overthrow of the State by the provocation of rebellion, he replied, 'My Lords, that be far from me; for we teach that, reforming things amiss, if the prince will not consent, the weapons that subjects are to fight withall are repentance and prayers, patience and tears.' The judge offered him his life if he would recant; and added, that he was now ready to pronounce sentence of death. 'And I am ready to receive it,' exclaimed this magnanimous man; 'for I protest before God (not knowing that I am to live an hour), that the cause is good, and I am contented to receive sentence, so that I may leave it for posterity how I have suffered for the cause.' He was condemned to die; and being still urged to submit to the Queen, he willingly expressed his regret that any of his writings should have given her offence, and disclaimed any such wish or intention, but firmly refused to disown what he believed to be truth, or to renounce liberty of conscience. By the interest of some powerful friends, a conditional pardon was obtained for him; but before the terms of it could be adjusted, or the Queen prevailed on to sign it, he died in prison. Penry, Greenwood, Barrow, and Dennis, of whom the first two were clergymen, and the others laymen, were soon after tried on similar charges, and perished by the hands of the executioner. A pardon was offered to them if they would retract their profession; but inspired by a courage which no earthly motive could overcome, they clung to their principles, and left the care of their lives to Heaven. Some more were hanged for dispersing the writings and several for attending the discourses of the Brownists. Many others endured the torture of severe imprisonment, and numerous families were reduced to indigence by heavy fines."

The two cardinal principles enunciated by the Brownists were these: first, if the King, or the magistrate under the King, refused or demurred to reforming the Church, the people might sever themselves from the National Church, and for themselves individually undertake a reformation; and, secondly, a Church might be gathered by a number of believers coming together under a willing covenant made among themselves, without civil authority.

Among those accused of assisting to spread the doctrines of the Brownists were two persons named Copping and Thacker. Under the interpretation of the law laid down by the Lord Chief Justice of England, they were hanged for the felony of sedition. When Elizabeth was told of the calm piety of the martyrs, and their prayers for herself as they went to their death, her heart for a time relented. But the persecuting spirit soon returned again, and she had for her chief adviser Archbishop Whitgift, who governed the Church with a rod of iron, and insisted upon subscription to points which had hitherto remained in abeyance.

In the year 1593 a new and yet severer law was enacted against the Puritans. These religious reformers were not only increasing in numbers every day, but were furnishing so many votaries "of the Brownist or independent doctrines, that, in the debate which took place in the House of Commons on the introduction of this measure, Sir Walter Raleigh stated, that the numbers of professed Brownists alone then amounted to twenty thousand. The humane arguments, however, which he derived from this consideration were unavailing to prevent the passing of a law which enacted, that any person above sixteen years of age who obstinately refused, during the space of a month, to attend public worship in a legitimate parochial Church should be committed to prison; that, if he persisted three months in his refusal, he must abjure the realm; and that, if he either refused this condition or returned after banishment, he should suffer death as a felon. If this act was not more fortunate than its predecessors in accomplishing the main object of checking the growth of Puritan principles, it promoted at least the subordinate purpose of driving a great many of the professors of ecclesiastical independency out of England. A numerous society of these fugitives was collected about the close of the sixteenth century at Amsterdam, where they flourished in peace and piety for upwards of a hundred years. Others retired to various Protestant states on the Continent, whence with fond, delusive hopes they expected to be recalled to their native land on the accession of Elizabeth's successor. The remainder continued in England to fluctuate between the evasion and the violation of the law,—cherishing with their principles a stern impatience, generated by the galling restraints that impeded the free expression of them; and yet retained in submission by the hope which, in common with the exiles, they indulged of a mitigation of their sufferings on the demise of the Queen."

But the hopes indulged of James I. on his accession proved fallacious. There seemed nothing before the Puritans but emigration, in order to enjoy liberty of conscience. John Penry, the Welsh martyr, who had taken degrees both at Oxford and Cambridge, had prophetically said just before his death, "Take my poor desolate widow and my mess of fatherless and friendless orphans with you into exile; you shall yet find days of peace and rest, if you continue faithful." Francis Johnson, another persecuted clergyman, eventually gathered his exiled flock into a Church at Amsterdam, where it shone as an example for at least a century. William Brewster, of the Scrooby Manor-house, Nottinghamshire, procured good Puritan preachers, and sent them to all places in the vicinity of Scrooby at his own expense. He had held a small office under Queen Elizabeth, but he had been shocked by the tyranny of the bishops against godly preachers and people.

The Hampton Court Conference was held in January, 1604, when an attempt was made to arrive at an amicable understanding between the Church and the Puritans. But it proved abortive, for James strenuously upheld the complete authority of the Church of England. "I will have none of that liberty as to ceremonies," he said; "I will have one doctrine, one discipline, one religion in substance and in ceremony." The erewhile Presbyterian thus became at once a full-blown Episcopalian. When the Puritans desired permission to assemble occasionally, and to enjoy the liberty of free discussion, the King peremptorily stifled the request; and turning to the bishops, he remarked, "I will make them conform, or I will harry them out of the land, or else worse, only hang them; that's all." The necessity of subscription was enforced, and a time set within which all clergymen should conform, or be removed from their benefices.

Whitgift died six weeks after the close of the conference, and he was succeeded as Archbishop by Bancroft, who required conformity with unrelenting rigour, while the King issued a proclamation of equal severity. In the year 1604 alone three hundred

Puritan ministers were silenced, imprisoned, or exiled. Then, by the Canons of the Convocation of 1606, every doctrine of popular rights was denied, and the superiority of the King to the Parliament and the laws asserted. Church and monarch reigned for the time supreme.

But in this same year, 1606, "a poor people" in the north of England, "in towns and villages of Nottinghamshire, Lincolnshire, and the borders of Yorkshire, in and near Scrooby, had 'become enlightened by the Word of God. Presently they were both scoffed and scorned by the profane multitude; and their ministers, urged with the yoke of subscription,' were, by the increase of troubles, led 'to see further,' that not only 'the beggarly ceremonies were monuments of idolatry,' but also 'that the lordly power of the prelates ought not to be submitted to.' Many of them, therefore, 'whose hearts the Lord had touched with heavenly zeal for His truth,' resolved, 'whatever it might cost them, to shake off the anti-Christian bondage, and, as the Lord's free people, to join themselves by a covenant into a Church estate in the fellowship of the Gospel.' Of the same faith with Calvin, heedless of acts of Parliament, they rejected 'the offices and callings, the courts and canons,' of bishops; and renouncing all obedience to human authority in spiritual things, asserted for themselves an unlimited and never-ending right to make advances in truth, and 'walk in all the ways which God had made known or should make known to them.'

"'The Gospel is every man's right; and it is not to be endured that any one should be kept therefrom.

But the Evangel is an open doctrine; it is bound to no place, and moves along freely under heaven, like the star which ran in the sky to show the wizards from the East where Christ was born. Do not dispute with the prince for place. Let the community choose their own pastor, and support him out of their own estates. If the prince will not suffer it, let the pastor flee into another land, and let those go with him who will, as Christ teaches.' Such was the counsel of Luther on reading 'the twelve articles' of the insurgent peasants of Swabia. What Luther advised, what Calvin planned, was carried into effect by this rural community of Englishmen."

The Reformed Church chose as their leading minister John Robinson, a godly, modest, and learned man, while William Brewster was their ruling elder. They met to worship God as opportunity offered, but always under great hardships. At length they determined to go into exile, and Holland was chosen as a sanctuary. Brewster had once served as a diplomatist in the Low Countries. The first attempt of this Puritan band to leave England, in 1607, was circumvented, and a number of them were imprisoned.

In the spring of 1608 the design was renewed, an unfrequented heath in Lincolnshire, near the mouth of the Humber, being chosen as the place of meeting. The authorities again interfered, but in the end Robinson and Brewster and their followers were allowed to leave their native land. They arrived in Amsterdam in 1608; but even now their wanderings were not at an end. "They knew they were *Pilgrims*," and therefore possessed their souls in patience.

Removing to Leyden in 1609, the exiles at last found a resting-place, where they were permitted to establish themselves in peace under the ministry of their pastor, John Robinson. "Being 'careful to keep their word, and painful and diligent in their callings,' they attained 'a comfortable condition, grew in the gifts and grace of the Spirit of God, and lived together in peace and love and holiness.' 'Never,' said the magistrates of the city—'never did we have any suit or accusation against any of them'; and but for fear of offence to King James, they would have met with public favour. 'Many came there from different parts of England, so as they grew a great congregation.' 'Such was the humble zeal and fervent love of this people towards God and His ways, and their single-heartedness and sincere affection one towards another,' that they seemed to come surpassingly near 'the primitive pattern of the first Churches.' A clear and well-written apology of their discipline was published by Robinson, who, also, in the controversy on free-will, as the champion of orthodoxy, 'began to be terrible to the Arminians,' and disputed in the University with such power that, as his friends assert, 'the truth had a famous victory.'"

But the Arminian controversy continued to rage with such fury that the Grand Pensionary Barneveldt was barbarously executed, while the learned Grotius was imprisoned. The English exiles lamented the cruelty and intolerance by which the bigoted representatives of Calvinism were thus disgraced, and they came to the conclusion that they might combine the indulgence of their patriotic feelings as Englishmen with the propagation of their religious principles, by establishing themselves in some distant quarter of the British dominions. After many days of earnest prayer for the counsel and direction of Heaven, the Pilgrims unanimously determined to transport themselves and their families to North America.

How was the transport across the Atlantic to be accomplished? This was a matter of difficulty. They wished to go to the most northern parts of Virginia, and in 1617 John Carver and Robert Cushman went to England to obtain the consent of the London Company. They bore with them articles of religion, promising "obedience in all things, active if the thing commanded be not against God's Word, or passive if it be"; but they denied all power to ecclesiastical bodies, unless it were given by the temporal magistrate. They pledged themselves to preserve unity of spirit in peace with all men. They found encouragement from the London Company, and could have obtained a patent at once through the influence of Sir Edwin Sandys, had not the envoys decided first to consult the pilgrims at Leyden.

However, on the 15th of December, 1617, the latter transmitted a formal and almost unanimous request, through Robinson and Brewster. The messengers, fortified by their reception at the hands of the Virginia Company, now petitioned the King for liberty of religion, to be confirmed under the sovereign's broad seal. Unfortunately, they found a powerful opponent in the great philosopher and statesman, Lord Bacon. He had shown such favour to settlers in Ireland and Virginia, that the Pilgrims naturally looked to him for support. But Bacon the statesman was not so great a man as Bacon the scholar. He became a subservient courtier like the rest, and said, " Discipline by bishops is fittest for monarchy of all others. The tenets of separatists and sectaries are full of schism, and inconsistent with monarchy. The King will beware of Anabaptists, Brownists, and others of their kinds ; a like connivency sets them on fire."

So, when the envoys were asked at James's council-board who should make their ministers, and they replied " the Church," without episcopal ordination, their mission was in danger. The King liked the idea of extending British territory and British trade, but he liked not this religious independence at all, so referred the matter to the prelates of Canterbury and London. But in 1619 things became brighter. Sir Edwin Sandys was elected treasurer of the London Virginia Company, and a patent was granted to the Pilgrims. As it was made out in the name of one who failed to accompany the expedition, however, it was never of any service. Moreover, the Pilgrims had not sufficient capital to carry out their own schemes.

Various plans were suggested for the fitting out of the expedition. The Dutch were appealed to, but failed to respond. The West India Company then offered to transport the emigrants free of charge, if they would go out solely under their auspices. The Virginia Company were also willing to do what they could. Finally, the emigrants resolved to trust to their own resources and the help of private friends. "The fisheries," remarks Bancroft, " had commended

American expeditions to English merchants; and the agents from Leyden were able to form a partnership between their employers and men of business in London. The services of each emigrant were rated as a capital of £10, and belonged to the company; all profits were to be reserved till the end of seven years, when the whole amount, and all houses and lands, gardens and fields, were to be divided among the shareholders according to their respective interests. The London merchant, who risked £100, would receive for his money tenfold more than the penniless labourer for his services. This arrangement threatened a seven years' check to the pecuniary prosperity of the community; yet, as it did not interfere with civil rights or religion, it did not intimidate the resolved."

Everything was now made ready for the departure of the emigrants. Two vessels were provided, one of one hundred and eighty tons, bearing the now historic name of the *Mayflower*; and the other the *Speedwell*, of sixty tons. As the ships could not hold anything like all the colony at Leyden, Robinson remained at home with a considerable portion of the body; while Brewster, the governing elder, went forth to America, with such of the youngest and strongest as freely offered themselves.

There was a most affecting scene at Leyden, when the Pilgrims, as was their custom in everything, commended themselves to God, and held a solemn fast. Robinson delivered a farewell address, breathing such a noble spirit of Christian candour and liberality as was then almost unknown in the world.

"Brethren," said this truly great Christian—for such he was, having drunk deeply of his Master's spirit—"we are now quickly to part from one another; and whether I may ever live to see your faces on earth any more, the God of heaven only knows; but whether the Lord has appointed that or no, I charge you, before God and His blessed angels, that you follow me no farther than you have seen me follow the Lord Jesus Christ.

"If God reveal anything to you, by any other instrument of His, be as ready to receive it as ever you were to receive any truth by my ministry; for I am verily persuaded, I am very confident, the Lord has more truth yet to break forth out of His holy Word. For my part, I cannot sufficiently bewail the condition of the Reformed Churches, who are come to a period in religion, and will go at present no farther than the instruments of their reformation. The Lutherans cannot be drawn to go beyond what Luther said; whatever part of His will our good God has revealed to Calvin, they will rather die than embrace it; and the Calvinists, you see, stick fast where they were left by that great man of God, who yet saw not all things.

"This is a misery much to be lamented; for though they were burning and shining lights in their times, yet they penetrated not into the whole counsel of God; but were they now living, would be as willing to embrace farther light, as that which they first received. I beseech you remember it, 'tis an article of your Church covenant, *that you be ready to receive whatever truth shall be made known to you from the written Word of God.* Remember *that*, and every other article of your sacred covenant.

"But I must herewithal exhort you to take heed what you receive as truth. Examine it, consider it, and compare it with other Scriptures of truth before you receive it; for 'tis not possible the Christian world should come so lately out of antichristian darkness, and that perfection of knowledge should break forth at once.

"I must also advise you to abandon, avoid, and shake off the name of Brownist; 'tis a mere nickname, and a brand for the making religion, and the professors of it, odious to the Christian world."

The closing scene in Holland was thus described by Edward Winslow, one of the Pilgrims: "When the ship was ready to carry us away, the brethren that stayed at Leyden, having again solemnly sought the Lord with us and for us, feasted us that were to go, at our pastor's house, being large; where we refreshed ourselves, after tears, with singing of psalms, making joyful melody in our hearts, as well as with the voice, there being many of the congregation very expert in music; and indeed it was the sweetest melody that ever mine ears heard. After this, they accompanied us to Delft Haven, where we went to embark, and then feasted us again; and after prayer performed by our pastor, when a flood of tears was poured out, they accompanied us to the ship, but were not able to speak one to another for the abundance of sorrow to part. But we only, going abroad, gave them a volley of small shot and three pieces of ordnance; and so, lifting up our hands to each other, and our hearts for each other to the Lord our God, we departed."

Such were the good and brave men whom a bigoted King and a relentless hierarchy drove from their native land to seek freedom of conscience on alien shores.

The *Mayflower* and *Speedwell* made first for Southampton; and after waiting there for a fortnight for the completion of all arrangements in connection with the expedition, the vessels sailed from Southampton on the 5th of August, 1620, for America. The colonists numbered in all seventy-four men and twenty-eight women. It was found soon after starting that the smaller vessel needed repairs, and the expedition put into Dartmouth for that purpose. Again they set forth; but after eight days the captain of the *Speedwell* and his companions became discouraged by the dangers of the enterprise, and asserted that the ship was too weak for the service. The expedition put back into Plymouth, and the *Speedwell* was dismissed, which " was very grievous and discouraging." Then the resolute little band remaining, amounting in all to one hundred and two souls, went on board the *Mayflower*, and on the 6th day of September, 1620, the Pilgrims finally left Plymouth, and the shores of England, for a new world.

Hudson's River was the intended destination of the emigrants, who proposed to found their settlement upon its banks; but the Dutch claimed a prior right to this territory, and the English settlers were conducted to the most barren part of Massachusetts. On the 9th of November, after a boisterous voyage of sixty-three days, the *Mayflower* cast anchor in the harbour of Cape Cod. This region was not only beyond the precincts of their grant, but beyond the territories of the Company from which the grant was derived. Before landing, the emigrants discussed the form of their future government; and as there were some not too well affected towards unity and concord, on the 11th they formed themselves into a body politic by this solemn voluntary compact:

"In the name of God, amen; we, whose names are underwritten, the loyal subjects of our dread sovereign, King James, having undertaken, for the glory of God, and advancement of the Christian faith, and honour of our King and country, a voyage to plant the first colony in the northern parts of Virginia, do, by these presents, solemnly and mutually, in the presence of God and one of another, covenant and combine ourselves together into a civil body politic, for our better ordering and preservation, and furtherance of the ends aforesaid; and, by virtue hereof, to enact, constitute, and frame such just and equal laws, ordinances, acts, constitutions, and offices, from time to time, as shall be thought most convenient for the general good of the colony. Unto which we promise all due submission and obedience."

This instrument, which signalized the birth of constitutional liberty in the United States, was signed by all the men in the emigrant body, and John Carver was unanimously chosen governor for the first year.

The American orator, Edward Everett, in an eloquent centennial address, thus described the voyage and landing of the *Mayflower*:

"The feeble company of Pilgrims is not to be marshalled by gartered statesmen or mitred prelates. Fleets will not be despatched to convoy the little band, nor armies to protect it. Had there been honours to be won, or pleasures to be enjoyed, or plunder to be grasped, hungry courtiers, midsummer friends, godless adventurers, would have eaten out the heart of the enterprise. Silken Buckinghams and Somersets would have blasted it with their patronage. But, safe amidst their unenvied perils, strong in their inoffensive weakness, rich in their untempting poverty, the patient fugitives are permitted to pursue unmolested the thorny paths of tribulation; and, landed at last on the unfriendly shore, the host of God, in the frozen mail of December, encamp around the dwellings of the just.

Stern famine guards the solitary coast,
And winter barricades the realms of frost.

"While Bacon is attuning the sweetest strains of his honeyed eloquence to soothe the dull ear of a crowned pedant, and his great rival, only less obsequious, is on his knees to deprecate the royal displeasure, the future founders of the new Republic beyond the sea are training up for their illustrious mission, in obscurity, hardship, and weary exile in a foreign land.

"And now—for the fulness of time is come—let us go up once more, in imagination, to yonder hill, and look out upon the November scene. That single dark speck, just discernible through the perspective glass, on the waste of waters, is the fated vessel. The storm moans through her tattered canvas as she creeps, almost sinking, to her anchorage in Province-town Harbour, and there she lies with her treasures, not of silver and gold (for of these she has none), but of courage, of patience, of zeal, of high spiritual daring. As often as I dwell in imagination on this scene; when I consider the condition of the *Mayflower*, utterly incapable, as she was, of living through another gale; when I survey the terrible front presented by our coast to the navigator who, unacquainted with its channels and roadsteads, should approach it in the stormy season,—I dare not call it a mere piece of good fortune, that the general north and south wall of the shore of New England should be broken by this extraordinary projection of the cape, running out into the ocean a hundred miles, as if on purpose to receive and encircle the precious vessel. As I now see her, freighted with the destinies of a continent, barely escaped from the perils of the deep, approaching the shore precisely where the broad sweep of this most remarkable headland presents almost the only point at which, for hundreds of miles, she could, with any ease, have made a harbour, and this, perhaps, the very best on the seaboard, I feel my spirit raised above the sphere of mere natural agencies. I see the mountains of New England rising from their rocky thrones. They rush forward into the ocean, setting down as they advance; and there they range themselves as a mighty bulwark around the Heaven-directed vessel. Yes, the everlasting God Himself stretches out the arm of His mercy and His power, in substantial manifestations, and gathers the meek company of His worshippers as in the hollow of His hand."

The early history of the colonists was full of hardships. They seemed to be shut out from the whole world, for the nearest French settlement was at Port Royal, and the English plantation in Virginia was five hundred miles distant. The weather was already unusually severe, and winter was at hand. The vessel's shallop was unshipped, but it was found to need serious repairs. Weary of delay, Miles Standish and Bradford, with some others, made an unsuccessful expedition inland. The first voyage made by the shallop was likewise a failure, and some who went in her contracted their death through the intense cold and frost. A small quantity of Indian maize was discovered on shore, but little else except Indian graves and a few untenanted wigwams.

On the 6th of December the shallop again went out, with Carver, Bradford, Standish, Winslow, and fourteen or fifteen others, including seamen. The spray of the sea froze as it fell on the explorers, and made their clothes like coats of iron. At night they reached Billingsgate Point, at the bottom of the Bay of Cape Cod, on the western shore of Wellfleet Harbour. Next day the company divided, but no suitable place for a settlement was found, and the whole party met again at night, and encamped on the shore near Namskeket, or Great Meadow Creek.

Next day the settlers were attacked by the Indians, but no serious consequences ensued, and they pursued their journey along the coast for a distance of nearly fifty miles. After some hours a terrible storm arose, and the shallop was nearly cast away, while her inmates were almost blinded by snow and rain. The pilot nearly ran the boat into a cove full of breakers; but this danger was averted, and grateful shelter was found under the lee of a small neck of land. With some difficulty a fire was kindled on the shore, and the night passed in painful expectancy. As the day broke the place of shelter was seen to be a little island within the entrance of a harbour. Next day was the Christian Sabbath, and the Pilgrims passed it in all reverence.

Monday, the 11th of December, 1620, Old Style, is a day ever memorable in the history of the United States. On that date the Pilgrims landed at a place afterwards included within the province of Massachusetts, to which they gave the name of New Plymouth, in commemoration of the town with which their last recollections of England were associated. The rock first trodden by the emigrants now bears an inscription recording the fact, and the day of landing is annually honoured as the origin of New England and the planting of its institutions.

The site being found favourable for a settlement, the little *Mayflower* was safely brought into harbour on the 15th of December. The settlers had an onerous task before them ; but they were one in heart, and a thoroughly democratic and Christian body, with principles of government already well established. Daniel Webster, the great American orator, finely said on this head, in a discourse on the settlement of New England: " Our fathers came hither to a land from which they were never to return. Hither they had brought, and here they were to fix, their hopes, their attachments, and their objects. Some natural tears they shed as they left the pleasant abodes of their fathers, and some emotions they suppressed when the white cliffs of their native country, now seen for the last time, grew dim to their sight. They were acting, however, upon a resolution not to be changed. With whatever stifled regrets, with whatever occasional hesitation, with whatever appalling apprehensions, which must sometimes arise with force to shake the firmest purpose, they had yet committed themselves to Heaven and the elements; and a thousand leagues of water soon interposed to separate them for ever from the region which gave them birth. A new existence awaited them here; and when they saw these shores, rough, cold, barbarous, and barren as then they were, they beheld their country. That mixed and strong feeling, which we call love of country, and which is in general never extinguished in the heart of man, grasped and embraced its proper object here. Whatever constitutes country, except the earth and the sun, all the moral causes of affection and attachment which operate upon the heart, they had brought with them to their new abode. Here were now their families and friends, their homes and their property. Before they reached the shore, they had established the elements of a social system, and at a much earlier period had settled their forms of religious worship. At the moment of their landing, therefore, they possessed institutions of government and institutions of religion: and friends and families, and social and religious institutions, established by consent, founded on choice and preference, how nearly do these fill up our whole idea of country? The morning that beamed on the first night of their repose saw the

Pilgrims already established in their country. There were political institutions, and civil liberty, and religious worship. Poetry has fancied nothing in the wanderings of heroes so distinct and characteristic. Here was man indeed unprotected and unprovided for, on the shore of a rude and fearful wilderness, but it was politic, intelligent, and educated man. Everything was civilized but the physical world. Institutions containing in substance all that ages had done for human government were established in a forest. Cultivated mind was to act on uncultivated nature; and, more than all, a government and a country were to commence with the very first foundations laid under the divine light of the Christian religion. Happy auspices of a happy futurity! Who would wish that his country's existence had otherwise begun? Who would desire the power of going back to the ages of fable? Who would wish for an origin obscured in the darkness of antiquity? Who would wish for other emblazoning of his country's heraldry, or other ornaments of her genealogy, than to be able to say that her first existence was with intelligence, her first breath the inspirations of liberty, her first principle the truth of divine religion?"

Early in January, 1621, the colonists began to build, but their exertions to erect suitable dwellings were obstructed for a time by the hostile attacks of neighbouring Indians, who had not forgotten the provocations received from previous explorers. After the Indians had been successfully repulsed, sickness—caused by scarcity of provisions and the increasing horrors of the season—afflicted the colonists with a calamity more fatal to their health and security than the perils of war.

The historians Mather, Neal, Grahame, and others furnish painful pictures of the sufferings of the colonists. More than one-half of their number, including John Carver, their first governor, "perished by hunger or disease before the return of spring; and, during the whole of the winter, only a few were capable of providing for themselves, or rendering assistance to the rest. But hope and virtue survived, and, rising in vigour beneath the pressure of accumulated sufferings, surmounted and ennobled every circumstance of distress. Those who retained their strength became the servants of the weak, the afflicted, and the dying; and none distinguished himself more in this humane employment than Carver, the governor. He was a man of large estate, but more enlarged benevolence; he had spent his whole fortune on the colonial project; and now, willingly contributing his life to its accomplishment, he exhausted a feeble body in laboriously discharging the humblest offices of kindness and service to the sick. He was succeeded by William Bradford, who, inheriting the merit and the popularity of his predecessor, was re-elected to the same office for many successive years—notwithstanding his own earnest remonstrance, that, if his office were an honour, it should be shared by his fellow-citizens, and, if it were a burden, the weight of it should not always be imposed upon him. When the distress of the colony was at its height, the approach of a powerful Indian chief with his followers seemed to portend the utter destruction of the colonists; but, happily, in the train of this personage was the ancient guest and friend of the English, Squanto, who eagerly and successfully laboured to mediate a good understanding between them and his countrymen. He afterwards cancelled the merit of this useful service, and endeavoured to magnify his own importance by fabricating charges of plots and conspiracies against some of the neighbouring tribes, while at the same time he maintained an empire of terror over these tribes by secretly assuring them that the English were in possession of a cask filled with the plague, which only his influence prevented them from setting abroad for the destruction of the Indians. But before he resorted to this mischievous policy the colonists had become independent of his services. His friendship with the English was never entirely dissolved; and on his death-bed soon after, he desired Governor Bradford to pray for him, that he might go to the Englishman's God in heaven. Some of the neighbouring tribes from time to time made alarming demonstrations of hostility, but they were at length completely overawed by the courage and resolution of Captain Miles Standish, a gallant and skilful officer, who, with a handful of men, was always ready to encounter their strongest force, and anticipate their most rapid movements."

On the 22nd of March, 1621, Massassoit—the greatest Indian chief of the country, and sachem of the tribe possessing the land north of Narragansett Bay, between the rivers of Providence and Taunton—came to visit the Pilgrims, who, with their wives and children, were now only fifty in number. A friendly treaty was concluded, by which both parties promised to abstain from mutual injuries and to deliver up offenders. The colonists were to receive assistance if attacked, and to render it if Massassoit should be unjustly assailed. This is the oldest act of diplomacy recorded in New England annals, and it was sacredly kept for more than half a century. In July new emigrants arrived from England, and during the same month an embassy from the little colony of New Plymouth to Massassoit succeeded in ratifying the treaty of amity, and preparing the way for a trade in furs.

In September nine Indian chiefs subscribed an instrument of submission to King James, and the British settlers explored the Bay of Massachusetts and Boston Harbour. One important native chief, named Canonicus, still maintained a hostile attitude, and in 1622 sent a bundle of arrows, wrapped in the skin of a rattlesnake, as a message of hostility. He succumbed, however, and craved for peace when Bradford sent back the skin stuffed with powder and shot.

The summer months had brought back renewed health to the colonists, and their numbers were recruited from time to time by successive emigrations of oppressed Puritans from Europe. But the additions fell far short of their needs; and the colonists were unhappily disappointed in their expectation of the main reinforcement which they had looked for from the emigration of the remainder of the congregation at Leyden. Robinson, their beloved pastor, had unexpectedly passed away, and his stimulating example and counsel were no longer available. The surviving members of the congregation were dismayed by the accounts of the distresses sustained by their friends in

New England; and after the death of Robinson, the greater part of them joined the other English exiles at Amsterdam, and few had the courage to proceed to New Plymouth.

Meanwhile, the colony continued to deepen the roots of its existence. The settlers evinced a due respect for the natives by purchasing from them the territory over which their settlement extended, but at the same time they neglected no precautions to defend by force, if needs be, what they had acquired by justice. Alarmed at the tidings of the massacre of their countrymen in Virginia, they erected a timber fort, and adopted other necessary measures for their security.

Historical records show that the constitution of the Church which the emigrants established "was the same with that which had prevailed among them at Leyden; and their system of civil government was founded on those ideas of the natural equality of men to which their ecclesiastical policy, so long the main object of their concern, had habituated their minds. The supreme legislative body was composed at first of all the freemen who were members of the Church; and it was not until the year 1639 that they established a house of representatives. The executive power was committed to a governor and council annually elected by the members of the legislative assembly. Their jurisprudence was founded on the laws of England, with some diversity, however, in the appreciation and punishment of crimes, wherein they approximated more nearly to the Mosaic institutions. Considering the protection of morals more important than the preservation of wealth, they punished fornication with flogging and adultery with death, while on forgery they inflicted only a moderate fine. The clearing and cultivation of the ground, fishing, and the curing of fish for exportation formed the temporal occupations of the colonists. The peculiarity of their situation naturally led them, like the Virginians, for some time to throw all their property into a common stock, and, like members of one family, to carry on every work of industry by their joint labour for the public behoof. But the religious zeal which promoted this self-denying policy was unable to overcome the difficulties which must always attend it, and which are peculiarly aggravated in a society deriving its principle of increment not so much from internal growth as from the confluence of strangers. About three years after the foundation of New Plymouth, it was judged proper to introduce separation of possessions, though the full right of separate property was not admitted till a much later period; and even that change is represented as having produced a great and manifest improvement in the industry of the people. The slow increase which, for a considerable period of time, the population of the colony exhibited has been ascribed to the prolonged operation of this system of equality; but it seems more likely that the slowness of the increase (occasioned by the poverty of the soil, and the report of the hardships attending a settlement in New England) was itself the reason why the complete ascertainment of the rights of separate property was so long retarded."

The colonists ceased to suffer from a scarcity of food after the harvest of 1623. Each family now tilled its own quota of land, though the community owned the soil. In a very short time so much corn was raised that it became a profitable article of commerce, and the Indians purchased corn from the emigrants, or exchanged beaver skins, etc., for it. The gains from the fur trade stimulated the envy of one Thomas Weston, a London merchant, who had done much in fitting out the Plymouth expedition. He now obtained a patent for land near Weymouth, the first plantation in Boston Harbour, and sent over sixty men. The venture proved a disastrous failure, and the colonists threw themselves on the hospitality of the Plymouth people, while they alienated the Indians by their folly and injustice. An attempt was made to massacre Weston's band, but the friendly Indian chief Massassoit revealed it to the Plymouth settlers, and the Weymouth planters were saved by their English brethren, and chiefly through the bravery of Miles Standish, who performed his most gallant exploit on this occasion. A portion of the rescued men remained at New Plymouth, and the rest returned to England.

It is worthy of note that the colonists of New Plymouth never received a charter from the Crown. They had one from the grand council of the Plymouth Company, by which they were authorized to choose a governor, council, and general court for the enactment of laws, and some historians have mistaken this for a royal charter. As a matter of fact, however, the social community of New Plymouth was never incorporated with legal formalities as a public body, but remained a voluntary municipal association until it was united with the colony of Massachusetts. Owing to a variety of causes, the growth of the colony was small, and it only numbered three hundred persons altogether after an existence of ten years. One great difficulty arose out of their connection with the English adventurers. The latter endeavoured to force upon the colonists a clergyman favourable to the Established Church, and likewise oppressed them by heavy charges upon goods sent from England, and heavy usury for money lent. The consequence was that the emigrants at length bought out the English adventurers, after which the common property of the settlement was equitably divided, and agriculture placed on the sure basis of private possession. The cultivators of the soil became the owners of the freehold, and eight of the more substantial settlers assumed all the engagements of the colony in consideration of a trade monopoly for six years.

In 1626 an effort was made by the London Plymouth Company to establish in Massachusetts a colony similar to that of New Plymouth. An expedition was sent out under Captain Wollaston, and it was his followers who first taught the Indians of the district the use of fire-arms—a knowledge which the colonists of New England soon had reason to lament. Wollaston's efforts were unsuccessful, like those of several adventurers who had preceded him in the same field. The coast of Massachusetts Bay was the scene of these failures, but eventually a colony was actually founded in this locality upon the model of that of New Plymouth.

A few words must be added with regard to the

civil government of the Plymouth colony in its early days. The governor was chosen by the whole people; and in 1624, at the request of Bradford, his power was restricted by the nomination of a council of five to act with him, the number being increased to seven in 1633. When sitting in council, the governor had only a double vote, and no law could be made or impost laid without the consent of the freemen. The whole body of male inhabitants constituted the legislature for more than eighteen years; but in 1639, in consequence of the increase of population, the representative system was introduced, and each town sent its committee to the general court. Though the colonists were never betrayed into those excesses of religious persecution from which they had themselves suffered, they sometimes sanctioned a disproportion between crime and punishment. For example, in 1645, although a majority of the house of delegates were in favour of an act to "allow and maintain full and free toleration to all men that would preserve the civil peace and submit unto government—and there was no limitation or exception against Turk, Jew, Papist, Arian, Socinian, Nicolaitan, Familist, or any other"—the governor was afraid that such a law would "eat out the power of godliness," and declined to put the question, so that the law was lost.

But with all its defects, this little colony boasted of greater civil and religious freedom than existed in any other quarter of the civilized world. The New Englanders were pioneers in the noblest sense, and out of small beginnings evolved great issues. No wonder that their descendants hold their names in honour and reverence. It was no empty boast when an Englishman wrote of the Plymouth colony that "the memory of the adventurers to this plantation shall never die." As religious men, these early settlers "acknowledged no infallible head but God Almighty, and no patristic guides to faith and practice but the holy company of the Prophets and Apostles."

It seemed to James I. and his satellites that this small band of Puritans, when it went out to the inhospitable shores of Northern America, went to its extinction, and to the grave of oblivion. Yet there was in this obscure and insignificant band a vitality which was destined to assert itself long after the Stuarts had been swept from the throne of England. The successors of the Plymouth colonists have grown into a mighty nation, which is destined to carry aloft the torch of liberty, first lit at the fires of persecution in England, down to the latest ages of time in the history of the Anglo-Saxon race.

www.ingramcontent.com/pod-product-compliance
Lightning Source LLC
Chambersburg PA
CBHW030018240426
43672CB00007B/1003